KARMIC RELATIONSHIPS

Esoteric Studies

Vol. II

I0802004

RUDOLF STEINER

Sixteen lectures given at Dornach, Switzerland, between 6th April and 29th June, 1924

Translated by George Adams
with revisions by M. Cotterell, C. Davy
and D. S. Osmond

RUDOLF STEINER PRESS

Rudolf Steiner Press
Hillside House, The Square
Forest Row RH18 5ES

www.rudolfsteinerpress.com

First edition 1956
Second edition 1974
Reprinted 1997, 2004
Reprinted in paperback 2015

Originally published in German under the title *Esoterische Betrachtungen karmischer Zusammenhänge, Zweiter Band* (volume 236 in the *Rudolf Steiner Gesamtausgabe* or Collected Works) by Rudolf Steiner Verlag, Dornach. This authorized translation published by kind permission of the Rudolf Steiner Nachlassverwaltung, Dornach

A catalogue record for this book is available from the British Library

ISBN 978 1 85584 520 6

Printed and bound in the UK by 4edge Limited

Vol. II

SUMMARY OF CONTENTS

THE COSMIC FORM OF KARMA AND THE STUDY OF INDIVIDUAL KARMIC RELATIONSHIPS

EDITOR'S PREFACE

During the year 1924, before his illness in September, Rudolf Steiner gave over eighty lectures, published with the title *Karmic Relationships: Esoteric Studies*, to members of the Anthroposophical Society in the following places: Dornach, Berne, Zürich, Stuttgart, Prague, Paris, Breslau, Arnhem, Torquay and London. English translations of these lectures are contained in the following volumes of the series:

Vols. I to IV. Lectures given in Dornach (49).
Vol. V. Lectures given in Prague (4) and Paris (3).
Vol. VI. Lectures given in Berne (2) Zürich (1), Stuttgart (3) Arnhem (3).
Vol. VII. Lectures given in Breslau (9).
Vol. VIII. Lectures given in Torquay (3) and London (3).

All these lectures were given to members of the Anthroposophical Society only and were intended to be material for study by those already familiar with the fundamental principles of Anthroposophy. The following extract from the lecture of 22nd June, 1924 (see Vol. II) calls attention to the need for exactitude when passing on such contents:

"The study of problems connected with karma is by no means easy and the discussion of anything that has to do with the subject entails—or ought at any rate to entail—a sense of deep responsibility. Such study is in truth a matter of penetrating into the most profound mysteries of existence, for within the sphere of karma and the course it takes lie those processes which are the basis of the other phenomena of world-existence, even of the phenomena of nature.... These difficult and weighty matters entail grave consideration of every word and every sentence spoken here, in order that *the limits within which the statements are made shall be absolutely clear....*"

The attention of readers is called to the fact that the fundamental explanations given by Rudolf Steiner of the laws and conditions of karma are contained in Vol. I of the series. Knowledge of the earlier lectures should therefore be regarded as an essential basis for study of those contained in the later volumes.

I

We will now continue our study of karma. I have pointed out to you how the impulses in the souls of human beings work on and are transplanted, as it were, from one earthly life into another, so that the fruits of an earlier epoch are carried over to a later one by men themselves.

An idea such as this must not be received merely as a theory; it should take hold of our very hearts and souls. We should feel that we who are now here have been many times in earthly existence, and that in every life we assimilated the culture and civilisation then around us; we took it into our souls and carried it over into the next incarnation, after working upon it spiritually between death and a new birth. Only when we look back in this way do we really feel ourselves standing within the community of mankind.

In order to be able to feel this, in order that in the coming lectures we may pass on to questions which concern us more intimately and will bring home to us the actual effects of karmic connections, I have found it necessary to give concrete examples. And I have tried to show you by these examples how the effects of what a man experienced and achieved in olden times, remain, and continue to work into the present, inasmuch as his achievements and experiences form part of his karma.

I spoke, for example, of Haroun al Raschid, that illustrious follower of Mohammed in the 8th and 9th centuries, who was the figure-head of a wonderful life of culture far surpassing anything to be found in Europe in those days.* Such culture as existed in Europe at that time—it was during the reign of Charlemagne—was extremely primitive; whereas over in the East at the Court of Haroun al Raschid there

* See Vol. I, lecture X; also *Cosmic Christianity*, lecture II (given by Rudolf Steiner in Torquay, 14th August, 1924).

came together everything that an Asiatic civilisation fructified from Europe could produce—the fruits of Greek culture and of ancient Oriental culture in practically every domain of life and knowledge. Architecture, astronomy (in the form in which it was pursued in those days), philosophy, mysticism, the arts, geography, poetry—all these branches of culture flourished at the Court of Haroun al Raschid.

Haroun al Raschid gathered around him the best of those who were of real account in Asia at that time. For the most part they were men who had been trained and educated in the Initiate Schools. Let me tell you of one of these personalities at the Court of Haroun al Raschid. The East, too, had reached its own Middle Ages, and this personality had been able to assimilate, in a rather more intellectual way, wonderful treasures of the spirit that had been carried over from long past ages into those later times. In a much earlier period he had himself been an Initiate.

Now as I have told you, it may easily happen that a personality who was an Initiate in a former age does not appear as one when he reincarnates, because he is obliged to adapt himself to the body at his disposal and to the educational facilities available at the time. Nevertheless he bears within him all that he acquired and experienced during his life as an Initiate.

In the case of Garibaldi, we have seen how in that he became a kind of seer in his life of will, giving himself up to the circumstances of the immediate present, he lived out all that he had been as an Irish Initiate.* We can see that while participating in the events of the day he bears within him impulses of quite a different character from those which an ordinary man could have gained from his education and environment. The impulse of Garibaldi's Irish initiation was still active; it was merely under the surface. And when some special experience or stroke of destiny befell Garibaldi there may very probably have welled up in him in the form of Imaginations, all that he bore within him from his life as an Irish Initiate.

* See Vol. I, lectures XI and XII.

So it has always been; and so it is to this day. A man may have been an Initiate in a certain epoch, and because in a later epoch he must make use of a body unable to contain all the impulses that are alive in his soul, he does not appear as an Initiate; nevertheless the impulse of initiation is at work in his deeds or relationships in life. So it was in the case of the personality who lived at the Court of Haroun al Raschid. He had once been an Initiate of a very high degree. He was not able to carry over in outwardly perceptible form the whole content of his earlier initiation, but nevertheless he was a shining light in the Oriental culture of the 8th and 9th centuries. For he was, so to speak, the organiser of all the sciences and arts studied and practised at the Court of Haroun al Raschid.

We have already spoken of the path taken by the individuality of Haroun al Raschid in later times. When he passed through the gate of death there remained with him the urge to carry further into the West the Arabism that was already spreading in that direction. And, as you know, Haroun al Raschid, whose field of vision embraced all the several arts and sciences, reincarnated as Lord Bacon of Verulam, the famous reformer of modern philosophy and science. All that had been within Haroun al Raschid's field of vision came forth again, in a Western guise, in Bacon.

The spiritual path taken by Bacon led from Bagdad, his home in Asia, to England. And from England, Bacon's work for the sciences spread over Europe more widely and with greater force than is generally realised.

After they had passed through the gate of death, these two personalities, Haroun al Raschid and his great counsellor —the outstanding personality who had been a high Initiate in earlier times—separated, in order to carry out a common work. As I have told you, Haroun al Raschid himself, who had occupied a position of great power and splendour, chose the path which led to England, where, as Lord Bacon of Verulam, he accomplished what he did for science, for the sphere of knowledge in general. The other soul, the soul of the man who had been his counsellor chose the path leading to Middle Europe, in order to meet there what was coming over from Bacon. The dates do not, it is true, absolutely coincide; but that is not important in a matter where actual time means little. Impulses separated by hundreds of years may often work simultaneously in a later civilisation.

The counsellor of Haroun al Raschid chose the path through Eastern to Middle Europe—chose it during his life between death and a new birth. And he was born again in Middle Europe; he was born into the spiritual life of Middle Europe as *Amos Comenius.*

These are remarkable events, of profound significance in history. Haroun al Raschid goes through his later evolution in such a way as to lead over from West to East a stream of culture that is abstract and bound up with the outer senses; whereas Amos Comenius unfolds his activity from the East, from Siebenbürgen in what is now Czechoslovakia, coming to Germany and afterwards undergoing exile in Holland, bringing with him his profoundly significant impulses for the development of thought and knowledge. If you follow his life you will see how he comes forward as the champion of the new pedagogy and as the author and originator of the so-called *Pansophia.* What he had formerly brought from his initiation in very ancient times and developed at the Court of Haroun al Raschid—all this he now brought to the movements of the day. It was the time when the Order of the Moravian Brothers had been founded, when Rosicrucianism had already been at work for several centuries; it was the time, too, when the *Chymical Wedding* had appeared, and also the *Reformation of Science*, by Valentin Andreae. And into the midst of all these movements which sprang from the selfsame source, came Comenius, that significant figure of the 17th century, with his message and his impulse.

You have there three successive earthly lives of importance, and it is by studying the more significant incarnations that one can learn how to study those of less importance and finally begin to understand one's own karma.—Three significant earthly lives follow one another. First we see, far away in Asia, the very same individuality who afterwards appears in Amos Comenius; we see him receiving in the places of the ancient Mysteries all the wisdom possessed by Asia in far distant ages; we see him carrying this over into his next incarnation, living at the Court of Haroun al Raschid, becoming there the great organiser and administrator of all that flourished under the aegis and protection of Haroun al Raschid. And then he appears again, this time going forth as it were to meet Bacon, who is the reincarnated Haroun al Raschid; he meets him in European civilisation where the impulses which both of them had caused to flow into this European civilisation are at work.

What I am now saying, my dear friends, has really great point and meaning. For if you will study the letters that were written and that build, as it were, a road from Bacon to Comenius—naturally they do so in a roundabout way, as is also the case with letters to-day!—if you will study the letters that were exchanged between Baconians, or between people in very close connection with the Baconian culture and the followers of the Comenius school, of the Comenius wisdom, you will be able to discern in the writing and answering of these letters the very same event that I have sketched diagrammatically on the blackboard.

The letters that were written from West to East and from East to West represent the living confluence of the two souls who meet one another in this way, having themselves laid the foundation for this meeting when they worked together over in the East during the 8th and 9th centuries. Now they unite again, to work once more in co-operation; this time they work from opposite directions, yet no less harmoniously.

This is the way in which history should be studied in order to gain insight into the working of human forces and the part they play in history.

Again, let us take another case.—It happened that peculiar circumstances drew my attention to certain events that occurred in the region we should now call the north-east of France. These events also took place in the 8th–9th century—a little later, however, than the time of which we were just now speaking. It was before the formation of large States, in the days when events took place more within smaller circles of people.

In the region, then, which to-day we should call the north-east of France, lived a personality who was full of ambitions. He had a large estate and he governed it remarkably well, quite unusually systematically for the time in which he lived. He knew what he wanted; there was a strange mixture of adventurousness and conscious purpose in him. And he made expeditions, some of which were more and some less successful; he would gather soldiers and make predatory expeditions, minor campaigns carried out with a small troop of men with the object of plunder.

With such a band of men he once set out from north-east France. Now it happened that during his absence another personality, somewhat less of an adventurer than himself, but full of energy, took possession of all his land and property.—It sounds fictitious to-day, but such things actually happened in those days.—And when the owner returned home—he was all alone—he found another man in possession of his estate. In the situation that developed he was no match for the man who had seized his property. The new possessor was more powerful; he had more men, more soldiers. The rightful owner was no match for him.

In those times it did not happen that if anyone were unable to go on living in his own home and estate he immediately went away into some foreign country. The rightful owner was an adventurer, certainly, but emigration was not such an easy matter then; he had neither the wherewithal nor the facilities. And so he became a kind of serf, he with his followers—a kind of serf attached to his own estate. His own property had been wrested from him and he, together with a number of those who once used to accompany him on adventures were forced to work as serfs.

In all these people who were now serfs where formerly they had been masters, a certain attitude of mind began to assert itself, an attitude of mind most derogatory to the principle of overlordship. On many a night in those well-wooded parts, fires were burning, and round the fires these men came together and hatched all manner of plots against those who had taken possession of their property.

In point of fact, the dispossessed owner, who from being the master of a large estate had become a serf, more or less a slave, filled all the rest of his life—as much of it as he was not compelled to give to his work—with making plans for regaining his property. He hated the man who had seized it from him.

And then, when these two personalities passed through the gate of death, they experienced in the spiritual world between death and rebirth, all that souls have been able to experience since that time, shared in it all, and came again to earth in the 19th century. The man who had lost home and property and had become a kind of slave, appeared as *Karl Marx*, the founder of modern socialism. And the man who had seized his estate appeared as his friend *Engels*. The actions which had brought them into conflict were metamorphosed in the course of the long journey between death and a new birth into an impulse and urge to balance out and set right what they had done to one another.

Read what went on between Marx and Engels, observe the peculiar configuration of Marx's mind, and remember at the same time what I have told you of the relationship between these two individuals in the 8th–9th century, and you will find a new light falling upon every sentence written by Marx and Engels. You will not be in danger of saying, in abstract fashion: This thing in history is due to this cause, and the other to the other cause. Rather will you see the human beings who carry over the past into another age, in such a way that although admittedly it appears in a somewhat different form, there is nevertheless a certain similarity.

And what else could be expected? In the 8th–9th century, when men sat together at night around a fire in the forest, they spoke in quite a different style from that customary in the 19th century, when Hegel had lived, when things were settled by dialectic. Try all the same to picture to yourselves the forest in north-eastern France in the 9th century. There sit the conspirators, cursing, railing in the language of the period. Translate it into the mathematical-dialectical mode of speech of the 19th century, and you have what comes to expression in Marx and Engels.

Such things lead us away from sensationalism—which creeps all too easily into ideas relating to the concrete facts of reincarnation—towards a true understanding of history. And the best way to steer clear of sensationalism is, instead of giving way to a feverish desire to know the details of reincarnation, instead of that, to try to understand in the light of the repeated earthly lives of individual human beings, those things in history that bring weal or woe, happiness or grief to mankind.

It was this point of view that while I was still living in Austria—although in Austria one is really within the German world—I was particularly interested in a certain personality who was a Polish member of the Reichstag. Those of you who have been attending lectures for a long time will remember that I have often spoken of Otto Hausner, the Austrian-Polish member of the Reichstag who was so active in the seventies of last century. Truth to tell, ever since I heard and saw Otto Hausner in the Austrian Reichstag about the end of the seventies and beginning of the eighties, the picture of this remarkable man has been before my mind's eye. He wore a monocle; he looked at you sharply with the other eye, but all the time the eye behind the monocle was watching for the weak points in his opponent. And while he spoke, he was looking to see whether the dart had struck home.

Now Hausner had a remarkable moustache—in my autobiography I did not want to go into all these details—and he used to accompany what he said with his moustache, so that the moustache made a kind of Eurythmy of the speech he poured out against his opponents!

It is interesting when you picture it all.—Extreme Left, Left, Middle Party, Czech Club (as it was called) and then Extreme Right, Polish Club. Here stood Hausner, and over on the extreme Left were his opponents. That was where all of them were.

The curious thing was that when, over the question of the occupation of Bosnia, Hausner was on the side of Austria, he received tumultuous applause from these people on the Left. When, later, he spoke about the building of the Arlberg railway, the most vehement opposition came from the same people on the extreme Left. And the situation remained so, in regard to everything he said after that.

Very many warnings and prophetic utterances made by Otto Hausner in the seventies and eighties have, however, since proved true. One often has occasion nowadays to look back in thought to what Otto Hausner used to say.

Now there was one feature that appeared in almost every speech Otto Hausner made, and this, among other less significant details in his life, gave me the impulse to investigate the course of his karma. Otto Hausner could hardly make a speech without uttering a kind of panegyric, as it were in parenthesis, on Switzerland. He was forever holding up Switzerland to Austria as a pattern. Because in Switzerland three nationalities get on well together, are indeed quite exemplary in this respect, he wanted the thirteen nationalities of Austria to take example from Switzerland and live together in the same federal unity as do the three nationalities of Switzerland. Again and again he would come back to this theme. It was quite remarkable.

In Hausner's speeches there was irony, there was humour, there was logic—not always, but very often—and there was the panegyric on Switzerland. It was perfectly clear that this panegyric arose out of a pure feeling of sympathy; this feeling gripped hold of him; he wanted to say these things. And moreover he knew how to shape his speech so that no one, except a group of German-Liberals on the Left, was seriously provoked or offended by it.

It was most interesting to see how, when some Left Liberal member had spoken, Otto Hausner would get up to oppose him, and with his monocled eye never turn his gaze aside for a moment but pour upon the Left Wing a perfectly incredible torrent of abuse and scorn. There were men of importance and standing among them, but he spared none. And there was always breadth of view in what he said; he was one of the most cultured members of the Austrian Reichstag.

The karma of such a man may readily arouse interest. I took my start from this passion of his for returning again and again to praise of Switzerland, and further, from the fact that once in a speech subsequently published as a brochure, *German Culture and the German Empire*, he collected together in a spirit of impishness and yet at the same time with nothing short of genius, all there was to be said *for* German culture and the German people and *against* the German Empire. There was really something grandly prophetic about this speech that was made in the early eighties, scuttling the German Empire as it were, saying all manner of harsh things about it, calling it the wrecker and destroyer of the true being and nature of the Germans. That was the second thing—this singular 'loving hatred', if I may put it so, and 'hating love' for all that is truly German, and for the German Empire.

And the third thing was the extraordinary interest which made itself manifest when Hausner spoke of the Arlberg Tunnel, of the plan to build the Arlberg railway from Austria to Switzerland and thus unite Middle Europe with the West. Needless to say, here too he introduced his song of praise for Switzerland, for the railway was to run into Switzerland. But when he spoke of this railway—and his speech was well-seasoned, though delivered with perfect delicacy—one really had the feeling: the man is basing it all on tendencies and proclivities he must have acquired in some remarkable way in a former earthly life.

Everyone was talking in those days of the enormous advantages that would accrue to European civilisation from the alliance of Germany with Austria. At that very time Hausner was developing in the Austrian Parliament his idea of the Arlberg railway; he was saying, and naturally all the others were going for him hammer and tongs about it, that the Arlberg railway must be built, because a State as he pictured Austria, uniting thirteen nations after the pattern of Switzerland, must have a choice of allies; when it suits her, Austria has Germany, and when it suits her she must also have a strategic route from Middle Europe to the West, so that she may be able to have France for an ally when she wishes. Naturally, when such an opinion was expressed in the Austria of those times, it received short answer! It was reported that Hausner was ironed out flat! In truth, however, it was a marvellous speech, highly spiced and full of poignancy. And this speech, I would have you note, pointed in the direction of the West.

Holding these three things together in mind, I discovered that the individuality of Otto Hausner had wandered across Europe from West to East at the time when Gallus and Columbanus* were journeying in the same direction. He set out with men who had been inspired by the Irish initiation, for the purpose of bringing Christianity to those regions. In company with them, his aim was to carry Christianity to the East. On the way, somewhere in the neighbourhood of the Alsace of to-day, he found himself extraordinarily attracted by the relics of ancient Germanic paganism, by the old memories of the gods, the old forms of worship, the figures and statues of the gods that he found in Alsace, and also in Germany and Switzerland. He received all this into his heart and mind in a deeply significant way.

Afterwards there developed in him, on the one hand, a liking for the Germanic nature and, on the other hand a counterforce which came from the feeling that he had gone too far in that past life. He underwent a drastic inner change, an inner metamorphosis, and this showed itself in the wide and comprehensive outlook he possessed in this later incarnation. He could speak of the German people and culture and of the German Empire like one who has once had close and intimate contact with these things, and yet who feels all the time that he ought not to have been

* Not St. Columba, but a slightly younger Irish monk—St. Columbanus (sometimes called Columba the Younger).

influenced by them. He should have been spreading Christianity. He had come into these parts while his duty lay elsewhere.—One could hear it in the very tone of his speeches.—And he wanted to go back and make good again! Hence his passion for Switzerland; hence his passion for the building of the Arlberg railway. Even in outward appearance, he did not really look Polish. Hausner himself used often and often to say that he was not a Pole at all by physical descent but only by civilisation and education, and that 'Raetian-German' blood flowed in his veins. He had brought over from an earlier incarnation the tendency to look towards the region where once he had been, whither he had accompanied St. Columbanus and St. Gallus with the resolve to spread Christianity, but where, instead, the old Germanic religion and culture had captured him and held him fast. And so it came about that he did his best, as it were, to be born again in a family as little Polish as possible, far away from the land in which he had lived in his earlier life, far removed from it and yet so that he could look longingly towards it.

These are examples which I wanted to unfold before you to-day in order to show you how strange and remarkable is the path of karmic evolution.—In the next lecture we shall consider the question of how good and evil develop through successive incarnations of human beings, and through the course of history. By studying in this way the more important and significant examples that meet us in history, we shall be able to throw light on relationships belonging more to everyday life.

II

It is a little difficult to continue what has been given in the last lectures, because so many friends who have not taken part in these studies are here to-day. On the other hand it is hardly possible to make a new beginning, for many things contained in the previous lectures have still to be completed. Friends who have just arrived will have to realise that if some of our thoughts to-day prove somewhat difficult to understand, it is because they are connected—inwardly, though not outwardly—with preceding lectures. At Easter we shall have a self-contained course, but to-day I must continue what has gone before. We did not expect so many friends at this date, although needless to say we are extremely glad that they have come.

In recent lectures we have been speaking of definite karmic relationships—not with the object of finding anything sensational in the successive earthly lives we have studied, but in order to arrive step by step at a really concrete understanding of the connections of destiny in human life.

I have described successive earthly lives of certain historic figures, in order to call forth an idea of how one earthly life works on into the next—and that is not an easy matter.

Again and again it must be emphasised that a new trend has come into the Anthroposophical Movement since the Christmas Foundation Meeting at Dornach. Of this I should now like to say a few introductory words.—You know, my dear friends, that since the year 1918 there have been all manner of undertakings within the Anthroposophical Society. Their origin is clear. When the Anthroposophical Society was founded, this question was really being asked, out of a deep occult impulse: Would the Anthroposophical Society continue to evolve by virtue of the inner strength which (in its members) it had acquired until then? There was only one way to make the test. Until then, I, as General Secretary, had had the leadership of the German Section, which was the form in which the Anthroposophical Movement had existed within the Theosophical Society. The only way now was for me no longer to take in hand the leadership of the Anthroposophical Society but to watch and see how this Society would evolve through its own inherent strength.

You see, my dear friends, that is something quite different from what the position would have been if already at that time (as at our Christmas Foundation Meeting) I had said that I would undertake the leadership of the Society. For the Anthroposophical Society, if led by me, must naturally be an altogether different thing than if led by someone else. Moreover, for certain deep reasons, the Society might have been led all the better if I myself had not had the administrative leadership. Many things might have been done if human hearts had spoken—things which in fact remained undone, or which were even done from outside, often enough under resistance from the anthroposophists.

During the War, of course, we had little opportunity to unfold our forces in all directions. So it came about that after the year 1918, the prevailing state of affairs was taken advantage of by those from many quarters who wanted to do this or that. If I had said at the time, "No, these things shall not be done", then of course we should hear it said to-day: "If this or that had only been allowed, we should now have numbers of flourishing undertakings."

For this very reason it was the custom at all times for the leaders of occult movements to let those who wanted to do something try it out and see what became of it, so that convictions might be called forth by the facts themselves. For that is the only way to call forth conviction. And so it had to be in our case too.

The upshot of it all has been that since the year 1918, opposition to our Movement has grown rife, and has brought about the present state of affairs, when it is impossible for me, for instance, to give public lectures in Germany.

At the present moment these facts must in no way be concealed from the Anthroposophical Movement. We must face them with all clarity. As long as we work with unclear situations we shall make no progress.

As you know, all manner of experiments were made in the hope of being 'truly scientific'—shall we say? Quite naturally so, in view of the characters of those concerned! Scientists who also partake in our Society naturally like to be scientific. But that is the very thing that annoys our opponents. When we say to them, "As scientists we can prove this or that truth", they come forward with all their so-called scientific claims, and then of course they become furious. We should be under no illusions on this point. Nothing has annoyed our opponents more than the fact that our members have tried to speak on the same subjects as they themselves do, and in the same manner, only—as these our members often used to say—"letting a little Anthroposophy flow into it." It was precisely this which called forth our opponents in such overwhelming numbers.

Again, we offend most strongly against the life-conditions of Anthroposophy if we give ourselves up to the illusion that we can win over the adherents of various religious communities by saying the same or similar things as they, only once more "letting Anthroposophy flow into it."

But now, since the Christmas Foundation Meeting, an entirely new element must come into all that is being done in the field of Anthroposophy. Those of you who have observed the way Anthroposophy is now being presented here, or the way it was presented at Prague and again at Stuttgart, will have observed that impulses are now at work which call forth something altogether new, even where our opponents are concerned. If we try to be 'scientific' in the ordinary sense of the word—as, unfortunately, many of our members have tried to be—then we are presuming, so to speak, that it is possible to enter into discussion with them. But now take the lectures that have been given here, or the lectures at Prague, or the single lectures at Stuttgart—can you believe for a single moment that there can be any question of entering into discussion with our opponents on these matters? It goes without saying: we can enter into no discussion with our opponents when we speak of these things. How, for example, should we discuss with any representative of the civilisation of to-day the statement, for example, that the soul of Muavija appeared again in the soul of Woodrow Wilson?*

Thus in the whole Anthroposophical Movement there is now a prevailing quality which can tend to nothing else than this.—We must take it at last in real earnest that there can be no question of entering into discussion or argument with our opponents. For if we do so, it will in any case lead nowhere. Thus we must realise that, with regard to our opponents, it can only be a question of refuting calumnies, untruths and lies. We must not give up ourselves to the illusion that these things can be discussed. They must expand by their own inherent power; they cannot be decided by any dialectic.

Through the whole tenor of the Anthroposophical Movement as it has been since Christmas last, this will perhaps be realised increasingly, even by our members. Henceforth the Anthroposophical Movement will take this attitude: It will no longer pay heed to anything other than what the spiritual world itself requires of it.

It is from this standpoint that I have placed before you various thoughts on karma. Those of you who were here, or who heard my last lecture at Stuttgart, will remember that I tried to show how the individualities who lived in the 8th and 9th centuries A.D. at the Court of Haroun al Raschid in Asia, having continued to evolve after death in different directions, played certain definite parts in their new incarnations. At the time of the Thirty Years' War (and a short time before) we have on the one hand the individuality of Haroun al Raschid, reincarnated in the Englishman, Bacon of Verulam. And a great organiser at the Court of Haroun al

* See Vol. I, lecture X.

Raschid, who had lived at the Court—not indeed as an Initiate, but as the reincarnation of an Initiate—this individuality we found again as Amos Comenius, whose field of action was rather in Middle Europe. From these two streams, much in the spiritual part of modern civilisation flowed together. In the spiritual and intellectual aspect of modern civilisation, the Near East—as it was in the time immediately after Mohammed—lived again, on the one hand through the reincarnated Haroun al Raschid, Bacon of Verulam; and on the other hand through Amos Comenius, who had been his counsellor.

In the present lecture I wish to emphasise the following fact:—The evolution of man does not merely take place when he is here on earth, but also when he is between death and a new birth. Bacon as well as Amos Comenius, having fastened Arabism—so to speak from two different sides—on to the civilisation of Europe, died again and passed into the life between death and a new birth. And there they were together with many souls who came down to earth after their time. Bacon and Amos Comenius, having died in the 17th century, lived on in the spiritual world. Other souls, who came down to earth in the 19th century, were in the spiritual world together with the souls of Bacon and Amos Comenius from the 17th to the 19th. On the one hand there were souls who gathered mainly around the soul of Bacon—Bacon whose work became so dominant. Then there were the souls who gathered around Amos Comenius. And though this is rather a pictorial way of speaking, we must not forget that there are 'leaders' and 'followers'—albeit under quite different conditions—even in the spiritual world which men pass through between death and a new birth. Such individualities as Bacon or Amos Comenius worked not only through what they brought about on earth—through their writings, for example, or through the traditions of them which lived on on earth. No, these leading spirits were also working through the souls whom they sent down, or the souls with whom they were together and who were then sent down; they worked by causing certain tendencies to germinate in these souls in the spiritual world. Thus among the men of the 19th century we find souls who had become dependent already in their evolution in the pre-earthly life on one or other of these two spirits—the discarnate Amos Comenius, and the discarnate Bacon.

As I said, I want to lead you more and more into the concrete way in which karma works. Therefore I will now draw your attention to two personalities of the 19th century whose names will be known to most of you. One of them was especially influenced in his pre-earthly life by Bacon, and the other by Amos Comenius.

If we observe Bacon as he stood in earthly civilisation—in his earthly life as Lord Chancellor in England—if we observe him there, we find that his working was such that an Initiate stood behind him. The whole Bacon-Shakespeare controversy, as it is outwardly pursued by the historians of literature, is appallingly barren. All manner of arguments are brought forward which are supposed to show that Shakespeare the actor did not really write his dramas, but that they were written by Bacon the philosopher and Lord Chancellor, and so on . . .

All these things—working with external methods, seeking out similarities in the way of thought in Shakespeare's dramas and Bacon's philosophic works—all these are barren superficialities. They do not get at the real truth. For the truth is that at the time when Bacon, Shakespeare, Jacob Boehme, and a fourth were working on the earth, there was one Initiate who really spoke through all four. Hence their kinship, for in reality it all goes back to one and the same source. Of course, these people who dispute and argue do not argue about the Initiate who stood behind, especially as this Initiate—like many a modern Initiate—is described to us in history as a rather intolerable fellow. But he was not merely so. No doubt he was so sometimes in his external actions, but he was not merely so. He was an individuality from whom immense forces proceeded, and to whom were really due Bacon's philosophic works as well as

Shakespeare's dramas and the works of Jacob Boehme, and also the works of the Jesuit, Jacob Balde.

If we bear this in mind, then we must see in Bacon, in the philosophic realm, the instigator of an immense and far-reaching stream of the time.

It is most interesting to observe what could become of a soul who lived throughout the two centuries, in the life beyond the earth, under the influence of the dead Bacon. We must turn our attention to the way in which Bacon himself lived after his death. For our studies of human history it will in fact be more and more important to observe the human beings who have lived on earth not only until the moment of their death but in their working beyond death, where they work on and on upon those souls who are afterwards to descend to earth. This applies especially to those who have themselves been responsible for great spiritual achievements.

No doubt these things may be somewhat shocking for men of the present time. So for instance I remember—if I may make this digression—I remember on one occasion I was standing at the entrance to the railway station in a small German University town with a well-known doctor who went in a great deal for occultism. Around us stood many other people. Presently he warmed up to his subject and out of his enthusiasm said to me in a loud voice, so that many of those who were around could hear him: "I will make you a present of the biography of Robert Blum; but that is a biography which begins only after his death." Spoken loudly as it was, one could well observe the shock it gave to those who were standing around us! One cannot say without more ado to the people of to-day, "I will make you a present of the biography of a man, but it begins only after his death."

For the rest—apart from this two-volumed biography of Robert Blum, which begins not with his birth but with his death—little has yet been done in the way of relating the biographies of men after their death. Biographies generally begin at birth and end at death; there are not yet many works that begin with a man's death.

Yet, for the real happenings of the world, what a man

does after his death is immensely important, notably when he passes on the results of what he did on earth—translated into the spiritual—to the souls who come down after him. We cannot understand the age which succeeds a given age if we do not observe this side of life.

Now I was specially interested in observing those individualities who surrounded Bacon after his death. Among them were individualities who were subsequently born as natural scientists. But there were also others who were born as historians; and if we observe the influence of the dead Lord Bacon on these souls, we see how the materialism which he founded upon earth—the mere researching into the world of sense (for, as you know, everything else was for him an 'idol')—translated into the spiritual, reverts into a kind of radicalism. And so indeed, in the very midst of the spiritual world, these souls received impulses which worked on in such a way that after their birth, having descended to the earth, they would attach no value to anything that was not a concrete fact visible to the senses.

I will now speak in a somewhat popular form, but I beg you not to take my words too literally, for if you do so it will of course be only too easy to say: 'How grotesque!' Among these souls there were also some who, by their former tendencies—derived from former earthly lives—were destined to become historians. And among them was one who was the greatest. (I am still speaking of the pre-earthly lives of all these souls). One among them was the greatest. Under the influence of Lord Bacon's impulses, all these souls said to themselves, in effect: It is no longer permissible to write history as it was written in former times, to write it with Ideas, investigating the inner connections. Only the actual facts must now be the object of our research.

Now I ask you, what does this mean? Are not the intentions of men the most important thing in history?—and they are *not* outwardly real! These souls, however, no longer permitted themselves to think in this way; and least of all did the soul who afterwards appeared again as one of the greatest historians of the 19th century—*Leopold von Ranke*.

Leopold von Ranke was a pre-earthly disciple of Lord Bacon.

Study the earthly career of Leopold von Ranke as a historian. What is his principle? Ranke's principle as a historian is this: nothing must be written in history save what is to be read of in the archives. We must compile all history from the archives—from the actual transactions of the diplomats.

If you read Ranke you will find it so. He is a German and a Protestant, but with his sense of reality this has no effect on him. He works objectively—that is to say, with the objectivity of the archives. So he writes his History of the Popes—the best that has ever been written from the pure standpoint of archives. When we read Ranke we are irritated, nay dreadfully so. It is a barren prospect to imagine the old gentleman—quick and alert as he was until a ripe old age—sitting forever in the archives and merely piecing together the diplomatic transactions. That is no real history. It is history which reckons only with the facts of the sense-world—that is to say, for the historian, with the archives.

And so indeed, precisely by taking into account the life beyond the earth we have the possibility to understand why Ranke became what he was.

But now we can also look across to Amos Comenius, and observe how he worked on the pre-earthly willing of souls who afterwards descended to the earth. For just as Leopold von Ranke became the greatest disciple of Bacon—of Bacon after his death—so did *Schlosser* become the greatest disciple of Comenius after his death.

Read Schlosser's History; observe the prevailing tone, the fundamental note he strikes. On every page there speaks the moralist—the moralist who would fain seize the human heart and soul—whose object is to speak right into the heart. Often he scarcely succeeds, for he is still rather a pedant. He speaks, in effect, like a pedant speaking to the heart. Nevertheless, being a pre-earthly disciple of Amos Comenius, he has absorbed something of the quality that was in Comenius himself, who was so characteristic by virtue of the peculiar quality of his spirit. For after all, Comenius too came over from Mohammedanism. Though he was very different from the spirits who gathered around Lord Bacon, nevertheless Comenius too, in his incarnation as Comenius, concentrated on the real, outer world. Everywhere he demanded visibility, objectivity, in education. There must always be an underlying picture. He demands vision—object lessons, as it were; he too lays stress on the sense-perceptible, though in quite another way. For Amos Comenius was also one of those who at the time of the Thirty Years' War believed most enthusiastically in the coming of the so-called Millennium. In his *Pansophia* he wrote down great and world-embracing ideas. He wanted to work for human education by a great impulsive power. This too worked on Schlosser. It is there in Schlosser.

I mention these two figures—Ranke and Schlosser—in order to show you how we can understand what appears as the spiritually productive power in man only if we also take into account his life beyond the earth. Only then do we understand it—just as we have also learnt to understand many things by taking into account repeated lives on earth. For in the thoughts which I have recently placed before you, we have observed this marvellous working across from one incarnation to another. As I said, I give these examples in order that we may then consider how a man can think about his own karma. Before we can dwell on the way in which good and evil—or illnesses or the like—work over from one incarnation to another, we must first learn to perceive how that which afterwards emerges in the spiritual and intellectual life of civilisation also works across from one incarnation to another.

Now my dear friends, I must admit that for me one of the most interesting personalities in modern spiritual life, with regard to his karma, was *Conrad Ferdinand Meyer*. Anyone who observes him closely will see that his most beautiful works depend on a peculiar fact, namely this: Again and again, in his whole human constitution, there was a kind of tendency for the Ego and astral body to flee from the physical and the etheric bodies.

Morbid conditions appear in Conrad Ferdinand Meyer, bordering very nearly on dementia. But these morbid conditions only express in a rather more extreme form what was always present in him in a nascent state. His soul-and-spirit tends to go out—holds to the physical and etheric only by a very loose thread. And in this condition—the soul-and-spirit holding to the physical and etheric by a very loose thread only—the most beautiful of his works originate; I mean the most beautiful of his longer works and of his shorter poems too. Conrad Ferdinand Meyer's most beautiful poems may even be said to have originated half out of the body. There was a peculiar relationship between the four members of his nature. Truly there is a great difference between such a personality and an average man of the present time. With an average man of this materialistic age we generally find a very firm and robust connection of the soul-and-spirit with the physical and etheric. The soul-and-spirit is deeply immersed in the physical and etheric—'sits tight', as it were. But in Conrad Ferdinand Meyer it was not so. He had a very tender relation of the soul-and-spirit to the physical and etheric. To describe his psyche is really one of the most interesting tasks one can undertake when studying the developments of modern spiritual life. Many things that emerge in Conrad Ferdinand Meyer appear almost like a dim, cloudy recollection—a recollection which has however grown beautiful in growing dim. When Conrad Ferdinand Meyer writes we always have the feeling: He is remembering something, though not quite exactly. He changes it—but changes it into something beautiful and form-perfected. We can observe this wonderfully, piece by piece, in certain of his works.

Now it is characteristic of the inner karma of a human being when there is such a definite relationship of the four members of his nature—physical body, etheric body, astral body and Ego. And in Conrad Ferdinand Meyer's case, when we trace back this peculiarly intimate connection, we are led, first of all, to the time of the Thirty Years' War. This was the first thing clear to me in his case: there is something of a former earthly life at the time of the Thirty Years' War. And then there is a still earlier life on earth going back into the pre-Carlovingian age, going back quite evidently into the early history of Italy.

When we endeavour to trace Conrad Ferdinand Meyer's karma, the peculiar, intangible fluidity of his being (which none the less expresses itself in such perfection of form)—the peculiar, intangible fluidity of his life somehow communicates itself to our investigation, until at length we feel: We are getting into confusion. I have no other alternative but to describe these things just as they happened in the investigation.

We go back into the time of the 6th century in Italy. There we have the feeling: We are getting into an extraordinarily insecure element. We are driven back again and again, and only gradually we observe that this is not due to ourselves but to the object of our research. There is really in the soul—in the individuality—of Conrad Ferdinand Meyer something that brings us into confusion as we try to investigate him. We are driven to return again and again into his present incarnation or into the one immediately before it. Again and again we must 'pull ourselves up' and go back again.

The following was the result.—You must remember, all that has lived in a human soul in former incarnations becomes manifest in the most varied forms—in likenesses which are often quite imperceptible to outer observation. This you will have seen from other instances of reincarnation given here.

So at length we come to an incarnation in Italy in the early Christian centuries—at the end of the first half of the first millennium A.D. Here we come to a halt. We find a soul living in Italy, to a large extent at Ravenna, at the Roman Court. But now we come into confusion. For we must ask ourselves: What was living in that soul? The moment we ask ourselves this question (in order to call forth the further occult investigation), the whole thing is extinguished once again.

We become aware of the experiences which this soul underwent while living at the Court at Ravenna—at the Roman Court. We enter into these experiences and we think we have them, and then again they are extinguished—blotted out from us; and we are driven back again to Conrad Ferdinand Meyer as he lived on earth in the immediate past. At length we perceive that in this later life he obliterates from our vision the content of his soul in the former life. Only after long trouble do we perceive at length how the matter really stands. Conrad Ferdinand Meyer—or rather the individuality who lived in him—was living at that time in a certain relationship to one of the Popes who sent him, among others, to England on a Roman Catholic, Christian Mission.

The individuality who afterwards became Conrad Ferdinand Meyer had first absorbed all that wonderful sense of form which it was possible to absorb in Italy at that time. The Mosaic art of Italy bears witness to it; also the old Italian painting, the greater part, nay practically the whole of which has been destroyed. This art did not continue.

And then he went on a Roman Catholic Christian Mission to the Anglo-Saxons. One of his companions founded the Bishopric of Canterbury. What afterwards took place at Canterbury began essentially with this foundation. The individuality, however, who afterwards appeared as Conrad Ferdinand Meyer, was only there as a witness, so to speak. Nevertheless, he was a very active person, and he called forth the ill-will of an Anglo-Saxon chieftain, at whose instigation he was eventually murdered. That is what we find to begin with.

But while he lived in England there was something in the soul of this Conrad Ferdinand Meyer which robbed him of real joy in life. His soul was deeply rooted in the Italian art of his time—or, if we will call it so, in the Italian spiritual life. He gained no happiness in the execution of his missionary work in England. Yet he devoted himself to it with great intensity—so much so that his assassination was a reaction to it.

This constant unhappiness—being repelled from something which he was none the less doing with all force and devotion out of another impulse in his heart—worked on in such a way that when he passed through his next earthly life there ensued a cosmic clouding-over of his memory. The inner impulse was there but it no longer coincided with any clear concept.

And so it came about that in his subsequent incarnation as Conrad Ferdinand Meyer, an undefined impulse was at work in him, to this effect: 'I was once working in England. It is connected somehow with Canterbury. I was murdered owing to my connection with Canterbury.'

So indeed the outer life of Conrad Ferdinand Meyer in this incarnation takes its course. He studies outer history, he studies Canterbury, studies what happened in Canterbury, in connection with the history of England. He comes across Thomas à Becket, Chancellor of King Henry II in the 12th century. He learns of the strange destiny of Thomas à Becket, who from being the all-powerful Chancellor of Henry II, was murdered virtually at his instigation. And so in this present incarnation as Conrad Ferdinand Meyer, his own half-forgotten destiny appears to him in Thomas à Becket. It comes before him, half-forgotten in his subconsciousness, for I am speaking of course, of the subconscious life which comes to the surface in this way. So he describes his own fate in a far distant time. But he describes it in the story of what actually happened in the 12th century between King Henry II and Thomas à Becket of Canterbury, whose fate he recounts in his poetic work *Der Heilige* (The Saint). So indeed it is—only all this takes place in the subconscious life which embraces successive incarnations. It is as though within a single earthly life a man had experienced something in his early youth in connection with a certain place. He has forgotten it. He experienced it maybe in the second or third year of his life. It does not emerge, but some other similar destiny emerges. The very same place is named, and as a result he has a peculiar sympathy for this other person's destiny. He feels it differently from one who has no 'association of ideas' with the same place.

Just as this may happen within one earthly life, so it took place in the concrete instance I am now giving you. There was the work in Canterbury, the murder of a person connected with Canterbury (for Thomas à Becket was Archbishop of Canterbury), the murder of Thomas à Becket at the instigation of the King of England. All of these schemes work in together. In the descriptions in his poem he is describing his own destiny.

But now the thing goes on—and this is most interesting in Conrad Ferdinand Meyer's case. He was born as a woman about the time of the Thirty Years' War—a lively woman, full of spiritual interest in life, a woman who witnessed many an adventure. She married a man who first took part in all the confused events of the Thirty Years' War, but then grew weary of them and emigrated to Switzerland, to Graubünden (Canton Grisons), where he lived a somewhat philistine existence. But his wife was deeply affected and impressed by all that took place in the Graubünden country under the prevailing conditions of the Thirty Years' War.

This too is eclipsed, as though with another layer. For it is so with this individuality: That which is living in him is easily forgotten in the cosmic sense, and yet he calls it forth again in a transmuted form, where it becomes more glorious and more intense. For out of what this woman observed and experienced in that incarnation there arises the wonderful characterisation of *Jürg Jenatsch*, the man of Graubünden, in Conrad Ferdinand Meyer's historic novel. Observing Conrad Ferdinand Meyer in this incarnation, we have indeed no explanation of his peculiarity if we cannot enter into his karma. I must say—speaking with a grain of salt—that I envy the people who 'understand' him so light-heartedly. Before I knew his reincarnations, all that I understood was that I did not understand him. This wonderful inner perfection of form, this inner joy in form, this purity of form, all the strength and power that lives in *Jürg Jenatsch*, and the wonderful personal and living quality in *The Saint*,—a good deal of superficiality is needed to imagine that one understands all this. Observe his beautiful forms—there is something of clear line in them, almost severe; they are painted and yet not painted. Here live the mosaics of Ravenna. And in *The Saint* there lives a history which was undergone once upon a time by this individuality himself; but a mist of the soul has spread over it, and out of the mist it emerges in another form.

And again one needs to know: All that is living in his romance of Graubünden, *Jürg Jenatsch*, was absorbed by the heart and mind of a woman; while in the momentum, the driving power that lives in this romance there lives again the swashbuckler of the Thirty Years' War. The man was pretty much of a philistine, as I said, but he *was* a swashbuckler. And so, all that comes over from former experiences on earth comes to life again in a peculiar form in Conrad Ferdinand Meyer. Only now do we begin to understand him. Now we say to ourselves: In olden times of human evolution, men were not ashamed to speak of Spirits from beyond descending to the earth, or of earthly human beings finding their way upward and working on from spiritual worlds. All this must come again, otherwise man will not get beyond his present outlook of the earthworm. For all that the natural-scientific conception of the world contains, it is the world-outlook of the earth-worm. Men live on earth as though only the earth concerned them, as though it were not true that the whole Cosmos works upon all earthly things and lives again in man. As though it were not true that earlier epochs of history live on, inasmuch as we ourselves carry into later times what we absorbed in former times.

We do not understand karma by talking theoretic concepts about successive earthly incarnations. To understand karma is to feel in our hearts all that we *can* feel when we see what existed ages ago flowing into the later epochs in the souls of men themselves. When we begin to see how karma works, human life gains quite a new content. We feel ourselves quite differently in human life.

Such a spirit as Conrad Ferdinand Meyer feels his former earthly lives like an undertone—an undertone that sounds from far away. We understand what appears in him only when we develop an understanding for this undertone. The progress of mankind in spiritual life will depend on its ability to regard life in this way, to observe in all detail what flows across from former epochs of the world's evolution into later epochs through the human beings themselves. Then we shall cease, in the childish way of psycho-analysts, to explain the peculiarities of souls by speaking of 'hidden underlying regions' and the like. After all, one can ascribe anything one likes to what is 'hidden'. We shall look for the real causes. In some respects, no doubt, the psycho-analysts do quite good work. But these pursuits remind us of the story of how someone heard that in the year 1749 a son was born to a certain patrician. Afterwards this son emerged as a very gifted man. To this day we can point to the actual birth-place in Frankfurt of the man who afterwards came forth as Wolfgang Goethe. 'Let us make excavations in the earth and see by dint of what strange emanations his talents came about'. Sometimes the psycho-analysts seem to me just like that. They dig into the earth-realm of the soul, into the hidden regions which they themselves first invent by their hypotheses, whereas in reality one ought to look into the preceding lives on earth and lives between death and a new birth. Then if we do so, a true understanding of human souls is opened out to us. Truly the souls of men are far too rich in content to enable us to understand their content out of a single life alone.

III

I should like during these few days to say something rather especially for the friends who have come here to attend the Easter Course,* and who have not heard much of what has been given in recent lectures here on the subject of karmic connections. Those who were present at the lectures before Easter may find some repetitions but the circumstances make this inevitable.

I have been laying particular emphasis on the fact that study of the historical development of the life of mankind must lead on to study of the human being himself. All our endeavours aim in the direction of placing man at the centre of our study of the world. Two ends are attained thereby. Firstly, it is only in this way that the world can be studied as it truly is. For all that man sees spread around him in nature is only a part—gives as it were one picture of the world only: and to limit study of the world to this realm of nature is like studying a plant without looking beyond root, green leaf and stem, and ignoring flower and fruit. This kind of study can never reveal the whole plant. Imagine a creature that is always born at a particular time of the year, lives out its life during a period when the plant grows as far as the green leaves and no further, dies before the plant is in blossom and appears again only when roots and green leaves are there.—Such a creature would never have knowledge of the whole plant; it would regard the plant as something that has roots and leaves only.

The materialistic mind of to-day has got itself into a similar position as regards its approach to the world. It considers only the broad foundations of life, not what blossoms forth from the totality of earthly evolution and

* *Easter as a Chapter in the Mystery-Wisdom of Man.* Dornach, 19th–22nd April, 1924.

earthly existence—namely, man himself. The real way of approach must be to study nature in her full extent, but in such a way as all the time to realise that she must needs create man out of herself. We shall then see man as the microcosm he truly is, as the concentration of all that is to be found outspread in the far spaces of the cosmos.

As soon, however, as we study history from this point of view, we are no longer able to regard the human being as a resultant of the forces of history, as a single, self-contained being. We must take account of the fact that he passes through different earthly lives: one such life occurs at an earlier time and another at a later. This very fact places man at the centre of our studies, but now in his whole being, as an individuality. This is the one end that is attained when we look in this way at nature and at history.

The other is this.—The very fact of placing man at the centre of study, makes for humility. Lack of humility is due to nothing else than lack of knowledge. A penetrating, comprehensive knowledge of man in his connection with the events of the world and of history will certainly not lead to excessive self-esteem; far rather it will lead the human being to look at himself objectively. It is precisely when a man does not know himself that there rise up in him those feelings which have their source in the unknown regions of his being. Instinctive, emotional impulses make themselves felt. And it is these instinctive, emotional impulses, rooted as they are in the subconscious, that make for arrogance and pride. On the other hand, when consciousness penetrates farther and farther into those regions where man comes to know himself and to recognise how in the sequence of historical events he belongs to the whole wide universe—then, simply by virtue of an inner law, humility will unfold in him. The recognition of his place in universal existence invariably calls forth humility, never arrogance. All genuine study pursued in Anthroposophy has its ethical side, carries with it an ethical impulse.

Unlike modern materialism, Anthroposophy will not lead to a conception of life in which ethics and morality are a mere adjunct; ethics and morality emerge, as if inwardly impelled, from all genuine anthroposophical study.

I want now to show you by concrete examples, how the fruits of earlier epochs of history are carried over into later epochs through human beings themselves. A certain very striking example now to be given, is associated with Switzerland.

Our gaze falls upon a man who lived about a hundred years before the founding of Christianity.—I am relating to you what can be discovered through spiritual scientific investigation.—At this period in history we find a personality who is a kind of slave overseer in southern Europe.

We must not associate with a slave overseer of those times the feelings that the word immediately calls up in us now. Slavery was the general custom in days of antiquity, and at the time of which I am speaking it was essentially mild in form; the overseers were usually educated men. Indeed the teachers of important personages might well be slaves, who were often versed in the literary and scientific culture of the time. So you see, we must acquire sounder ideas about slavery—needless to say, without defending it in the least degree—when we are considering this aspect of the life of antiquity.

We find, then, a personality whose calling it is to be in charge of a number of slaves and to apportion their tasks. He is an extraordinarily lovable man, gentle and kind-hearted and when he is able to have his own way he does everything to make life easier for the slaves. In authority over him, however, is a rough, somewhat brutal personality. This man is, as we should say nowadays, his superior officer. And this superior officer is responsible for many things that arouse resentment and animosity in the slaves. When the personality of whom I am speaking—the slave overseer—passes through the gate of death, he is surrounded in the time between death and a new birth by all the souls who were thus united with him on earth, the souls of the slaves who had been in his charge. But as an individuality he is very strongly connected with the one who was his superior officer.

The fact that he, as the slave overseer, was obliged to obey this superior officer—for in accordance with the prevailing customs of the time he always did obey him, though often very unwillingly—this fact established a strong karmic tie between them. But a deep karmic tie was also established by the relationship that had existed in the physical world between the overseer and the slaves, for in many respects he had been their teacher as well.

We must thus picture a further life unfolding between death and rebirth among all these individualities of whom I have spoken.

Afterwards, somewhere about the 9th century A.D., the individuality of the slave overseer is born again, in Central Europe, but now as a woman, and moreover, because of the prevailing karmic connection, as the wife of the former superior officer who reincarnated as a man. The two of them live together in a marital relationship that makes karmic compensation for the tie that had been established away back in the first century before the founding of Christianity, when they had lived as subordinate and superior officers respectively. The superior officer is now, in the 9th century A.D., in a commune in Central Europe where the inhabitants live on very intimate terms with one another; he holds some kind of official position in the commune, but he is everyone's servant and comes in for plenty of knocks and abuse.

Investigating the whole matter further, we find that the members of this rather extensive commune are the slaves who once had their tasks allotted to them in the way I told you. The superior officer has now become as it were the servant of them all, and has to experience the karmic fulfilment of many things which, through the instrumentality of the overseer, his brutality inflicted upon these people.

The wife of this man (she is the reincarnated overseer), suffers with a kind of silent resignation under all the impressions made by the ever-discontented superior officer in his new incarnation, and one can follow in detail how karmic destiny is here being fulfilled.

But we see, too, that this karma is by no means completely adjusted. A part only is adjusted, namely the karmic relationship between the slave overseer and his superior officer. This has been lived out and is essentially finished in the medieval incarnation in the 9th century; for the wife has paid off what her soul had experienced owing to the brutality of the man who had once been the superior officer and is now her husband.

This woman, the reincarnation of the former slave overseer, is born again, and what happens now is that the greater number of the souls who had once been slaves and had then come together again in the large commune—souls in whose destiny this individuality had twice played a part—came again as the children whose education this same individuality in his new incarnation has deeply at heart. For in this incarnation he comes as *Pestalozzi*. And we see how Pestalozzi's infinite humanitarianism, his enthusiasm for education in the 18th century, is the karmic fulfilment in relation to human beings with whom he had already twice been connected—the karmic fulfilment of the experiences and the sufferings of earlier incarnations.

What comes to view in single personalities can be clear and objectively intelligible to us only when we are able to see the present earthly life against the background of earlier earthly lives.

Traits that go back not merely to the previous incarnation, but often to the one before that, and even earlier, sometimes show themselves in a man. We see how what has been planted, as it were, in the single incarnations, works its way through with a certain inner, spiritual necessity, inasmuch as the human being lives not only through earthly lives but also through lives between death and a new birth.

In this connection, the study of a life of which I spoke to those of you who were in Dornach before Easter, is particularly striking and interesting—the life of *Conrad Ferdinand Meyer*.

Conrad Ferdinand Meyer presents a very special enigma to those who study the inner aspect of his life and at the same time greatly admire him as a poet. There is such wonderful harmony of form and style in his poems that we cannot help saying: what lives in Conrad Ferdinand Meyer always hovers a little above the earthly—in respect of the style and also in respect of the whole way of thinking and feeling. And if we steep ourselves in his writings we shall perceive how he is immersed in an element of spirit-and-soul that is always on the point of breaking away from the physical body. Study the nobler poems, also the prose-poems, of Conrad Ferdinand Meyer and you will say to yourselves: There is evidence of a perpetual urge to get right away from connection with the physical body. As you know, in his incarnation as Conrad Ferdinand Meyer, it was his lot to fall into pathological states, when the soul-and-spirit separated from the physical body to a high degree, so much so that insanity ensued, or at any rate conditions resembling insanity. And the strange thing is that his most beautiful works were produced during periods when the soul-and-spirit had loosened from the physical body.

Now when we try to investigate the karmic connections running through the life of Conrad Ferdinand Meyer, we are driven into a kind of confusion. We cannot immediately find our bearings. We are led, first, to the 6th century A.D., and then again we are thrown back into the 19th, into the Conrad Ferdinand Meyer incarnation. The very circumstances we are observing, mislead us. I want you to realise the extraordinary difficulty of a genuine search for knowledge in this domain. If you are satisfied with phantasy, then it is naturally easy, for you can make things fit in as you like. For one who is not satisfied with phantasy but carries his investigation to the point where he can rely upon the faculties of his own soul not to play him false—for him it is no easy matter, especially when he is investigating these things in connection with an individuality as complex as that of Conrad Ferdinand Meyer. In investigating karmic connections through a number of earthly lives it is no great help to look at the particularly outstanding characteristics. What strikes you most forcibly in a man, what you see at once when you meet him or learn of him in history—these characteristics are, for the most part, the outcome of his earthly environment. A man as he confronts us is a product of his earthly environment to a far greater extent than is generally believed. He takes in through education what is present in his earthly environment. It is the more intangible, more intimate traits of a man which taken quite concretely, lead back through the life between death and a new birth into former earthly lives.

In these investigations it may be more important to observe a man's gestures or some habitual mannerism than to consider what he has achieved perhaps as a figure of renown. The mannerisms of a person, or the way he will invariably answer you—not so much *what* he answers but *how* he answers—whether, for example, his first tendency is always to be negative and only when he has no other alternative, to agree, or whether again in quite a good-humoured way he is rather boastful . . . these are the kind of traits that are important and if we pay special attention to them they become the centre of our observations and disclose a great deal. One observes, for instance, how a man stretches out his hand to take hold of things; one makes an objective picture of it and then works upon it in the manner of an artist; and at length one finds that it is no longer the mere gesture that one is contemplating, but around the gesture the figure of another human being takes shape.

The following may happen.—There are men who have a habit, let us say, of making a certain movement of the arms. I have known men who simply could not begin to do anything without first folding their arms. If one visualises such a gesture quite objectively, but with inner, artistic feeling, so that it stands before one as a plastic, pliable form, then one's attention is directed away from the man who is actually making the gesture. But the gesture does not remain as it is; it grows into another figure which is an indication, at least, of something in the previous incarnation or in the one before that. It may well be that the gesture is now used in connection with something that was not present at all in the previous incarnation—let us say it is a gesture used in picking up a book, or some similar action. Nevertheless, it is for gestures and habits of this kind that we must have an eye if we are to keep on the right track.

Now in the case of an individuality like Conrad Ferdinand Meyer, the point of significance is that while he is creating his poems there is always a tendency to a loosening of the soul-and-spirit from the physical body. There we have a starting-point but at the same time a point where we may easily go astray.

We are led, as I told you, to the 6th century A.D. We have the feeling: that is where he belongs. And moreover we find a personality who lived in Italy, who experienced a very varied destiny in that incarnation in Italy, who indeed lived a kind of double existence. On the one side he was devoted with the greatest enthusiasm to an art that has almost disappeared in this later age, but was then in its prime; it is only in the remaining examples of mosaics that we are still able to glimpse this highly developed art. And the individuality to whom we are first impelled, lived in this milieu of art in Italy at the end of the 5th and the beginning of the 6th century A.D.—That is what presents itself, to begin with.

But now this whole picture is obscured, and again we are thrown back to Conrad Ferdinand Meyer. The darkness that obscures vision of the man of the 6th century now overshadows the picture of Conrad Ferdinand Meyer in the 19th; and we are compelled to look very closely into what Conrad Ferdinand Meyer does in the 19th century.

Our attention is then drawn to the fact that his tale *Der Heilige* (The Saint), deals with Thomas à Becket, the Chancellor of Henry II of England. We feel that here is something of peculiar importance. And we also have the feeling that the impression received from the earlier incarnation has driven us up against this particular deed of Conrad Ferdinand Meyer. But now again we are driven back into the 6th century, and can find there no explanation of this. And so we are thrown to and fro between the two incarnations, the problematic one in the 6th century and the Conrad Ferdinand Meyer incarnation—until it dawns upon us that the story of Thomas à Becket as told in history, came up in Conrad Ferdinand Meyer's mind owing to a certain similarity with an experience he had himself undergone in the 6th century, when he went to England from Italy as a member of a Catholic mission sent by Pope Gregory. There we have the second aspect of Conrad Ferdinand Meyer in his previous incarnation. On the one side he was an enthusiastic devotee of the art that subsequently took the form of mosaic.—Hence his talent for form, in all its aspects. On the other side, however, he was an impassioned advocate of Catholicism, and for this reason accompanied the mission. The members of this mission founded Canterbury, where the bishopric was then established.

The individuality who afterwards lived in the 19th century as Conrad Ferdinand Meyer was murdered by an Anglo-Saxon courtier, in circumstances that are extraordinarily interesting. There was something of legal subtlety and craftiness, albeit still in the rough, about the events connected at that time with the murder.

You know very well, my dear friends, how even in ordinary life the sound of something remains with you. You may once have heard a name without paying any particular attention to it . . . but later on a whole association of ideas is called up in your mind when this name is mentioned. In a similar way, through the peculiar circumstances of this man's connection with what later became the archbishopric of Canterbury—the town of Canterbury, as I said, was founded by the mission of which he was a member—these experiences lived on, lived on, actually, in the sound of the name Canterbury. In the Conrad Ferdinand Meyer incarnation the sound of this name—Canterbury—came to life again, and by association of ideas his attention was called to Thomas à Becket, (the Lord Chancellor of Canterbury under Henry Plantagenet) who was treacherously murdered. At first, Thomas à Becket was a favourite of Henry II, but was afterwards murdered, virtually through the instigation of the King, because he would not agree to certain measures.

These two destinies, alike in some respects and unlike in

others, brought it about that Conrad Ferdinand Meyer transposed, as it were, into quite different figures taken from history, what he had himself experienced in an earlier incarnation in the 6th century—experienced in his own body, far from what was at that time his native land. Just think how interesting this is! Once we have grasped it, we are no longer driven hither and thither between the two incarnations. And then, because again in the 19th century, Conrad Ferdinand Meyer has a kind of double nature, we see how his soul-and-spirit easily separates from the physical. Because he has this double nature, the place of his own, actual experiences is taken by another experience in some respects similar to it . . . just as pictures often change in the play of human imagination. In a man's ordinary imagination during an earthly life, the picture changes in such a way that imagination weaves in freedom; in the course of many earthly lives it may be that some historical event which is connected with the person in question as a picture only, takes the place of the actual event.

Now this individuality whose experience in an earlier life worked on through two lives between death and rebirth and then came to expression in the story *Thomas à Becket, the Saint*,—this individuality had had another intermediate earthly life as a woman at the time of the Thirty Years' War. We have only to envisage the chaos prevailing all over Central Europe during the Thirty Years' War and it will not be difficult to understand the feelings and emotions of an impressionable, sensitive woman living in the midst of the chaos as the wife of a pedantic, narrow-minded man. Wearying of life in the country that was afterwards Germany, he emigrated to Graubünden in Switzerland, where he left the care of house and home to his wife, while he spent his time sullenly loafing about. His wife, however, had opportunity to observe many, many things. The wider historical perspective, no less than the curious local conditions at Graubünden, worked upon her; the experiences she underwent, experiences that were always coloured by her life with the bourgeois, commonplace husband, again sank down into the foundations of the individuality, and lived on through the life between death and a new birth. And the experiences of the wife at the time of the Thirty Years' War are imaginatively transformed in Conrad Ferdinand Meyer's tale, *Jürg Jenatsch.*

Thus in the soul of Conrad Ferdinand Meyer we have something that has gathered together out of the details of former incarnations. As a man of letters, Conrad Ferdinand Meyer seems to be an individuality complete in itself, for he is an artist with very definite and fixed characteristics. But in point of fact it is this that actually causes confusion, because one's attention is immediately directed away from these very definite characteristics to the elusive, double nature of the man.

Those who have eyes only for Conrad Ferdinand Meyer the poet, the famous author of all these works, will never come to know anything of his earlier lives. We have to look through the poet to the man; and then, in the background of the picture, there appear the figures of the earlier incarnations.

Paradoxical as it will seem to the modern mind, the only way in which human life can be understood in its deeper aspect is to centre our study of the course of world-events around observation of man himself in history. And man cannot be taken as belonging to one age of time only, as living in one earthly life only. In considering man, we must realise how the individuality passes from one earthly life to another, and how in the interval between death and a new birth he works upon and transforms that which has taken its course more in the subconscious realm of earthly life but for all that is connected with the actual shaping of the destiny. For the shaping of destiny takes place, not in the clear consciousness of the intellect, but in what weaves in the subconscious.

Let me now give you another example of how things work over in history through human individualities themselves.

In the first century A.D., about a hundred years after the founding of Christianity, we have an exceedingly significant

Roman writer in the person of *Tacitus*. In all his work, and very particularly in his 'Germania', Tacitus proves himself a master of a concise, clear-cut style; he arrays the facts of history and geographical details in wonderfully rounded sentences with a genuinely epigrammatic ring. We may also remember how he, a man of wide culture, who knew everything considered worth knowing at that time—a hundred years after the founding of Christianity—makes no more than a passing allusion to Christ, mentioning Him as someone whom the Jews crucified but saying that this was of no great importance. Yet in point of fact, Tacitus is one of the greatest Romans.

Tacitus had a friend, the personality known in history as *Pliny the Younger*, himself the author of a number of letters and an ardent admirer of Tacitus.

To begin with, let us consider Pliny the Younger. He passes through the gate of death, through the life between death and a new birth, and is born again in the 11th century as a Countess of Tuscany in Italy, who is married to a Prince of Central Europe. The Prince has been robbed of his lands by Henry the Black of the Frankish-Salic dynasty and wants to secure for himself an estate in Italy. This Countess Beatrix owns the Castle of Canossa where, later on, Henry IV, the successor of Henry III the Black, was forced to make his famous penance to Pope Gregory.

Now this Countess Beatrix is an extraordinarily alert and active personality, taking keen interest in all the conditions and circumstances of the time. Indeed she cannot help being interested, for Henry III who had driven her husband, Gottfried, out of Alsace into Italy before his marriage to her, continued his persecution. Henry is a man of ruthless energy, who overthrows the Princes and Chieftains in his neighbourhood one after the other, does whatever he has a mind to do, and is not content when he has persecuted someone once, but does it a second time, when the victim has established himself somewhere else.—As I said, he was a man of ruthless vigour, a 'great' man in the medieval style of greatness. And when Gottfried had established himself in

Tuscany, Henry was not content with having driven him out but proceeded to take the Countess back with him to Germany.

All these happenings gave the Countess an opportunity of forming a penetrating view of conditions in Italy, as well as of those in Germany. In her we have a person who is strongly representative of the time in which she lives, a woman of keen observation, vitality and energy, combined with largeness of heart and breadth of vision.

When, later on, Henry IV was forced to go on his journey of penance to Canossa, Beatrix's daughter Mathilde had become the owner of the Castle. Mathilde was on excellent terms with her mother whose qualities she had inherited, and was, in fact, the more gifted of the two. They were splendid women who because of all that had happened under Henry III and Henry IV, took a profound interest in the history of the times.

Investigation of these personalities leads to this remarkable result: the Countess Beatrix is the reincarnated Pliny the Younger, and her daughter Mathilde is the reincarnated Tacitus. Thus Tacitus, a *writer* of history in olden times, is now an *observer* of history on a wide scale—(when a woman has greatness in her she is often wonderfully gifted as an observer)—and not only an observer but a direct participant in historical events. For Mathilde is actually the owner of Canossa, the scene of issues that were immensely decisive in the Middle Ages. We find the former Tacitus now as an observer of history.

A deep intimacy develops between these two—mother and daughter—and their former work in the field of authorship enables them to grasp historical events with great perspicacity; subconsciously and instinctively they become closely linked with the world-process, as it takes its course in nature as well as in history.

And now, still later on, the following takes place.—Pliny the Younger, who in the Middle Ages was the Countess Beatrix, is born again in the 19th century, in a milieu of romanticism. He absorbs this romanticism—one cannot exactly say with enthusiasm, but with aesthetic pleasure. He has on the one hand this love for the romantic, and on the other—due to his family connections—a rather academic style; he finds his way into an academic style of writing. It is not, however, in line with his character. He is always wanting to get out of it, always wanting to discard this style.

This personality (the reincarnated Pliny the Younger and the Countess Beatrix) happens on one occasion brought about by destiny, to be visiting a friend, and takes up a book lying on the table, an English book. He is fascinated by its style and at once feels: The style I have had up till now and that I owe to my family relationships, does not really belong to me. This is *my* style, this is the style I need. It is wonderful; I must acquire it at all costs.

As a writer he becomes an imitator of this style—I mean, of course, an artistic imitator in the best sense, not a pedantic one—an imitator of this style in the artistic, aesthetic sense of the word. And do you know, the book he opened at that moment, reading it right through as quickly as he possibly could and then afterwards reading everything he could find of the author's writings—this book was Emerson's *Representative Men*. And the person in question adopted its style, immediately translated two essays from it, conceived a deep veneration for the author, and was never content until he was able to meet him in real life.

This man, who really only now found himself, who for the first time found the style that belonged to him in his admiration for the other—this reincarnation of Pliny the Younger and of the Countess Beatrix, is none other than *Herman Grimm*. And in *Emerson* we have to do with the reincarnated Tacitus, the reincarnated Countess Mathilde.

When we observe Herman Grimm's admiration for Emerson, when we remember the way in which Herman Grimm encounters Emerson, we can find again the relationship of Pliny the Younger to Tacitus. In every sentence that Herman Grimm writes after this time, we can see the old relationship between Pliny the Younger and Tacitus emerging. And we see the admiration that Pliny the Younger had for Tacitus, nay more, the complete accord and understanding between them, coming out again in the admiration with which Herman Grimm looks up to Emerson.

And now for the first time we shall grasp wherein the essential greatness of Emerson's style consists, we shall perceive that what Tacitus displayed in his own way, Emerson again displays in his own special way. How does Emerson work? Those who visited Emerson discovered his way of working. There he was in a room; around him were several chairs, several tables. Books lay open everywhere and Emerson walked about among them. He would often read a sentence, imbibe it thoroughly and from it form his own magnificent, free-moving, epigrammatic sentences. That was how he worked. There you have an exact picture of Tacitus in life! Tacitus travels, takes hold of life everywhere; Emerson observes life in *books*. It all lives again!

And then there is this unconquerable desire in Herman Grimm to meet Emerson. Destiny leads him to *Representative Men* and he sees at once: *this* is how I must write, this is my true style. As I said, he had already acquired an academic style of writing from his uncle Jacob Grimm and his father Wilhelm Grimm, and he then abandons it. He is impelled by destiny to adopt a completely different style.

In Herman Grimm's writings we see how wide were his historical interests. He has an inner relationship of soul with Germany, combined with a deep interest in Italy. All this comes out in his writings.

These are things that go to show how the affairs of destiny work themselves out. And how is one led to perceive such things? One must first have an impression and then everything crystallizes around it. Thus we had first to envisage the picture of Herman Grimm opening Emerson's *Representative Men*. Now Herman Grimm used to read in a peculiar manner. He read a passage and then immediately drew back from what he had read: it was a gesture as though he were swallowing what he had read, sentence by sentence. And it was this inner gesture of swallowing sentence by sentence that made it possible to trace Herman Grimm to his earlier incarnation. In the case of Emerson it was the walking to and fro in front of the open books, as well as the rather stiff, half-Roman carriage of the man, as Herman Grimm saw him when they first met in Italy—it was these impressions that led one back from Emerson to Tacitus. Plasticity of vision is needed to follow up things of this kind.

My dear friends, I have given you here another example which should indicate how our study of history needs to be deepened. This deepening must really be evident among us as one of the fruits of the new impulse that should take effect in the Anthroposophical Society through the Christmas Foundation Meeting. We must in future go bravely and boldly forward to the study of far-reaching spiritual connections; we must have courage to reach a vantage-point for observation of these great spiritual connections. For this we shall need, above all, deep earnestness. Our life in Anthroposophy must be filled with earnestness.

And this earnestness will grow in the Anthroposophical Society if those who really want to do something in the Society give more and more thought to the contents of the News Sheet that is sent out every week into all circles of Anthroposophists as a supplement to the weekly periodical, *Das Goetheanum.* A picture is given there of how one may shape the life in the Groups in the sense and meaning of the Christmas Meeting, of what should be done in the members' meetings, how the teaching should be given and studied. The News Sheet is also intended to give a picture of what is happening among us. Its title is: 'What is going on in the Anthroposophical Society', and its aim is to bring into the whole Society a unity of thought, to spread a common atmosphere of thought over the thousands of Anthroposophists everywhere. When we live in such an atmosphere, when we understand what it means for all our thinking to be stimulated and directed by the 'Leading Thoughts', and when we understand how the Goetheanum will thus be placed in the centre as a concrete reality through the initiative of the esoteric Vorstand—I have emphasised again and again that we now have to do with a Vorstand which conceives its task to be the inauguration of an esoteric impulse—when we understand this truly, then that which has now to flow through the Anthroposophical Movement will be carried forward in the right way. For Anthroposophical Movement and Anthroposophical Society must become one. The Anthroposophical Society must make the whole cause of Anthroposophy its own.

And it is true to say that if once this 'thinking in common' is an active reality, then it can also become the bearer of comprehensive, far-reaching spiritual knowledge. A power will come to life in the Anthroposophical Society that really ought to be in it, for the recent developments of civilisation need to be given a tremendous turn if they are not to lead to a complete decline.

What is said concerning successive earthly lives of this or that individual may at first seem paradoxical, but if you look more closely, if you look into the progress made by the human beings of whom we have spoken in this connection, you will see that what is said is founded on reality; you will see that we are able to look into the weaving life of gods and men when with the eye of spirit we try in this way to apprehend the spiritual forces.

This, my dear friends, is what I would lay upon your hearts and souls. If you take with you this feeling, then this Easter Meeting will be like a revitalising of the Christmas Meeting; for if the Christmas Meeting is to work as it should, then all that has developed out of it must be the means of revitalising it, of bringing it to new life just as if it were present with us.

May many things grow out of the Christmas Meeting, in constant renewal! May many things grow out of it through the activity of courageous souls, souls who are fearless representatives of Anthroposophy. If our meetings result in strengthening courage in the souls of Anthroposophists, then there will grow what is needed in the Society as the body for the Anthroposophical soul: a courageous presentation to the world of the revelations of the Spirit vouchsafed in the age of Light that has now dawned after the end of Kali-Yuga; for these revelations are necessary for the further evolution of man. If we live in the consciousness of this we shall be inspired to work courageously. May this courage be strengthened by every meeting we hold. It can be so if we are able to take in all earnestness things that seem paradoxical and foolish to those who set the tone of thought in our day. But after all, it has often happened that the dominant tone of thought in one period was soon afterwards replaced by the very thing that was formerly suppressed. May a recognition of the true nature of history, and of how it is bound up with the onward flow of the lives of men, give courage for anthroposophical activity—the courage that is essential for the further progress of human civilisation.

IV

Studies that are concerned with the karma of human beings must be undertaken with deep earnestness and inwardly assimilated. For it is not the mere knowledge of some particular karmic connection that is important. What is really important is that such studies should quicken the whole of man's nature, enabling him to find his bearings in life.

Such studies will never be fruitful if they lead to greater indifference towards human beings than is otherwise the case; they will be fruitful only if they kindle deeper love and understanding than are possible when account is taken merely of the impressions of a single life.

Anyone who reviews the successive epochs in the evolution of mankind cannot fail to realise that in the course of history very much has changed in man's whole way of thinking and perception, in all his views of the world and of life. Generally speaking, man is less interested in the past than in the future, for which the foundations have yet to be laid. But anyone who has a sufficiently clear grasp of how the souls of men have changed in the course of the earth's evolution will not shrink from the necessity of having himself to undergo the change that will lead him to study, not merely the single earthly life of some individual, but the succession of earthly lives, in so far as these can be brought within the range of his vision.

I think that the examples given in the last lecture—Conrad Ferdinand Meyer, Pestalozzi, and others—can show how understanding of a personality, love for this personality, can be enhanced when the latest earth-life is viewed against the background of other lives of which it is the outcome.

And now, in order that our studies may be really fruitful, I want to return to a question to which, as many of those present here will know, I have already alluded. Reference is often made in spiritual science to the existence in olden times of Initiates possessed of clairvoyant vision, personalities who were able to communicate the secrets of the spiritual world. And from this the question quite naturally arises: Where are these Initiates in our own time? Have they reincarnated?

To answer this question it is necessary to point out how greatly a later earth-life may differ from a preceding one in respect of knowledge and also in respect of other activities of the soul. For when in the time between death and a new birth the moment approaches for the human being to descend to the earth and unite with a physical-etheric organisation, a very great deal has to take place. The direction towards family, race and so forth, has indeed long been determined, but the resolve to undergo this tremendous change in the form of existence, the change involved in the transition from the world of soul-and-spirit into the physical world—this resolve is a stupendous matter. For as you can well imagine, circumstances are not as they are on earth, where the human being grows weaker as he approaches the end of his normal life; after all his experiences on earth he will actually have little to do with the decision to enter into a different form of existence when he passes through the gate of death. The change, in this case, comes upon him of itself, it breaks in upon him.

Here on earth, death is something that breaks in upon man. The descent from the spiritual world is completely different. It is a matter, then, of fully conscious action, a deliberate decision proceeding from the deepest foundations of the soul. We must realise what a stupendous transformation takes place in the human being when the time comes for him to exchange the forms of life in the pre-earthly existence of soul-and-spirit for those of earthly existence. The descent entails adaptation to the prevailing conditions of civilisation and culture and also to the bodily constitution which a particular epoch is able to provide. Our own epoch does not readily yield bodies—let alone conditions of culture and civilisation—in which Initiates can live again as they lived in the past. And when the time approaches for the soul of some former Initiate to use a physical body once again, it is a matter of accepting this body as it is, and of growing into the environment and the current form of education. But what once was present in this soul is not lost; it merely comes to expression in some other way. The basic configuration of the soul remains but assumes a different form.

Now in the 3rd and 4th centuries A.D. it was still possible for the soul to acquire a deep knowledge of Initiation truths, because at that time, especially in Southern Europe and Asia Minor, *body followed soul*, that is to say, the bodily functions were able to adapt themselves inwardly to the soul. One who may have lived in the early Christian centuries as an Initiate, with a soul wholly inward-turned and full of wisdom, is obliged to descend to-day into a kind of body which, owing to the intervening development, is directed pre-eminently to the external world, lives altogether in the external world. The result is that owing to the bodily constitution, the inner concentration of soul-forces that was still possible in the 3rd or 4th century of our era, is so no longer. And so the following could take place in the course of evolution.—I am telling you of things that reveal themselves to inner vision.

There was a certain Mystery-centre in Asia Minor, typical of all such institutions in that part of the world in the early Christian centuries. Traditions were everywhere alive in those olden days when men were deeply initiated into these Mysteries. But everywhere, too, men were more or less aware of the rules that must be imposed on the soul in order to acquire knowledge leading to its own deep foundations, as well as out into the cosmic All. And in the early Christian centuries these very Mysteries of Asia Minor were occupied with a momentous question.

Boundless wisdom had streamed through the sanctuaries of the Mysteries. If you will read what was described in my book *Christianity as Mystical Fact*—as far as description was possible in a printed publication at that time—you will see that the ultimate aim of all this wisdom was an understanding of the Mystery of Golgotha. And in these Mysteries of Asia Minor the great question was: How will the sublime content of the Mystery of Golgotha, the reality of what has streamed into the earth through the Mystery of Golgotha—how will it evolve further in the hearts and minds of men? And how will the ancient, primeval wisdom—a wisdom that encompassed the Beings who have their habitations in the stars and the manifold orders of Divine-Spiritual Beings who guide the universe and the life of man—how will this primeval wisdom unite with what is concentrated in the Mystery of Golgotha? How will it unite with the Impulse which, proceeding from a sublime Sun-Being, from the Christ, is now to pour into mankind?—That was the burning question in these Mysteries of Asia Minor.

There was one personality who with his Mystery-wisdom and Mystery-experiences felt this question with overwhelming intensity. It is in truth a shattering experience when in the search for karmic connections one comes upon this man who was initiated in one of these Mysteries in Asia Minor in the early Christian centuries. It is a shattering experience, for with his Initiation-knowledge he was aware in every fibre of his being of the need to grasp the meaning and import of the Mystery of Golgotha, and he was faced with the problem: What will happen now? How will these weak human souls be able to receive it?

Weighed down in soul by this burning question concerning the destiny of Christianity, this Initiate was walking one day in the wider precincts of his Mystery-centre, when an experience came to him of an event that made an overwhelming impression—the treacherous murder of Julian the Apostate. With the vision and insight of Initiation he lived through this event.

It was known to him that Julian the Apostate had attained a certain degree of Initiation in the ancient Mysteries, that he wanted to preserve for the spiritual life of mankind, the impulses that had been cultivated in the ancient Mysteries, to ensure their continuance, in short to unite Christianity with the wisdom of the Mysteries. He knew that Julian the Apostate proclaimed, in the sense of the Mystery-wisdom, that as well as the physical Sun there is also a Spiritual Sun, and that whoever knows the Spiritual Sun, knows Christ. But this teaching was regarded as evil in the days of Julian the Apostate and led to his treacherous murder on his journey to Persia. This most significant, symptomatic event in world-history was lived through by the Initiate of whom I am speaking.

Those of you who for many years have been listening to what has been said on the subject of karmic connections in world-history, will remember that in the lectures I once gave in Stuttgart on certain chapters of occult history—reference was also made to the same theme at the Christmas Foundations Meeting*—I spoke of the deep tragedy of Julian the Apostate's position in the history of humanity.

His death was felt and experienced by the Initiate to whom I am now referring, whose Initiate-knowledge, received in a Mystery-centre in Asia Minor, was shadowed by the question: What will become of Christianity? And through these symptomatic events there came to him the crystal-clear realisation: A time will come when Christianity will be misunderstood, will live only in traditions, when men will no longer know anything of the glory and sublimity of Christ, the Sun-Spirit Who dwelt in Jesus of Nazareth.

All this lay like a weight upon the soul of the Initiate. And for the rest of his life at that time he was heavy-hearted and sorrowful in regard to the evolution of Christianity. He experienced the consternation and dismay which a symptomatic event of the kind referred to must inevitably cause in an Initiate. It made an overwhelming, shattering impression upon him.

And then we go further.—The impression received by this Initiate was bound to lead to a reincarnation comparatively soon afterwards—in point of fact at the time of the Thirty Years' War, when very many outstanding, interesting

* Lecture-Course XVI. *Occult History.* Stuttgart, December 27th–31st, 1910 and January 1st, 1911.

World-History in the light of Anthroposophy. Dornach. December 24th–31st, 1923.

incarnations took place, incarnations that have played an important part in the historical evolution of mankind.

The Initiate was born again as a woman, at the beginning of the 17th century, before the actual outbreak of the Thirty Years' War. She lived on into the time of the conflict and was in contact with certain attempts that were made from the side of Rosicrucianism to correct the tendencies of the age and to make preparation in a spiritual way for the future. This work, however, was largely overshadowed and submerged by the savagery and brutality prevailing during the Thirty Years' War. Think only of the *Chymical Wedding of Christian Rosenkreuz* which appeared shortly before its outbreak. And many other significant impulses came into the life of mankind at that time, before being stamped out or brutalised by the War.

This personality, who as an Initiate had experienced the deeply symptomatic event connected with Julian the Apostate and had then passed through the incarnation as a woman in the 17th century, was born again in the 19th century. All that had become even more inward during the incarnation as a woman, all that had formerly been present in the soul—not the Initiation-wisdom but the horror caused by the terrible event—all this, in the last third of the 19th century, poured into a peculiarly characteristic view of the world which penetrated deeply into the prevailing incongruities of human existence.

The whole tenor and trend of the present age is such that it is difficult for one who has carried over ancient Initiation-wisdom from an earlier earth-life into the life of the 19th and 20th centuries, to work effectively through deeds. And so, in this case, what was brought over—deeply transformed and apparently externalised, though in reality still inward—pressed its way from the heart—the seat of the old Initiation-wisdom—towards the senses and sense-observation, striving to find expression in poetry, in literature.

That is the reason why recent times have produced so many really splendid examples of literature. Only they are incoherent, they are simply not intelligible as they stand. For they have been created not only by the personality who was present on earth at the end of the 19th or beginning of the 20th centuries, but an additional factor has been some experience in a past life such as I have related, an experience that had such a shattering effect upon an Initiate—albeit an Initiate in Mysteries already decadent. This shattering experience in the soul works on, streams into artistic, poetic qualities of soul—and what, in this case, comes over in so characteristic a way, lives itself out in the personality of *Ibsen.*

When this vista is open to one, the secrets of the evolution of humanity light up from writings which appeared at the end of the 19th century and which cannot be the work of a single man but of a man through whom and in whom earlier epochs are also coming to expression.

In approaching a theme like this, we shall certainly not lose respect either for the course taken by world-history or for the single personality who stands before us with greatness and distinction. In very truth, the experiences that come upon one in this domain are shattering—that is to say when such matters are pursued with the necessary earnestness.

Now you will often have heard tell of an alchemist who lived in a comparatively early period of the Middle Ages: Basilius Valentinus (Basil Valentine), a Benedictine monk. His achievements in the spheres of medicine and alchemy were of momentous significance and to study him in connection with karmic relationships in world-history leads to remarkable results, results which show very clearly how difficult it is to understand the age in which we ourselves are living.

Many things in our time are not only incomprehensible but often repellent, disagreeable, horrifying in a certain respect, and if we look at life merely as it is perceptible to the senses, it is impossible not to feel indignation and disgust.

It is different, however, for one who can perceive the human and historical connections. Things are by no means what they seem! Traits may show themselves in life to-day for which the onlookers have, quite understandably, nothing but censure and indignation. And yet all the time, even in the unpleasant elements themselves, there may be something that is intensely fascinating. This will be the case more and more frequently.

As I said, there in the early Middle Ages we find Basilius Valentinus, a Benedictine monk, engaged in the pursuit of medicine and alchemy in his cellars in the monastery and making a number of important investigations. There are others with him who are his pupils and they write down what Basilius Valentinus has said to them. Consequently there are hardly any original writings of Basilius Valentinus himself; but there are writings of pupils which contain a great deal that is genuinely his wisdom, his alchemical wisdom.

Now when, at a certain time of my life, one of the pupils of Basilius Valentinus who especially interested me came into my field of vision, I realised: This pupil is again in incarnation, but spiritually there has been a remarkable metamorphosis. He has come again in the 19th century and beginning of the 20th century.

But the alchemical activity, directed without co-ordination towards the senses, manifested outwardly as a view of life in which alchemical concepts are always, so to speak, being welded into sense-observations. In this later incarnation the man observes external facts—how people act, how things happen among them, how they talk to one another—and he groups it all together in a way that is often repellent. But the explanation lies in the fact that the personality in question had, in an earlier incarnation, worked at alchemy under Basilius Valentinus. And now he jumbles everything together—the relationships between people, how they behave to one another, what they say, what they do and so forth. He does not look at these things with the eyes of a modern philistine—far from it!—but with the eye of a soul in which impulses from his former alchemical pursuits are still alive. He jumbles up events that occur among men, makes dramas out of them, and becomes: *Frank Wedekind.*

These things must of course be studied in pursuance of a longing for a genuine understanding of man. When this is the case, life becomes, not poorer, but infinitely richer. Take Wedekind's '*Hidalla*' or any other of his dramas which make the brain reel when one attempts to find the thread connecting what comes first with what comes later. Yet there is something fascinating about it for anyone who can look beyond the surface, and the commonplace judgments of the critics sitting in the stalls will leave him untouched. From their own standpoint, of course, these critics are justified—but that is of no account. The real point is that world-history has here produced a strange and remarkable phenomenon.—Alchemical thinking, flung as it were across centuries, is now applied to human life and human deeds; these, together with human rules and standards are all jumbled into a hotchpotch, just as once in alchemical kitchens—at a time when alchemy was already on the decline—substances and their forces were mixed in retorts and tests made of their effects.

Even in respect of the point of time at which they occur on earth, the lives of men are determined by connections of destiny and karma. Let me give you another example in corroboration of this.

We turn our gaze back to the time when the Platonic School flourishes in Greece. There was Plato, surrounded by a number of pupils. In their characters these pupils differed greatly from one another and what Plato himself depicts in the Dialogues, where characters of the most varied types appear and converse together, is in many respects a true picture of his School. Very different characters came together in this School.

In the School there were two personalities in particular who imbibed, each in a very different way, all that fell from Plato's lips, bringing such sublime illumination to his pupils, and that he also carried further in conversations with them.

One of these two pupils was a personality of rare sensitiveness and refinement. He was particularly receptive to everything that Plato did, through his teaching on the Ideas, to lift men's minds and hearts above the things of earth. Everywhere we find Plato affirming that over against the transitoriness of the single events in man's life and environment, stand the *Eternal Ideas*. The material world is transitory; but the material world is only a picture of the Idea which—itself eternal—passes in perpetual metamorphoses through the temporal and the transitory. Thus did Plato lift his pupils above the transitory things belonging to the external world of sense to contemplation of the eternal Ideas which hover over them as the heavens hover over the earth.

But in this Platonic treatment of the world, man in his true being fares rather badly. For the Platonic conceptions and mode of thinking cannot properly be applied to man, in whom the Idea itself becomes alive in objective reality. Man is too individual. The Ideas, according to Plato, hover above the things. This is true in respect of the minerals, crystals and the other phenomena of the lifeless sense-world; Goethe too, while on the track of the archetypal plant (the '*Urpflanze*') was observing the varying *types;* and the same applies in the case of the animals. With man, however, it is a matter of seeking the living Idea within each single human individuality. It was Aristotle—not Plato—who taught that the Idea as *entelechy* has entered into the human being.

The first of the two pupils shared with whole-hearted fervour in this heavenward flight in Platonism. With his spiritual vision he could accompany Plato in this heavenward flight, in this soaring above the earth, and words of mellowed sweetness would fall from his lips in the Platonic School on the sublimity of the Ideas that hover over and above the things of earth. In his soul he soared to the Ideas. When he was not lingering in his world of vision but living again in his heart and mind, going about among the Greeks as he loved to do, he took the warmest interest in every human being with whom he came into contact. It was only when he had come down as it were to everyday life that his heart and feelings could be focused upon the many whom he loved so well, for his visions drew him away from the earth. And so in this pupil there was a kind of split between the life of heart when he was among living human beings and the life of soul when he was transported to the Eternal Ideas, when he was listening in the Academy to Plato's words or was himself formulating in words full of sweetness, the inspirations brought by Platonism. There was something wonderfully sensitive about this personality.

Now a close and intimate friendship existed between this man and another pupil in the Platonic School. But in the course of it, a different trend of character which I will now describe, was developing in the friend, with the result that the two grew apart. Not that their love for one another cooled, but in their whole way of thinking they grew apart; life separated them. They were able, at first, to understand one another well, but later on even this was no longer possible. And it led to the one I have described becoming irritable and 'nervy' as we should say to-day, whenever the other spoke in the way that came naturally to him.

The second pupil was no less ready than the first to look upwards to the Eternal Ideas which were the inspiration of so much living activity in the School of Plato. This pupil, too, could be completely transported from the earth. But the deep, warm-hearted interest in numbers of his fellow human beings—that he lacked. On the other hand he was intensely attracted by the myths and sagas of the ancient gods which were extant among the people and were well-known to him. He interested himself deeply in what we to-day call Greek Mythology, in the figures of Zeus, Athene and the rest. It was his tendency more or less to pass living human beings by, but he took a boundless interest in the gods whom he pictured as having lived on earth in a remote past and as being the progenitors of humanity.

And so he felt the urge and the strong desire to apply the inspiration experienced in his life of soul to an understanding of the profound wisdom contained in the sagas of the gods and heroes. Men's relation to such sagas was of course completely different in Greece from what it is to-day. In Greece it was all living reality, not merely the content of books or traditions.

This second personality who had been on terms of intimate friendship with the first, also grew out of the friendship—it was the same with them both. But as members of the Platonic School there was a link between them. Now the Platonic School had this characteristic.—Its pupils developed forces in themselves which tended to separate them from one another, to drive them apart after the School had for a time held them close together. As a result of this, individualities developed such as the two I have described, individualities who in spite of their different natures belonged together and who then grew apart.

These two individualities—they were born again as women in Italy in the days of the Renaissance—came again to the earth in modern times; the first too early and the second rather too late. This is connected with the strong resolution that is required before making the descent to incarnation.

Having passed through the gate of death, the one I described first, who had soared in spirit to super-earthly realms but without the fullness of human nature which expressed itself only in his heart and feelings, was able between death and rebirth to apprehend what pertains to the First Hierarchy, the Seraphim, Cherubim and Thrones; to some extent he could also apprehend the Second Hierarchy, but not the Hierarchy immediately above man, not, therefore, the Hierarchy through which one learns how the human body is built up and organised here on earth.

He thus became a personality who in pre-earthly existence had developed little insight into the constitution and nature of the human body; hence, when he was born again, he did not take into himself the final impulse. He made a partial, not a full descent into the body, did not come right down into it, but always hovered a little above it.

His friend from the Platonic School waited before descending to incarnation. The reason for the waiting was that had the two of them met, had they been actual contemporaries, they would not have been able to tolerate one another. And yet, for all that, the one who had been wont to speak at such length about his intercourse with men, recounting it with such charm and sweetness to the other—who did not go among his fellows but was engrossed in the myths and sagas of the gods—this first personality was destined to make a deep impression upon the other, to precede him. The second followed later.

This second personality, having steeped himself in Imaginations of the gods, had now developed a high degree of understanding of all that has to do with man. Accordingly he wanted to extend his time in the spiritual world and gather impulses that would enable him to take deep hold of the body. And what actually happened was that he took hold of the body too forcefully, he sank too deeply into it.

Thus we have here two differing configurations of destiny. Of two members of the Platonic School, one takes too slight a hold of the body in the second incarnation afterwards and the other takes too strong a hold. The one cannot completely enter his body; he is impelled into it in his youth but out of it again soon afterwards and is obliged to remain outside. This is *Hölderlin.*

The other is carried so deeply into his body that he enters with too much force into his organs and suffers almost lifelong illness. This is *Hamerling.*

Thus we have before us great human destinies stretching through the ages of time, and the impulses which gave rise to these destinies; and we are now able to divine how the spiritual impulses work. For we must place this fact in all clarity before our souls: an individuality like Hölderlin, who has come from the Platonic School and who cannot enter fully into his body but has to remain outside it, such an individuality experiences in the dimness of insanity, impulses that work in preparation for coming earthly lives, impulses that destine him for greatness. And it is the same with the other, Robert Hamerling.

Illness and health appear in quite a different light when considered in the setting of destiny than when they are observed within the bounds of the single earthly life.

I think it can surely be said that reverence will arise in

men's hearts and minds when life is treated in this way—reverence and awe for the mysterious happenings brought about by the spiritual world. Again and again I must emphasise that these things are not being told in order to satisfy cravings for sensation, but to lead us more and more deeply into a knowledge and understanding of the spiritual life. And it is only through this deeper penetration into the spiritual life that the external, sense-life of man can be explained and illumined.

V

We have now studied a number of examples showing how destiny unfolds, examples which can explain and illumine the life and history of mankind. The purpose of these studies has been to show that individuals themselves carry into later epochs of earthly existence what they have experienced and assimilated in earlier times. Connections have come to light which enable us to understand how certain decisive actions of men have their roots in moral causes created by themselves in the course of the ages.

It is not this kind of causal connection only that the study of karma can disclose to us. Many other things, too, become intelligible, which to external observation seem at first obscure and incomprehensible. But if we are to participate in the great change in thinking and perception that is essential in the near future if civilisation is to progress and not fall into decline, it is incumbent upon us to develop, in the first place, a sense for what in ordinary circumstances is beyond our grasp and the understanding of which requires insight into the deeper relationships of existence. A man who finds everything comprehensible may, of course, see no need to know anything of more deeply lying causes. But to find everything in the world comprehensible is a sign of illusion and merely indicates superficiality. In point of fact the vast majority of things in the world are incomprehensible to the ordinary consciousness. To be able to stand in wonder before so much that is incomprehensible in everyday life—that is really the beginning of a true striving for knowledge.

A call that has so often gone out from this platform is that anthroposophists shall have *enthusiasm* in their seeking, enthusiasm for what is implicit in Anthroposophy. And this enthusiasm must take its start from a realisation of the wonders confronting us in everyday life. Only then shall we be led to reach out to the causes, to the deeper forces underlying existence around us.

This attitude of wonder towards the surrounding world can spring both from contemplation of history and from observation of what is immediately present. How often our attention is arrested by events in history which seem to indicate that human life here and there has lost all rhyme and reason. And human life does indeed lose meaning if we focus our attention upon a single event in history and omit to ask: How do certain types of character emerge from this event? What form will they take in a later incarnation?... If such questions remain unasked, certain events in history seem to be entirely meaningless, irrelevant, pointless. They lose meaning if they cannot become impulses of soul in a subsequent life on earth, find their balance and then work on into the future.

Now there is certainly something that really does not make sense in the phenomenon of a personality such as the Roman Emperor *Nero*. No reference has yet been made to Nero in lectures in the Anthroposophical Movement.

Think of all that history recounts of Nero. In face of such a personality it seems as if life could be mocked and scorned with impunity, as if the utterly flippant disregard for life displayed by one in a position of great power and authority, brought no consequences. Anyone hearing of Nero's deeds must be dull-witted if he is not driven to ask: What becomes of a soul such as this, who scorns the whole world, who regards the life of other men, nay even the existence of a whole city, as something he can play with? "What an artist is lost in me!" is a saying attributed to Nero, and it seems to be in line with his whole attitude and tenor of mind. Utmost flippancy, an intense desire and urge for destruction, acknowledged even by himself—and the soul actually taking pleasure in it all!

One can only be repelled by the story, for here is a personality who literally radiates destruction. And the question forces itself upon us: What becomes of such a soul?

Now we must be quite clear on this point: Whatever is discharged, as it were, upon the world, is reflected in the life between death and a new birth, and discharged in turn upon the soul who has been responsible for the destruction. A few centuries later, that is to say, a comparatively short time afterwards, Nero appeared again in the world in an unimportant form of existence. During this incarnation a certain balance was brought about in respect of the mania for destruction, the enthusiasm for destruction in which he had indulged as a ruler, simply out of an inner urge. In that next life on earth something of this was balanced out, for the same individuality was now in a position where he was obliged to destroy; he was in a subordinate position, acting under orders. The soul had now to realise what it is like when such acts are *not* committed out of free will while in a position of supreme power.

Matters of this kind must be studied quite objectively and all emotion avoided—that is absolutely essential. In a certain respect, such a destiny calls for pity—for to be as cruel as Nero, to have a mania for destruction as great as his, is, after all, a destiny. There is no need for hatred or censure; moreover such an attitude would prevent one from experiencing all that is required in order to understand the further developments. Insight into the things that have been spoken of here is possible only when they are looked at objectively, when no hostile judgment is passed but when human destiny is really understood. Things disclose themselves quite clearly, provided one has the faculty for understanding them... That this Nero-destiny came vividly before me on one occasion was attributable to what seemed to be chance—but it was only seemingly chance.

One day, when a terrible event had occurred, an event of which I shall speak in a moment and which had a shattering effect throughout the region concerned, I happened to be visiting a person frequently mentioned in my autobiography: Karl Julius Schröer. When I arrived I found him profoundly shocked, as numbers were, by what had happened. And the word "Nero" fell from his lips—apparently without reason—as though it burst from dark depths of the spirit. To all appearances the word came entirely out of the blue. But later on it became quite clear that in reality the Akashic Record was here being voiced through human lips. The event referred to was the following.—

The Austrian Crown Prince had always been acclaimed as a brilliant personality, and great hopes were entertained for the time when he would ascend the Throne. Although all kinds of things were known about the behaviour of the Crown Prince Rudolf, they were accepted as almost inevitable in the case of one of such high rank; nobody dreamt for a moment that the things told about him might lead to any serious, tragic conflicts. It was therefore an overwhelming shock when it became known in Vienna that the Crown Prince Rudolf had met his death in mysterious circumstances near the Convent of the Holy Cross, outside Baden, near Vienna. Details gradually came to light and at first there was talk of a "fatal accident"—indeed this was officially announced. Then, after the official announcement, it became known that the Crown Prince had gone to his hunting lodge accompanied by the Baroness Vetsera and that there they had both met their death.

The details are so well-known that there is no need to recount them here. All that followed made it impossible for anyone acquainted with the circumstances to doubt that this was a case of suicide. For what happened first of all was that after the issue of the official announcement of the fatal accident, the Prime Minister of Hungary, Koloman Tisza, took exception to this version, and obtained from the then Emperor of Austria the promise that this incorrect statement should not be allowed to stand. The Hungarian Prime Minister refused to be responsible for making this announcement to his people, and he was very emphatic in his refusal. Besides this, there was a man on the medical staff who was one of the most courageous doctors in Vienna at the time and who was to assist at the post-mortem examination; and this man said that he would sign nothing that was not corroborated by the objective facts.

Well, the objective facts were a clear indication of suicide; this was officially admitted and the earlier announcement corrected. And if there were no other circumstances than the admission of suicide by a family as fervently Catholic as that of the Austrian Emperor, that alone would have precluded the slightest shadow of doubt.

Nobody who can judge the facts objectively will think of doubting it, but there is one very obvious question: How was it possible that anyone with such a brilliant future should turn to suicide when faced with circumstances which, in his position, could easily have remained concealed? Obviously, there was no objective reason why a Crown Prince should commit suicide on account of a love affair—I mean that there was no objective reason attributable to external circumstances.

There was no objective reason for such an action, but the fact was that this heir to a Throne found life utterly worthless—a state of mind which had, of course, a psycho-pathological basis. This itself needs to be understood, for a pathological condition of the soul is also connected with destiny. And the fundamental fact here is that one to whom a brilliant future was beckoning, found life utterly worthless.

This, my dear friends, is one of those phenomena in life which seem to be wholly inexplicable. And in spite of all that has been written or said about the whole affair, a true judgment can be formed only by one who says to himself: This single human life, this life of Crown Prince Rudolf of Austria, gives no clue to the suicide or to the causes of the preceding pathological state of mind; something else must be at the bottom of it all.

And now, if you picture to yourself the Nero soul, having subsequently experienced what I described and passing at length into that heir to a Throne who does away with himself, who forces the consequences by means of suicide . . . then the whole setting is altered. Within the soul there is a tendency which originates in preceding earthly lives; in the time between death and rebirth the soul perceives in direct vision that nothing but forces of destruction have issued from it—and now the 'grand reversal', as I will call it, has to be experienced.

And how is it experienced?—A life abounding in things of external value reflects itself inwardly in such a way that its bearer considers it utterly worthless, and commits suicide. The soul becomes sick, half demented, seeking an external entanglement in the love affair, and so forth. But these things are merely the consequences of the soul's endeavour as it were to direct against itself all the arrows which in the past had been directed to the world. And then, when we have insight into these relationships, we perceive the unfolding of an overwhelming tragedy, but for all that a righteous, just tragedy. The two pictures are co-ordinated.

As I have said so often, it is the underlying details that make real investigation possible in such domains. Many factors in life must work together here.

I told you that when this shattering event had just occurred, I was on my way to Schröer. The event itself was not the reason for my visit—I happened to be on the way to him and he was the first person to whom I spoke about the matter. He said: "Nero! . . ."—quite out of the blue, and I could not help asking myself: Why does he think of Nero just at this moment? He actually introduced the conversation with the mention of Nero. This amazed me at the time. But the shattering effect was all the greater in view of the particular circumstances in which the word "Nero" was uttered. Two days previously—all this was public knowledge—a Soirée had been held at the house of Prince Reuss, then German Ambassador in Vienna. The Austrian Crown Prince was present, and Schröer too, and the latter saw how the Crown Prince was behaving on that occasion—two days before the catastrophe. The strange behaviour at the Soirée, the suicide two days later, all of it described so dramatically by Schröer—this, in connection with the utterance of the name "Nero", made one realise that there was good reason for further investigation.

Now why did I often follow up things that happened to fall from Schröer's lips? It was not that I simply took anything he said as a pointer, for he, of course, knew nothing of such matters. But many things he said, especially those which seemed to shoot out of the blue, were significant for me because of something that once came to light in a curious way.

A conversation I had with Schröer on one occasion led to the subject of phrenology. Not humorously, but with the seriousness with which he was wont to speak of such things, employing a certain solemnity of language even in everyday matters, Schröer said to me: "I too was once examined by a phrenologist. He felt my head all over and discovered up there the bump of which he said: 'There's the theosophist in you'."—Remember that this was in the eighties of last century when there was as yet no talk of Anthroposophy. It was Schröer, not I, who was examined by the phrenologist who said: "There's the theosophist in you." Now Schröer, outwardly, was far from being a theosophist—my autobiography makes that abundantly clear. But it was just when he spoke of things without apparent motive that his utterances were sometimes profoundly significant. And so there seemed to be a certain connection between the utterance of the word 'Nero' and the outer confirmation of his theosophical trend. This was what made him a personality to whose spontaneous utterances one paid heed.

And so investigation into the Nero destiny shed light on the subsequent Meyerling destiny and it was found that in the personality of the Austrian Crown Prince Rudolf one actually had to do with the Nero soul.

This investigation—which has taken a long time, for in matters of this kind one must be extremely cautious—presented special difficulties to me because I was continually being diverted by the fact that all kinds of people—you may believe it or not—were claiming with fanatical insistence that they themselves had been Nero! So it was a matter, first of all, of combating the subjective force emanating from these alleged reborn Neroes. One had to get through a kind of thicket.

But what I am telling you now, my dear friends, is much

more important because it has to do with an historical phenomenon, namely, *Nero himself*. And to understand the further development is much more important than to understand, let us say, the actual catastrophe at Meyerling. For now we see how things which, to begin with, arouse horror and indignation—as does the life of Nero—live themselves out according to a perfect world-justice; we see how this world-justice is fulfilled and how the wrong returns, but in such a way that the individuality is himself involved in creating the balance.—That is what is so stupendous about karma.

Still more can become clear when such wrong is balanced out in the course of particular earthly lives. In this case the balance will be almost complete, for you will realise how closely the fulfilment is bound up with the compensatory deed. Just think of it . . . a life which considers itself worthless, so worthless that a whole Empire (Austria was then a great Empire) and the rulership of it are abandoned! The suicide in such circumstances bears the consequence that after death it all has to be lived through in direct spiritual vision. This is the fulfilment, albeit the terrible fulfilment, of what may be called the righteous justice of destiny, the balancing out of the wrong.

But on the other hand, leaving all this aside, there was a tremendous force in Nero—a force which must not be lost for humanity. This force must of course be purified and we have spoken of the purification. If this has been accomplished, such a soul will carry its forces into later epochs of the earth's existence with salutary effects. When we apprehend karma as righteous compensation, we shall never fail to see how it tests the human being, puts him to the test even when he takes his place in life in a way that horrifies us. The just compensation is brought about, but the human forces are not lost. What has been committed in one life may, under certain circumstances, and provided the righteous justice has taken effect, even be transformed into a power for good. That is why a destiny such as the one described to-day is so profoundly moving.

This brings us to the consideration of good and evil, viewed in the light of karma: good and evil, fortune and misfortune, happiness and sorrow—as man experiences them breaking into, shining into, his individual life.

In regard to perception of a man's moral situation there was far greater sensitivity in earlier epochs of history than is to be found in modern humanity. Men of the present age are not really sensitive at all to the problem of destiny. Now and again, of course, one comes across someone who has an inkling of the onset of destiny; but real understanding of its problems is shrouded in darkness and bewilderment in our modern civilisation, which regards the single earthly life as something complete in itself. Things happen—and that is that. A disaster that befalls a man is commented on but not really pursued in throught. This is pre-eminently the case when through something that seems to be pure chance, a man who to all appearances is thoroughly good and who has committed no wrong, either perishes, or perhaps does not actually perish but has to endure terrible suffering on account of some injury, or other cause. No thought is given to why such a fate should cut in this way into a so-called innocent life.

Humanity was not always so obtuse and insensitive with regard to the problem of destiny. We need not go very far back in time to find that blows of destiny were felt to strike in from other worlds—even the destiny a man has brought upon himself.

What is the explanation of this? The explanation is that in earlier times men were not only endowed with instinctive clairvoyance but even when this had faded, its fruits were still preserved in traditions; moreover external conditions and customs did not conduce to such a superficial, commonplace view of the world as prevails to-day, in the age of materialism. There is much talk nowadays of the harmfulness of purely materialistic-naturalistic thinking which has become so universal and has even crept into the various creeds—for the religions too have become materialistic. In no single domain is outer civilisation sincerely desirous of knowing anything about the spiritual world and although men talk in theory of the need to fight this trend, a theoretical battle against materiailstic ideas achieves very little. The point of salient importance is that by reason of the conception of the world which has led men to freedom, which will do so still more, and which constitutes a transitional period in the history of human evolution—by reason of this conception of the world, a certain means of healing that was available in earlier epochs for outer sense-observation has been lost.

In the early centuries of Greek civilisation—in fact it was so for a considerable time—men saw in nature around them the outer, phenomenal world. The Greek, as well as modern man, looked out at nature. True, the Greek saw nature in a rather different aspect, for the senses themselves have evolved—but that is not the point here. The Greek had a remedy wherewith to counteract the organic harm that is caused in man when he merely gazes out into nature.

We do not only become physiologically long-sighted with age as the result of having gazed constantly at nature, but this gives our soul a certain configuration. As it gazes at nature, the soul realises inwardly that not all the demands of vision are being satisfied. Unsatisfied demands of vision remain. And this holds good for the process of perception in general—hearing, feeling, and so forth. Certain elements in the perceptive process remain unsatisfied when we gaze out into nature. It is more or less the same as if a man in physical existence wished to spend his whole life without taking adequate food. Such a man deteriorates physically. But when he merely gazes at nature, the perceptive faculty in his life of soul deteriorates. He gets a kind of 'consumption' of soul in his sense-world. This was known in the old Mystery-wisdom.

But it was also known how this 'consumption' in the life of soul can be counteracted. It was known that the *Temple Architecture*, where men beheld the equipose between down-bearing weight and upbearing support, or when, as in the East, they beheld forms that were really plastic representations of moral forces, when they looked at the architectural forms confronting the eye and the whole of the perceptive process, or experienced the musical element in these forms—it was known that here was the remedy against the consumption which befalls the senses when they merely gaze out into nature. And when the Greek was led into his temple where he beheld the pillars, above them the architrave, the inner composition and dynamic of it all, then his gaze was bounded and completed. When a man looks at nature his gaze is really no more than a stare, going on into infinity, never reaching an end. In natural science too, every problem leads on and on in this way, without coming to finality. But the gaze is bounded and completed when one faces a work of great architecture created with the aim of intercepting the vision, rescuing it from the pull of nature. There you have one feature of life in olden times: this capturing of the outward gaze.

And again, when a man turns his gaze inwards to-day, it does not penetrate to the innermost core of his being. If he practises self-knowledge, what he perceives is a surging medley of all kinds of emotions and outer impressions, without clarity or definition. He cannot lay hold of himself inwardly; he lacks the strength to grasp this inner reality in imaginations, in pictures—as he must do before he can make any real approach to the inmost kernel of his being.

It is here that cult and ritual enacted reverently before men take effect. Everything of the nature of cult and ritual, not the external rites only but *comprehension of the world expressed in imagery and pictures*, leads man towards his innermost being. As long as he strives for self-knowledge with abstract ideas and concepts, nothing is achieved. But when he penetrates into his inmost being with pictures that give concrete definition to experiences of soul, then he achieves his aim. The inmost kernel of his being comes within his grasp.

How often have I not said that man must meditate in *pictures*, in *images*. This has been dealt with at ample length, even in public lectures.

And so, looking at man in the past, we find on the one side that his gaze and perception, when directed outwards, are as it were bounded, intercepted, by architectonic forms; on the other side, his inward-turned gaze is bounded and held firm by picturing his soul-life; and this can also be presented to him through the imagery of cult and ritual.

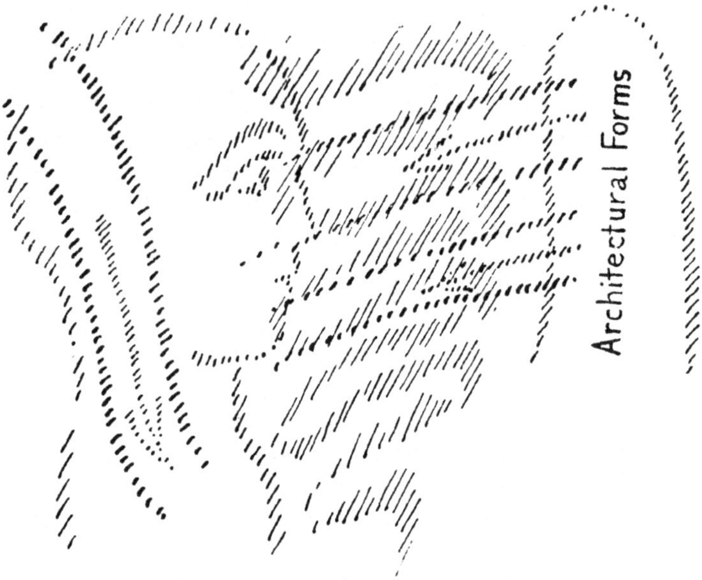

On the one side, therefore, there is the descent into the inmost being; on the other, the outward gaze lights upon the forms displayed in sacred architecture. A certain union is thereby achieved. Between what comes alive within and that upon which the gaze falls, there is an intermediate domain, imperceptible to man in his everyday consciousness because his outward gaze is not captured by forms of architecture born of deep, inner knowledge, nor is his inward gaze given definition by pictures and imaginations. But there is this intermediate domain . . . if you let *that* work in your life, if you go about with inner self-knowledge deepened through imagination, and with sense-perceptions made whole and complete through forms created and inspired by a real understanding of man's nature . . . then your feeling in regard to strokes of destiny will be the same as it was in olden times. By cultivating the domain that lies between the experience of true architectonic form and the experience of true, symbolic imagery along the path inwards, a man becomes sensitive to the strokes of destiny. He feels that what befalls him comes from earlier lives on earth.

This again is an introduction to the studies which we shall be pursuing and which will include consideration of the good and the evil in connection with karma.

But what is of salient importance is that within the Anthroposophical Movement there shall be right thinking. The architecture that would have fulfilled the needs of modern man, that would have been able to capture his gaze in the right way and to have led naturalistic perception, which veils and obscures the vision of karma, gradually into real vision—this architecture did once exist, in a certain form. And the fact that anthroposophical thoughts were uttered in the setting of those forms, kindled the inner vision. Among its other aspects the Goetheanum Building, together with the way in which Anthroposophy would have been cultivated in it, was in itself an education for the vision of karma. And that is what must be introduced into modern civilisation: education for the vision of karma.

But needless to say, it was in the interests of those who are opposed to what ought now to enter civilisation, that such a Building should fall a prey to the flames . . . There, too, it is possible to look into the deeper connections. But let us hope that, before very long, forms that awaken a vision of karma will again stand before us, at the same place.

This is what I wanted to say in conclusion to-day, when so many friends from abroad are still with us after our Easter Meeting.

VI

We have considered a series of karmic relationships in the historical development of mankind, and have observed how one or other relationship flows over from one earthly life into another. We will now pass on to the consideration of karmic relationships from a fresh point of view, and you will find that it is one which leads still more directly into life. For the study of karma has real value only when it flows into the moral character of our life, into the whole mood and tenor of our life and soul; so that in taking our place in the world as human beings we can experience through the study of karma an invigoration as well as a deepening of our life. Life has many riddles, and it is wrong to regard them all as insoluble. If that were so, man would gradually be torn right out of his true being. Were the riddles of the nature of man to remain quite unknown to him, he would have to pass through existence like an unconscious being. But it is the task of man to grow ever more and more conscious. And this he can do only when he learns to penetrate with some degree of insight into all that is connected with him, all that is connected with his soul and his spirit.

As karma is a component part of our whole life and existence, it goes without saying that the study of karma is a study that has directly to do with the very foundations of human life. Nevertheless, it is very difficult for us in our present-day consciousness to undertake a study of karma in its direct application to life. For any at all adequate study of the working of karma in actual life, the life in which we ourselves are immersed, calls for a far more objective outlook than is possible for the kind of consciousness which arises from present-day conditions of living and education. In these conditions there is much that *hides* karmic connections, makes them invisible; for this reason, the very things that would make life comprehensible from the point of view of karma and destiny are extraordinarily difficult to observe.

Present-day man is very little inclined to detach himself from his own being and to give himself wholly to some other being or object. Modern man lives very strongly within himself. And the strange thing is that when he strives towards the spirit, when he receives into himself the spiritual, he runs great danger of living all the more within himself! For what do we find when someone begins to enter more deeply into anthroposophical life? Many a person who in the course of his life has come into the Anthroposophical Movement will be able to say to himself: As long as I lived in the outside world I had these or those relations with life: they absorbed me and I accepted them as belonging intimately to me. I prized this or that; I believed that this or that was necessary for living. Moreover, I had friends with whom I was on terms of intimacy by virtue of the habits and circumstances of daily life. Then came the time when I found Anthroposophy. Since that moment, much in my life has come to a stop. I have moved right away from many of the old connections; or at least they no longer have the same value for me. Many things that I enjoyed doing have become repulsive to me; I can no longer regard them as things with which I want to remain connected.

And if, having embarked on these reflections, he carries his thought a little farther, and tries to find what it is that has taken the place of these things, he will very quickly discover that his egoism has not decreased. I do not say this reproachfully, no, not even with the faintest shadow of reproach; I merely wish to state it as a fact which anyone is quite well able to observe in himself. His egosim has, in fact, increased; he pays far more heed now to the special way in which he himself is constituted. He asks more than he ever did before: "What sort of impression does my neighbour make on me?" Previously he had been accustomed to take the actions of another person more or less for granted. Now he enquires about the impression they have made on himself. Or, again, he may have been placed within some connection of life which used to seem quite satisfactory. He fulfilled his duties, and so forth. *Now* his duties become repulsive to him; he would like to quit them because he feels they are not sufficiently spiritual, and so forth.

Thus it is that spiritual endeavour within Anthroposophy may very easily lead into a kind of egoism; a man tends to attach far greater importance to himself than he did before.

But it all rests on the fact that, in such a case, there has been no *expansion of interest* towards the outside world; on the contrary, interest has been thrust back within. I have often pointed out that one who grows in a true and right way into anthroposophical life, does not take *less* interest in external life; rather does he, by reason of his Anthroposophy, take far more interest. Everything outside himself begins to be far more interesting to him than before; it has far more value for him. For this, however, it is necessary that he should not withdraw from external life, but perceive, rather, the spirituality in it.

This of course means that certain things begin to show themselves in other human beings which had not been noticed before. But then we must also have the courage to notice these things, and not to overlook them. For consideration of life from the point of view of karma, it is absolutely necessary that we acquire in some measure the power to go out of ourselves and into the other man.

Naturally, this is peculiarly difficult when the other person becomes a means for karmic adjustments in life which are unpleasant, and possibly even painful to us! But unless we are able to go out of ourselves, even in matters which are disagreeable and painful to us, no true and valid study of karma is possible. For let us remind ourselves:—what are the conditions that have to exist in the world for karma to be brought into being?

We are each placed within a certain human life. In the course of it we act, think, and feel in one way or another. We enter into certain relationships with other human beings and within these relationships things happen. We think, feel, will and do things that call for a karmic adjustment. We enter into relationships with other men, and again things happen which demand a karmic adjustment. Try to survey from this point of view one human earthly life and then observe how at the end of it a man passes through the portal of death into the spiritual world. He now lives within the spiritual world. In the spiritual world it is not as in the physical world. In the physical world you stand outside the other man. You stand outside even those people with whom you come in close contact. Between you and the other man there is at least air, and each one has his own skin! So that when you approach another ever so closely, you can always in a certain measure keep yourself to yourself. This, however, is no longer possible when you have gone through the portal of death and dwell in the spiritual world. Let us take a typical case. You have done something to another man which calls for a karmic compensation. You go on living with him, after you have both passed through the portal of death. You live then *within the other man;* and this not by virtue of your good will or your inner perfection, but compulsorily, if I may put it so.

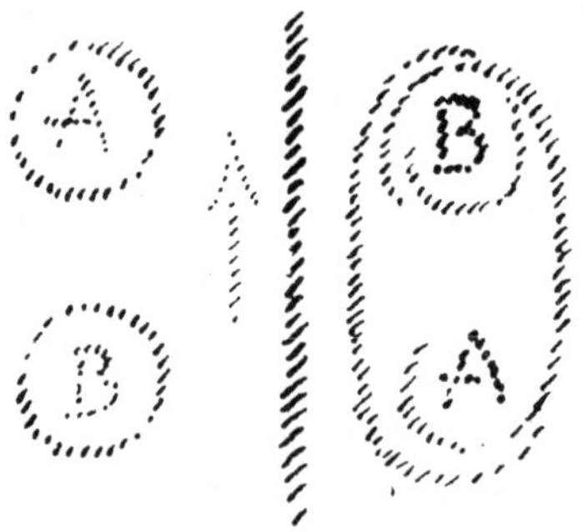

Suppose A and B go through the portal of death. Afterwards they are in the spiritual world. They confront one another in the spiritual world. Yet, whereas here B lived within himself and A lived within himself, after death A lives in B as well as in himself, and B lives in A as well as in himself. In the spiritual world, men live entirely within one another; and in so doing they are maintained by the forces which they have stored up in their lives on earth. After death we do not enter into relation with just any kind of men; we enter into relation with those with whom we have already established a connection for good or for ill. And it is these connections which bring it about that we live not merely within ourselves but within the other. Now imagine, you have done something to another man,—or, let us say, B has acted towards A in a way which demands karmic compensation. When B passes through the portal of death, then after death, in the passage through the world between death and a new birth, he lives in A. He experiences, within A, what he did to A. And while he is thus living outside himself, he provides for the karmic compensation to be brought about. Thus all that is to be brought to pass as karmic compensation during the next earthly life, you yourself cause by living in the other man. It is only on descending again to the physical world that A makes what you have put into him *into his own deed.* In the next earthly life he comes to meet you with what you really have willed to inflict upon yourself through him.

When, therefore, in the next earthly life, something is inflicted on me by another man as a karmic compensation, this happens because I laid it into him during the time I lived within him between death and a new birth. At that time it was not his deed at all; it becomes his deed only as he descends again into earth-life. Thus the conditions for the working of karma in the course of evolution arise from the fact that karmically-connected human beings dwell within one another in the time between death and rebirth.

Now when we consider ordinary life on earth, we do not really penetrate very deeply into it. As far as the other man is concerned, we are extraordinarily little aware of him, consciously. For instance, how little we notice any slight difference in the behaviour of another man in relation to ourselves! Suppose we meet a man in life, and he behaves towards us in a certain way. We are aware of it, but we use very little discrimination. We do not observe what entirely different motives and impulses may account for his behaviour. A man, let us say, is antagonistically disposed towards me. This antagonism may be caused by the mere fact that my existence irritates him, because he is attuned to something quite different in life. Therefore he treats me in a certain way. This treatment can be of such a nature that only in the next life is it karmically balanced. In such a case the antagonism can be quite original, not in the least conditioned by preceding earthly lives.

But I may also receive a similar, perhaps even identical, treatment from another man, into whom I myself implanted bit by bit all that comes to me with this treatment, in the time between death and rebirth.

The feeling which can differentiate between two such kinds of treatment, externally similar, is very little developed to-day; it must show itself again, in order that the *moral tenor of life* may become purer, and man's moral perception stronger. In earlier epochs—in epochs not even very remote from us—such a distinction lay within human comprehension. One felt, e.g. towards one man: He hates me and does this or that out of hate for me; while with another man one had the feeling; he must do something against me, he simply cannot help it, he is inwardly predestined to act in this way.

This feeling, which can be subtly discerned in the facts of life, must again become more general. It will give to life many fine nuances which are of great importance.

There is another difference we must learn to observe. You will readily admit that when a man comes into relation with other men, all manner of things are connected with this relationship, things which do not interest him as much as the relationship itself. Again, I will take a characteristic instance. Suppose you enter a society—I am not thinking now of the Anthroposophical Society; I exclude it for reasons that will emerge in the course of these lectures. The reason why you enter this society may be that you have a karmic link with one or two persons, perhaps with only one person in the society; but you have to participate in everything connected with the society in order to approach this one person as closely as your karmic relations with him demand. While from the point of view of karma the relation to this one man only is important, you share in everything that you come up against in this society, through the people you meet there, etc. So we have to recognise that life confronts us in such a way that the relations into which it brings us are of the most varied shades; quite indifferent relationships may stand side by side with the most significant, in the deepest sense of the word.

But note in this connection, how true it is that external life is frequently only Maya, is in many respects the Great Illusion. Thus it can happen—I will again construct a hypothetical case—that you enter a society, and the relation to the one person, which is well determined karmically, has difficulty in establishing itself. You have to link on to all sorts of people in order to approach that one man. With these other men you make connections which—let us say—appear extremely important to a more rough-and-ready consideration of life; yes, it may be, they make themselves very strongly felt, whereas perhaps the connection which you approach last of all, and which is of real karmic importance, takes its course gently, softly, unobtrusively.

Thus it can really be that the karmically important element in some connection of life appears like a little mount beside giant mountains, which are in reality of lesser importance. To a spiritualised consideration, however, the little hillock reveals itself in its right significance. The events which occur in life cause us many illusions. As a rule we do not know how to judge them if we take only one earthly life into consideration. It is only when we perceive other earthly lives in the background that we can estimate correctly the one earthly life in all its events.

I should like to illustrate this by an example. Strange personalities have appeared in our time. Apart from those of whom I have spoken to you in our studies on karma, a number of quite remarkable personalities have appeared here and there. External study often does not lead at all into karmic connections; we need a study which is able to take note of incisive moments in life. Then we come to see, in all clarity, just those facts which make us realise how illusory external life is unless it is considered on the basis of the spiritual. Recently I mentioned here an example which may have appeared to you very strange, the example of an alchemist of the school of Basil Valentine, who reappeared again as Frank Wedekind.

My starting-point for the observation of this strange karma—the starting-point is not always significant in itself; if afterwards the starting-point has led on to inner clarity, then naturally the whole thing changes—the starting-point in this case was the circumstance that I had hardly ever before seen such hands as Frank Wedekind's, and I saw Frank Wedekind gesticulate with those hands of his when he acted in his own "Hidalla". The whole apparent chaos of this play (which, as I recently mentioned, is a perfect horror from the ordinary, conventional point of view) connected itself with the impression of his hands that I had had before, and conjured up before my vision the chemical manipulations on which, in a former life, he had been engaged. On the basis of his "Hidella", in connection with these strange hands, appeared the earlier incarnation which one could then follow further.

You will see from this how one must develop an eye for what is of real significance in a human being. There are men in whom the countenance is the most characteristic element. But there are also men in whom the most important characteristic is not the face at all, but, for instance, the hands; from the face of such a man one can infer nothing, only from the hands. When you pass on from the individual to the general, precisely in the example which I have just brought forward, you can realise quite clearly how it stands. For these medieval alchemists were of course obliged to acquire extraordinary dexterity with their hands.

In earlier lectures I have spoken of how nothing is suffered to remain of all that man has developed in his head. But that which he bears in the rest of his organism is subsequently brought to expression in the (next) head. Now in childhood the whole forming of the body takes its start from the head. Above all, such expressive organs as the hands are shaped in accordance with the most intimate impulses of the head. We may therefore expect that something very characteristic will appear in the hands or feet of one who has worked in the manner of alchemists.

I say all this to show you how important it is to take one particular thing in its full significance, and to regard as insignificant what frequently presents itself in the sense-world as the most evident, the most essential, the greatest, etc. In our time, as I said, there have appeared many strange and remarkable personalities who stand before us without our being able to arrive at any complete survey of the karmic connections. Just in the case of such personalities it is a question of observing in them what is striking and significant. The fact that somebody was a great artist, for example, is something which may possibly be determined only in the very smallest measure by his karma. But *what* exactly he does in his art, how he conducts himself in it, these are things that are specially determined in karma. Thus, the very things which, one may say, make life really poetic, reveal themselves to a study of karma.

Let us suppose we can look back on a man's previous incarnations. In respect of the present incarnation they are remarkably illuminating in certain points. But we can never understand how to find our way intelligently in these investigations as long as we make use of the ordinary criteria for understanding and interpreting life. Life becomes a reality in quite a different sense when one resolves to pursue a study of karma in all earnestness.

Let me give you an example. I will in the first place relate quite simply what happened. I was walking one day along a street and I had a picture before me. I see a ship-wrecked man. His ship is far away, and sinking. The man is in a lifeboat, hurrying towards a fairly large island. His gaze is directed strangely, considering that he is still in doubt whether his boat will reach land and his life be safe! He is looking at the bubbling, foaming billows. I am impressed by the fact that he can still gaze at the waves, even though he is liable at any moment to be drowned. A disturbed and shaken soul, but in the shock—and so in a body-free manner—deeply united with Nature.

While still on the same walk—the picture had of course no connection whatever with my surroundings—my way led me to an Art Exhibition where I saw for the first time Boecklin's "Toteninsel" (Island of the Dead). I mention this only that you may see how in approaching these things we must take a wider outlook. It is not simply a matter of meditating upon all one can think and feel about Boecklin from the starting-point of his picture, "Island of the Dead". It need not be so at all; it is quite possible that under certain circumstances one has to revert to something one has seen prophetically, and link that on to one's experience of the picture.

And so, too, when we meet a man in real life. Then, in order to find karmic connections, it is not only important to consider what we experience just in the moment of meeting him; it is often most illuminating to recall some intimate previous experience, for we may find that we understand it only when we see how it connects with what we afterwards perceive in him or through him.

The very things that prove so illuminating for karma are often things that throw their shadows in advance—or, we may also say, their *light*. We need a fine sense for the intimacies of life, which sometimes means that we not only connect the future with the past, but regard the past as something that elucidates the future. Unless we can learn to look at life in this intimate way, we shall not easily develop that inner mobility of soul which is necessary for a deeper penetration into karmic connections.

It is indeed a fact that when specially significant karmic events enter a man's life, they are connected with inner events in his life which may date from several years previously. We have to acquire in this way an expanded view of life.

For think of the following:— When you look at the thinking element in man, as it exists in ordinary consciousness, you find it related only to the past. When, however, you look at human feeling, with the many shades and nuances it receives from emotional and temperamental depths, then you come upon strange secrets of life. The course of a man's life can be very little gauged by the way he thinks; but very much by the way he feels. And when you observe such a life, let us say, as Goethe's, and ask yourself: How did Goethe feel in the year 1790?—then, through the peculiar stamp and character of Goethe's feeling in the year 1790 you get the entire later colouring of his life; it is all present as a nucleus in the feeling of 1790. As soon as we descend into the depths of the human soul we really perceive the peculiar colouring—not of course the details—of the subsequent life. A man might gain a great deal of illumination on his own life if he paid more attention to the inexplicable shades of feeling which are not caused from without but rise from the depths within.

Men will accustom themselves to taking this kind of thing specially into account if they pay attention to the points I have mentioned to-day. I shall have more to say about them: they are important for a consideration of life that intends to take note of karmic connections. And this holds good, whether one is dealing with karmic connections in one's own life, or with karmic connections of those who are dear to one. For you must understand that if one desires to consider karma, it is a question really of *looking through* a human being in a certain way. When no more than the ordinary physical human being stands in your field of vision, he stands there before you non-transparent. You look at his face, at the way he moves about and behaves, at the way he speaks, or perhaps even also at the way he thinks,—the latter being, on the whole, generally only a conventional reflection of his upbringing and experience. But so long as you look no further than this, the karma of this human being does not stand objectively before you.

When, however, a man becomes transparent for you, then at first you really have the feeling that he is hovering in the air. Gradually it comes about that you no longer think of him as walking or moving his arms and hands. You lose all sense of this. Understand me aright, my dear friends. In ordinary life what a man does with his arms and legs is extremely important. But this loses its importance when one wishes to observe the deeper elements in man. You must take what I am saying in its fullest meaning. Can you look right away from what a man achieves by means of his arms and hands, and see him hovering, as it were, not so much in respect of space as in respect of life? I mean, take no account of journeys he has made, of all his goings and comings, in short, of all he does with his legs; and attach equally little importance to the work he does with his hands. Watch rather his mood, his temperament; watch everything in him in which arms and legs take no part. Then you have, so to speak, the first transparency to which you can attain. And what will this first transparency show? Picture to yourselves, you have here an object. At first you see nothing but the object. Well and good. But then something is drawn upon the object. And now it is again erased. This is how it is with man when you arrive at the first transparency, when you look away from the man of ordinary life and completely disregard his arms and legs. You have to tear him right out of the connections into which he has come through the activity of his arms and legs. If you now observe him, something in him becomes transparent, and you look through to what was previously covered up by the activity of arms and legs.

And what is it you see? You begin to understand that behind the man the Moon appears. I will draw here diagrammatically the threefold man. Now suppose, *this* (i.e. the lower part) first becomes transparent; we disregard the arms and legs. Then the man no longer appears to us detached from the universe as he otherwise does; he begins to reveal behind him the Moon, with all the impulses which work in man from the Moon. We begin to say: "Yes, man has a certain power of phantasy,—whether it be developed or no, he has this power in him. He cannot help it. Moon forces are behind this. They are hidden from us only by the activity of

arms and legs. But now all that has vanished, and in the background appears before us the creative Moon."

We go on. We try to make man still more transparent. By a kind of suggestion, we think away all that makes man emotional, all that endows him with a certain temperament—in short, those features of his every-day life in which his soul-nature is chiefly expressed. Still more disappears; he becomes still more transparent. And we can go farther. We can disregard all that exists in man, because he has senses. First, you disregard everything that is in man by virtue of his having arms and legs. Now you ask yourself: what remains over from man, when I ignore the fact that he has ever perceived anything by means of his senses? There remains a certain direction of thought, a certain impulsive force of his thought, a tendency of life. At this point, however, the whole rhythmic system, the breast of man, becomes transparent. It vanishes, and in the background appears before you all that exists there as Sun-impulse (see diagram). You look through man and behold in reality the Sun, when you ignore all that man has perceived by means of his senses. You can try this on yourself. You can ask yourself: what do I owe to my senses? And then, when you look away from all this, you see through yourself and behold yourself as a Sun-being.

And when further you disregard man's thoughts, the direction of his thinking, then the head too disappears. Now the whole man is gone. You look through, and finally behold Saturn in the background. But in this moment, the man's karma, or your own karma, lies open before you. For in the moment when you observe the working of Saturn in a man, when a man has become entirely transparent to you, and you observe him so extensively that you behold him on the background of the whole planetary system—on the background of Moon, Sun and Saturn—in that moment the karma of the man lies open before you. And if one is going to speak of practical karma-exercises—I told you already that I wanted to do it at the beginning of the foundation of the Anthroposophical Society, but did not succeed at that time—then one must really begin in this way. One must say: It is a matter first of all of disregarding—in ourselves or in others—all that we are in life, inasmuch as we are beings endowed with arms and legs. Cut this right out of your thought. All you have ever attained through the fact that you are a being endowed with arms and legs—this you must ignore.

Then you will say: "Yes, but we fulfil our karma just because we have arms and legs!" So you do. So long, however, as you look at your arms and legs, you are not aware of what it is you fulfil through having arms and legs. This you see only when you no longer look at your arms and legs any more, but find in the activity of arms and legs the impulses of the Moon. Then it is a matter of going a step further, and disregarding all that man absorbs by means of his senses, what he has in his soul by means of his senses—whether you are practising the exercise with yourself or with others. You behold man then as Sun-being, you see the Sun-impulse in him. And again, you must disregard the fact that he has a certain tendency of thought, a certain tendency of soul—then you realise him to be a Saturn-being.

Should you arrive thus far, then you have man once more before you, but now—as a spirit. Now the legs move and the arms work, but spiritually, and they show us what they do. But they show us this according to the *forces* which work and rule in them. This is what we have to learn and experience.

When I do the most trifling thing, when I pick up the chalk here—as long as I merely see this fact, the picking-up of the chalk, then I know nothing of karma. I must do away with all this. I must bring it about that all this can reproduce itself in a picture, can appear again in a picture. Not in the strength that is contained in my muscles—this can explain nothing at all—but in the picture that takes the place of the act, appears the force that induces the hand to move, in order to pick up the chalk. And it appears as something coming from previous incarnations.

This is how it is, when I gradually do away with visible man in the above manner and see behind him his Moon-impulses, his Sun-impulses, and his Saturn-impulses. Then the image or picture of the man comes to meet me again from the cosmos. But it is not the man in his present incarnation; it is the man in one of his preceding incarnations or in several previous incarnations. I must first bring it about that the man who is walking here at my side, becomes transparent for me, ever more and more transparent, in that I put away from my vision his whole life. Then there comes to the same spot, but now proceeding from cosmic distances, the man as he was in his previous earthly lives.

Perhaps what has been placed before you to-day about these connections is not at once altogether clear and comprehensible. But I wanted to point the way prospectively, as it were, and in the coming lectures we shall enter into more and more detailed considerations of the nature of karma as it flows in human life from one incarnation to another.

VII

To-day we shall begin to consider the inner activities of the soul which can gradually lead man to acquire conceptions, to acquire thoughts, about karma. These thoughts and conceptions are such that they can ultimately enable a man to perceive, in the light of karma, experiences which have a karmic cause.

Looking around our human environment, we really see in the physical world only what is caused by physical force in a physical way. And if we do see in the physical world something that is not caused by physical forces, we still become aware of it through external physical substances, through external physical objects of perception. Of course, when a man does something out of his own will, this is not caused by physical forces, by physical causes, for in many respects it comes out of the free will. But all that we perceive outwardly is exhausted in the physical phenomena of the world we thus observe. In the entire sphere of what we can thus observe, the karmic connection of an experience we ourselves pass through cannot reveal itself to us. For the whole picture of this karmic connection lies in the spiritual world, is really inscribed in what is the etheric world, in what underlies the etheric world as the astral world, or as the world of spiritual beings who inhabit this astral outer world. Nothing of all this is seen, as long as we merely direct our senses to the physical world.

All that we perceive in the physical world is perceived through our senses. These senses work without our having much to do with it. Our eyes receive impressions of light, of colour, of their own accord. We can at most—and even that is half involuntary—adjust our gaze to a certain direction; we can gaze at something or we can look away from it. Even in this there is still much of the unconscious, but at all events a fragment of consciousness. And, above all, that which the eye must do inwardly in order to see colour, the wonderfully wise, inner activity which is exercised whenever we see anything—this we could never achieve as human beings if we were supposed to achieve it consciously. That would be out of the question. All this must, to begin with, happen unconsciously, because it is much too wise for man to be able in any way to help in it.

To attain a correct point of view as regards the knowledge possessed by the human being, we must really fill our thoughts with all the wisdom-filled arrangements which exist in the world, and which are quite beyond the capacity of man. If a man thinks only of what he can achieve himself, then he really blocks all paths to knowledge. The path to knowledge really begins at the point where we realise, in all humility, all that we are incapable of doing, but which must nevertheless come to pass in cosmic existence. The eye, the ear—yes, and the other sense-organs—are, in reality, such profoundly wise instruments that men will have to study for a long time before they will be able even to have an inkling of understanding of them during earthly existence. This must be fully realised. Observation of the spiritual, however, cannot be unconscious in this sense. In earlier times of human evolution this was possible even for observation of the spiritual. There was an instinctive clairvoyance which has faded away in the course of the evolution of humanity.

From now onwards, man must consciously attain an attitude to the cosmos through which he will be able to see through into the spiritual. And we must see through into the spiritual if we are to recognise the karmic connections of any experience we may have.

Now it is necessary for the observation of karma that we at least begin by paying attention to what can happen within us to develop the faculty of observing karmic connections. We, on our part, must help a little in order to make these observations conscious. We must do more, for example, than we do for our eye in order to become conscious of colour.

My dear friends, what we must learn first of all is summed up in one word: to wait. We must be able to wait for the inner experiences.

About this "being able to wait", I have already spoken. It was in the year 1889—I tell about this in the *Story of my Life*—that the inner spiritual construction of Goethe's "Fairy Tale of the Green Snake and the Beautiful Lily" first came before my mind's eye. And it was then, for the first time, that the perception as it were of a greater, wider connection than appears in the Fairy Tale itself presented itself to me. But I also knew at that time: I cannot yet make of this connection what I shall some day be able to make of it. And so what the Fairy Tale revealed to me at that time simply remained lying in the soul.

Then, seven years later, in the year 1896, it welled up again, but still not in such a way that it could be properly shaped; and again, about 1903, seven years later. Even then, although it came with great definition and many connections it could not yet receive its right form. Seven years later again, when I conceived my first Mystery Play, *The Portal of Initiation*—then only did the Fairy Tale reappear, transformed in such a way that it could be shaped and moulded plastically.

Such things, therefore, demand a real waiting, a time for ripening. We must bring our own experiences into relation with that which exists out there in the world. At a moment when only the seed of a plant is present, we obviously cannot have the plant. The seed must be brought into the right conditions for growth, and we must wait until the blossom, and finally the fruit, come out of the seed. And so it must be with the experiences through which we pass. We cannot take the line of being thrilled by an experience, simply because it happens to be there, and then forgetting it. The person who only wants his experiences when they are actually present will be doing little towards ultimate observation of the spiritual world. We must be able to wait. We must be able to let the experiences ripen within the soul.

Now the possibility exists for a comparatively quick

ripening of insight into karmic connections if, for a considerable time, we endeavour patiently, and with inner activity, to picture in our consciousness, more and more clearly, an experience which would otherwise simply take its course externally, without being properly grasped, so that it fades away in the course of life. After all, this fading away is what really happens with the events of life. For what does a man do with events and experiences, as they approach him in the course of the day? He experiences them, but in reality only half observes them. You can realise how experiences are only half observed if you sit down one day in the afternoon or in the evening—and I advise you to do it—and ask yourself: 'What did I actually experience this morning at half-past nine?' And now try to call up such an experience in all details before your soul, recall it as if it were actually there, say at half-past seven in the evening—as if you were creating it spiritually before you. You will see how much you will find lacking, how much you failed to observe, and how difficult it is. If you take a pen or pencil to write it all down, you will soon begin to bite at the pen or the pencil, because you cannot hit upon the details—and, in fine, you want to bite them out of the pencil!

Yes, but that is just the point, to take upon oneself the task of placing before the mind, in all precision, an experience one has had,—not at the moment when it is actually there, but afterwards. It must be placed before the soul as if one were going to paint it spiritually. If the experience were one in which somebody spoke, this must be made quite objectively real: the ring of the voice, the way in which the words were used, clumsily or cleverly—the picture must be made with strength and vigour. In short, we try to make a picture of what we have experienced. If we make a picture of such an experience of the day, then in the following night, the astral body, when it is outside the physical body and the etheric body, occupies itself with this picture. The astral body itself is, in reality, the bearer of the picture, and gives shape to it outside the body. The astral body takes the picture with it when it goes out on the first night. It shapes it there, outside the physical and etheric bodies.

That is the first stage (we will take these stages quite exactly): the sleeping astral body, when outside the physical and etheric bodies, shapes the picture of the experience. Where does it do this? In the external ether. It is now in the external etheric world; it does this in the external ether.

Now picture to yourself the human being: his physical and etheric bodies lie in bed, and the astral body is outside. We will leave aside the ego. There outside is the astral body, reshaping this picture that has been made. But the astral body does this in the external ether. In consequence of this the following happens—think of it: the astral body is there

outside, shaping this picture. All this happens in the external ether which encrusts, as it were, with its own substance that which is formed as a picture within the astral body. So the external ether makes the etheric form (dotted (dark) outline) into a picture which is clearly and precisely visualised by the eye of spirit.

In the morning you return into the physical and etheric bodies and bear into them what has been made substantial by the external ether. That is to say: the sleeping astral body shapes the picture of the experience outside the physical and etheric bodies. The external ether then impregnates the picture with its own substance. You can imagine that the picture becomes stronger thereby, and that now, when the astral body returns in the morning with this stronger substantiality, it can make an impression upon the etheric body in the human being. With forces that are derived from the external ether, the astral body now stamps an impression into the etheric body.

The second stage is therefore: The picture is impressed into the etheric body by the astral body.

There we have the events of the first day and the first night. Now we come to the second day. On the second day, while you are busying yourself with all the little things of life in full waking consciousness, there, underneath the consciousness, in the unconscious, the picture is descending into the etheric body. And in the next night, when the etheric body is undisturbed, when the astral body has gone out again, the etheric body elaborates this picture.

Thus in the second night the picture is elaborated by the man's own etheric body. There we have the second stage:—The picture is impressed into the etheric body by the astral body; and in the next night the etheric body elaborates the picture. Thus we have: the second day and the second night.

Now if you do this, if you actually do not give up occupying yourself with the picture you formed on the preceding day—and you can continue to occupy yourself with it, for a reason which I shall immediately mention—if you do not disdain to do this, then you will find that you are living on further with the picture. What does this mean—to continue occupying yourself with it? If you really take pains to shape such a picture, vigorously, elaborating it plastically in characteristic, strong lines on the first day after you had the experience, then you have really exerted yourself spiritually. Such things cost spiritual exertion. I don't mean what I am going to say as a hint—present company is, of course, always excepted in these matters!—but after all, it must be said that the majority of men simply do not know what spiritual exertion is. Spiritual exertion, true spiritual exertion, comes about only by means of activity of soul. When you allow the world to work upon you, and let thoughts run their course without taking them in hand, then there is no spiritual exertion. We should not imagine, when something tires us, that we have exerted ourselves spiritually. Getting tired does not imply that there has been spiritual exertion. We can get tired, for instance, from reading. But if we have not ourselves been productive in some way during the reading, if we merely let the thoughts contained in the book act on us, then we are *not* exerting ourselves. On the contrary, a person who has really exerted himself spiritually, who has exerted himself out of the inner activity of his soul, may then take up a book, a very interesting one, and just "sleep off" his spiritual exertion in the best possible way, in the reading of it. Naturally, we can fall asleep over a book if we are tired. This getting tired is no sign at all of spiritual exertion.

A sign of spiritual exertion, however, is this: that one feels—the brain is used up. It is just as we may feel that a demand has been made on the muscle of the arm when lifting things. Ordinary thought makes no such strong claims upon the brain. The process continues, and you will even notice that when you try it for the first time, the second, the third, the tenth, you get a slight headache. It is not that you get tired or fall asleep; on the contrary, you cannot fall alseep; you get a slight headache from it. Only you must not regard this headache as something baleful; on the contrary, you must take it as actual proof of the fact that you have exerted your head.

Well, the process goes on . . . it stays with you until you go to sleep. If you have really done this on the preceding day, then you will awake in the morning with the feeling: "There actually *is* something in me! I don't quite know what it is, but there is something in me, and it wants something from me. Yes, after all it is not a matter of indifference that I made this picture for myself yesterday. It really means something. This picture has changed. To-day it is giving me quite different feelings from those I had previously. The picture is making me have quite definite feelings."

All this stays with you through the next day as the remaining inner experience of the picture which you made for yourself. And what you feel, and cannot get rid of through the whole of the day—this is a witness to the fact that the picture is now descending into the etheric body, as I have described to you, and that the etheric body is receiving it.

Now you will probably experience on waking after the next night—when you slip into your body after these two days—that you find this picture slightly changed, slightly transformed. You find it again . . . precisely on waking the third day you find it again within you. It appears to you like a very real dream. But it has undergone a transformation. It will clothe itself in manifold pictures until it is other than it was. It will assume an appearance as if spiritual beings were now bringing you this experience. And you actually receive the impression: Yes, this experience which I had and which I subsequently formed into a picture, has actually been brought to me. If the experience happened to be with another human being, then we have the feeling after this has all happened, that actually we did not only experience it through that human being, but that it was really brought to us. Other forces, spiritual forces, have been at play. It was they who brought it to us.

The next day comes. This next day the picture is carried down from the etheric body into the physical body. The etheric body impresses this picture into the physical body, into the nerve-processes, into the blood-processes. On the third day the picture is impressed into the physical body. So the third stage is: The picture is stamped into the physical body by the etheric body.

And now comes the next night. You have been attending throughout the day to the ordinary little trifles of life, and underneath it all this important process is going on: the picture is being carried down into the physical body. All this goes on in the subconscious. When the following night comes, the picture is elaborated in the physical body. It is spiritualised in the physical body. First of all, throughout the day, the picture is brought down into the processes of the blood and nerves, but in the night it is spiritualised. Those who have vision see how this picture is now elaborated by the physical body, but it appears spiritually as an altogether changed picture. We can say: the physical body elaborates the picture during the next night.

1st Day and 1st Night:
When outside the physical and etheric bodies, the astral body shapes the picture of the experience. The outer ether impregnates the picture with its own substance.

2nd Day and 2nd Night:
The picture is stamped by the astral body into the etheric body. And the etheric body elaborates the picture during the next day.

3rd Day and 3rd Night:
The picture is stamped by the etheric body into the physical body. And the physical body elaborates the picture during the next night.

Now this is something of which you must make an absolutely correct mental picture. The physical body actually works up this picture spiritually. It spiritualises the picture. So that when all this has really been gone through, it does happen—when the human being is asleep—that his physical body works up the whole picture, but not in such a way that it remains within the physical body. Out of the physical body there arises a transformation, a greatly magnified transformation of the picture. And when you get up in the morning, this picture stands there, and in truth you hover in it; it is like a kind of cloud in which you yourself are. With this picture you get up in the morning.

So this is the third day and the third night. With this picture, which is entirely transformed, you get out of bed on the fourth day. You rise from sleep, enveloped by this cloud. And if you have actually shaped the picture with the necessary strength on the first day, and if you have paid attention to what your feeling conveyed to you on the second day, you will notice now that your will is contained in the picture as it now is. The will is contained in it! But this will is unable to express itself; it is as though fettered. Put into somewhat radical terms, it is actually as if one had planned after the manner of an incredibly daring sprinter, who might resolve to make a display of a bravado race: I will run, now I am running to Ober-Dornach, I make a picture of it already, I've got it within me. It is my will... But in the very moment when I want to start, when the will is strongest, somebody fetters me, so that I stand there quite rigidly. The whole will has unfolded, but I cannot carry out the will. Such, approximately, is the process.

When this experience of feeling yourself in a pillory develops—for it is a feeling of being in a pillory after the third night—when you again awake in it, feeling in a pillory as it were, with the will fettered through and through, then, if you can pay attention to it, you will find that the will begins to transform itself. This will becomes *sight*. In itself it can do nothing, but it leads to our seeing something. It becomes an eye of the soul. And the picture, with which one rose from sleep, becomes objective. What it shows is the event of the previous earth-life, or of some previous earth-life, which had been the cause of the experience that we shaped into a picture on the first day. By means of this transformation through feeling and through will, one gets the picture of the causal event of a preceding incarnation.

When we describe these things, they appear somewhat overpowering. This is not to be wondered at, for they are utterly unfamiliar to the human being of the present time. They were not so unknown to the men of earlier culture-epochs. Only, according to the opinion of modern men who are clever, those other men—in their whole way of living—were stupid! Nevertheless, those 'stupid' men of the earlier culture-epochs really had these experiences, only modern man darkens everything by his intellect, which makes him clever, but not exactly wise.

As I said, the thing seems somewhat tumultuous, when one relates it. But after all, one is obliged to use such words; for since the things are utterly unknown to-day, they would not appear so striking if they were worded more mildly. They must appear striking. But the whole experience, from beginning to end, throughout the three days, as I have described it to you, must take its course in inner intimacy, in rest and peace of mind. For so-called occult experiences—and these are such—do not take their course in such a way that they can be bragged about. When one begins to brag about them, they immediately stop. They must take their course in inner repose and quietude. And it is best when, for the time being, nobody at all notices anything of the consecutive experiences except the person who is having them.

Now you must not think that the thing succeeds immediately, from the outset. One always finds, of course, that people are pleased when such things are related. This is quite comprehensible . . . and it is good. How much there is that one can learn to know! And then, with a tremendous diligence people start on it. They begin . . . and it doesn't succeed. Then they become disheartened. Then, perhaps, they try it again, several times. Again it does not succeed. But, in effect, if one has tried it about 49 times, or, let us say, somebody else has tried it about 69 times, then the 50th or the 70th time it does succeed. For what really matters in all these things is the acquisition of a kind of habit of soul concerning them. To begin with, one must find one's way into these things, one must acquire habits of the soul. This is something that certainly ought to be carefully observed by the Anthroposophical Society which, since the Christmas Foundation, is intended to be a complete expression of the Anthroposophical Movement.

Really a very great deal has been given within the Anthroposophical Society. It is enough to make one giddy to see standing in a row all the Lecture-Courses that have been printed. But in spite of it, people come again and again, asking one thing or the other. In the majority of cases this is not at all necessary, for if everything that is contained in the Lecture-Courses is really worked upon, then most of the questions find their own answer in a much surer way. One must have patience, really have patience. Truly, there is a great deal in anthroposophical literature that can work in the soul. We must take to heart all that has to be accomplished, and the time will be well filled with all that has to be done. But, on the other hand, in regard to many of the things which people want to know, it must be pointed out that the Lecture-Courses exist, that they have been left lying there, and after they have been given many people trouble about them only inasmuch as they want a "new" Course; they just lay the old ones aside. These things are closely connected with what I have to say to-day.

One does not reach inner continuity in following up all that germinates and ripens in the soul, if there is a desire to hurry in this way, from the new to the new; the essential point is that things must mature within the soul. We must accustom ourselves to inner, active work of the soul, work in the spirit. This is what helps us to achieve such things as I have explained to you to-day; this alone will help us to have, after the third day, the inner attitude of soul in connection with some experience we may wish to see through in the light of karma.

This must always be the mode of procedure if we are to learn to know the spiritual. To begin with, we must say to ourselves: the first moment when we approach the spiritual in thought in some way, was the first beginning; it is quite impossible to have any kind of result immediately; we must

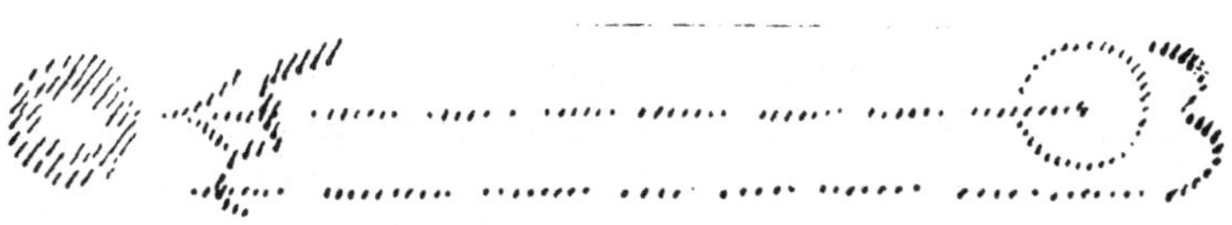

be able to wait. Suppose I have an experience to-day that is karmically caused in a preceding incarnation. I will make a diagrammatic sketch. Here I am, here is my experience, the experience of to-day (right). This is caused by the quite differently-constituted personality in the same ego in a previous earth-life (left). There it is. It has long ceased to belong to my personality, but it is stamped into the etheric world, or into the astral world, which lies behind the etheric world. Now I have to go back, to retrace the way backwards.

I told you that at first the thing appears as if some being were really bearing the experience towards me. This is so, on the second day. But after the third day it appears as if those who have brought it to me, those spiritual beings, withdraw, and I become aware of it as something of my own, which I myself, in a previous incarnation, laid down as cause. Because this is no longer within the present, because this is something I must behold in the past earth-life, I seem to be fettered. This state of being fettered ceases only when I have perceived the thing, when I have a picture of what was in the previous incarnation, and when I then look back to the event which I have not lost sight of through the three days. Then I become free, as I return, for now I can move about freely with the effect. As long as I am only within the cause, I cannot move about with the cause. Thus I go back into a previous incarnation, there become fettered as it were by the cause, and only when I now enter right into this present earth-life, is the thing resolved.

Now let us take an example: suppose somebody experiences at a certain time on a certain day that a friend says something to him that is not altogether pleasant—perhaps he had not expected it. This friend says to him something not altogether pleasant. He now ponders what he experiences in listening to what his friend says. He makes a vivid picture of what he has experienced, how he got a slight shock, and how he got vexed, perhaps he was also hurt, or the like. This is an inner working, and as such it must be brought into the picture. Now he lets the three days elapse. The second day he goes about and says to himself: 'This picture which I made yesterday has had a strange effect upon me. The whole day long I have had within me something like an acid, as it were, something that comes from the picture and makes me feel inwardly out of sorts . . .' At the end of the whole process, after the third day, he says to himself: 'I get up in the morning and now I have the definite feeling that the picture is fettering me. Then this event of the previous incarnation is made known to me. I see it before me. Then I pass over to the experience which is still quite fresh, which is still quite present. The fettering ceases, and I say to myself: 'So this is how it was in the previous earth-life! This is what caused it; now there is the effect. With this effect I can live again . . . now the thing is present again.'

This must be practised over and over again, for generally the thread is broken on the very first day, when we make the first effort. And then nothing comes.

It is particularly favourable to let things run parallel, so that we do not stop at one event, but bring a number of events of the day into picture-form in this way. You will say: 'Then I must live through the next day with the greatest variety of feelings.' But this is quite possible. It is not at all harmful. Only try it; the things go quite well together. 'And must I then be fettered so and so often after the third day?' This does not matter either. Nothing of this matters. The things will adjust themselves in time. What belongs, from an earlier incarnation, to a later one, will find its way to it. But it will not succeed at once; it will not succeed at the first attempt; the thread breaks. We must have patience to try the thing over and over again. Then we feel something growing stronger within the soul. Then we feel that something awakens in the soul, and we say to ourselves: 'Until now you were filled with blood. You have felt within you the pulsation of the blood and the breath. Now there is something within you besides the blood. You are filled with something.'

You can even have the feeling that you are filled with something of which you can say quite definitely that it is like a metal that has become aeriform. You actually feel something like metal, you feel it in you. It cannot be described differently; it really is so. You feel yourself permeated with metal, in your whole body. Just as one can say of certain waters, that they 'taste metallic', the whole body seems to 'taste' as if it were inwardly permeated by some delicate substance, which, in reality, is something spiritual.

You feel this when you come upon something which was, of course, always in you, but to which you only now begin to pay attention. Then, when you begin to feel this, you again take courage. For if the thread is always breaking and everything is as it was before—if you want to get hold of a karmic connection, but the thread is always breaking—you may easily lose courage. But when you detect within yourself this sense of being inwardly filled, then you get courage again. And you say to yourself: it will come right in time.

But, my dear friends, these things must be experienced in all quietude and calmness. Those who cannot experience them quietly but get excited and emotional, spread an inner mist over what really ought to happen, and nothing comes of it.

There are people to-day in the outside world who know of Anthroposophy only by hearsay. Perhaps they have read nothing at all of it, or only what opponents have written. It is really very funny now.—Many of the antagonistic writings spring out of the earth like mushrooms—they quote literature, but among the literature they quote there are none of my books at all, only the books of opponents! The authors admit that they have not really approached the original sources, that they know only the antagonistic literature. Such things exist to-day. And so there are people outside who say: "The Anthroposophists are mad." As a matter of fact, what one can least of all afford to be in order to reach anything at all in the spiritual world is to be mad. One must not be mad in the very slightest degree if one hopes to come to anything in the spiritual world. Even the tiniest fragment of madness is a hindrance to reaching anything. This simply must be avoided. Even a slight fancifulness, slight capriciousness, must be avoided. For all this giving way to the moods of the day, the caprices of the day, forms obstacles and handicaps on the way to progress in the spiritual world. If one desires to progress in the field of Anthroposophy, there is nothing for it but to have an absolutely sane head and an absolutely sane heart. With doting sentimentality (*Schwärmerei*) which is already the beginning of madness, one can achieve nothing.

Things such as I have told you to-day, strange as they sound, must be experienced in the light of absolute clarity of mind, of absolute soundness of head and heart. Truly, there is nothing that can more surely save one from very slight daily madness, than Anthroposophy. All madness would by means of Anthroposophy if people would only devote themselves to it with real intensity. If somebody were to set himself to go mad through Anthroposophy, this would certainly be an experiment with inadequate means!

I do not say this in order to make a joke, but because it must be an integral part of the mood and tenor of anthroposophical endeavour. This is the attitude that must be adopted towards the matter, as I have just explained to you, half in joke, if we want to approach it in the right way, with the right orientation. We must set out to be as sane as possible; then we approach it in the right spirit. This is the least we can strive for, and above all, strive for in respect to the little madnesses of life.

Once I was friends with a very clever professor of philosophy, now long since dead, who used to say on every occasion: "We all have some point or other on which we are a little mad!" He meant, all people are a little mad . . . but he was a very clever man. I always believed there was something behind his words, that his assertion was not altogether without foundation! He did not become an Anthroposophist.

We will continue, then, to-morrow.

VIII

To-day we shall begin a series of studies which will throw light on the unfolding of human karma from the side of the external bodily form as we encounter it in the physiognomy, the play of gestures, in all the external manifestations of the human being in the physical world. For in considering individual karmic connections, I have already drawn attention to the fact that it is precisely by observing apparently insignificant trifles in the human being that karmic connections may be perceived. It is also a fact that the external appearance of the human being gives in many respects a picture of his moral and spiritual tenor in his previous earthly life, or in a series of previous lives.

Along these lines certain types of human beings can be observed, and it will be found that a certain type leads back to a definite attitude and behaviour in one of the previous earthly lives. In order to avoid vague abstractions, let us consider examples.—Suppose, for instance, some human being's life on earth has been spent in occupying himself very closely with the things which confronted him in life; he has had intimate and real interest for many things, not passing by or missing anything about men, things or phenomena of the world. You will certainly have opportunity to observe this in human beings in the present life.

We may meet people who have a better knowledge—let us say—of the statesmen of ancient Greece than of the statesmen of our own time. If they are asked about somebody such as Pericles, Alcibiades or Miltiades, they know all about them, because they learnt it at school. If they are questioned about a person of the same kind belonging to the present day, they can hardly give any information. But the same thing exists in the sphere of the ordinary observation of life. In this connection I have often mentioned details which have certainly seemed strange to those who imagine that they are standing at the highest peak of idealism. There are men, for instance, who, in talking to you in the afternoon, will tell you that they saw a lady in the street in the morning. When you ask them what sort of dress she was wearing, they do not know! It is really incredible, but it is a fact—there are such people.

Now of course, such a thing can be interpreted in all sorts of different ways. It can be said: This is a case of such lofty spirituality that a man who happens to find himself in these circumstances considers it much too trifling to take notice of such things. But this is not a sign of a really penetrating spirituality. It may be lofty spirituality, but loftiness alone is not the point; what really matters is whether the spirituality is penetrating or superficial. There is not, in this case, any penetrating spirituality, because, after all, what a human being needs in the way of clothing *is* quite significant, and in a certain sense it is just as significant as, for instance, the type of nose or mouth he has. Again, there are human beings who are attentive to everything in life. They judge the world according to what they experience from it. Others go through the world as if nothing in it were of the slightest interest to them. They have taken in everything only as a kind of dream which quickly flows away again.

These are—I might say—two polar opposite types of human beings. But however you may judge of it, my dear friends, whatever opinion you may have about whether a man is at a high or low level because he does not remember the dress worn by the lady he saw in the morning—that is not the point. To-day we want to discuss what influence this has on the karma of the human being. It actually makes a great difference whether a man pays attention to things in life, whether he takes interest in every detail, or whether he does not pay attention to things. Details are of enormous importance for the whole structure of spiritual life—not because they are details, but because a detail like the one mentioned points to a very definite constitution of soul.

There was a professor who always lectured extremely well

and who, all the time he was lecturing, stared at one point—the upper part of the chest of someone in the audience; his eyes were riveted on this particular point. He never lost the thread of his lectures, which were always admirable. But one day he did lose the thread; he kept on looking and then turning away. Afterwards he went to the person in the audience and asked: "Why did you sew on the button that had always been missing? It has made me lose my head!" He had always been looking at the place of the missing button and this gave him concentration. Always to be looking at the place where a button is torn off or not, seems trifling, but as a matter of fact, so far as the inner attitude of soul is concerned it is significant whether such a thing is done or not. And when it is a question of observing the lines of karma, it is of extraordinarily great importance.

Let us therefore look a little more closely at these two types of human beings of whom I have been speaking. You need only remember what I have frequently told you about the passing over of the human being from one incarnation into the other. In earthly life man has his head, and he has, as well, the rest of his body. This part of his body, outside the head, contains a certain concatenation of forces. The physical body of the human being is finally given over to the elements. The physical substance, of course, is not carried over from one earthly life into the other. But the concatenation of forces which a man has in his organism, apart from his head, is carried through the life between death and a new birth and becomes the head of the next earthly life, whereas the head of the present incarnation has been formed out of the limb-system and the rest of the organism of the previous earthly life. Thus the non-head nature—if I may coin this expression—of the one earthly life transforms itself into the head of the following earthly life. The head is always the product of the non-head nature of the preceding earthly life. This holds good for the whole concatenation of forces in the constitution of the human being.

When somebody goes through life with great attentiveness to everything, he must, in the nature of things, move about a great deal. Human beings who lead an entirely sedentary life are very difficult to study to-day from the point of view of karma, because there was no such mode of life in earlier times. It remains to be seen what men with an exclusively sedentary mode of life will be like in the next earthly life, for sedentary existences have become customary only in this age. But when, in earlier times, a man was attentive to the things in his environment, he always had to *go* to them; he had to make his limbs mobile, to bring his limbs into activity. The whole body was active, not only the senses which belong to the head-system. Everything in which the whole body takes part, when the human being is attentive and observant, passes over into the structure of the head of the next earthly life, and has a definite effect. The head of the human being in the next earthly life is so constituted that he has then a very strong urge to send into the rest of his organism such forces as cause the forces of the earth to work very strongly into his organism. In the first seven years of life, everything contained in the organism, muscles, bones, etc., is formed from out of the head. The head sends out these forces. Every bone is shaped as it must be shaped, by means of the head. If, because of the type of incarnation which I have described to you, the head has the tendency to develop a strong relationship to the forces of the earth, what happens then? Then by the grace of the head—if I may put it so—the earth-forces are very much favoured during the formation of the human being in the embryonic period, but also, especially, in the life up to the change of teeth. The forces of the earth are very strongly propagated by the head. The result is that in such a human being there is a special development of everything that depends upon the forces of the earth. He gets big bones, strong bones, extremely broad shoulder-blades, for instance, and the ribs are well developed. Everything bears the stamp of good development.

But now, all that is connected with the carrying over of the faculty of attention from the past into the present earthly life, with the way the organism is formed—all this, it is true, proceeds *spatially* from the head, but nevertheless, in reality, from the soul and spirit. For in all these formative forces the soul and spirit participate; from such forces we can always look to the soul and spirit. In such human beings the head has become related to the earth as the result of the conditions in the previous earthly life which I have described. We can see this in the brow, which is not particularly loftly—for lofty brows are not allied to the earth—but it has definition, strength, and similar characteristics.

So we see that the human being develops in such a way that his bones are strongly formed. And the strange thing is: when these forces that are allied to the earth work forcefully over from the previous earthly life, the hair grows very quickly. In observing children whose hair grows very quickly we must always connect this with their powers of attention in the previous earthly life. It is a fact that out of his moral and spiritual attitude in any one incarnation the human being forms his body in the next earthly life.

Now we shall always find confirmation of how the forces of the soul and spirit participate in this shaping of the human being. A man whose karma it is, in the next earthly life, to have strong bones, well developed muscles, as the result of attentiveness to life—such a man, we shall see, goes through life with courage. Through this attentiveness he has also acquired the natural force belonging to a courageous life.

In times when men ceased to describe successive earthly lives, they still had the knowledge that really exists only when repeated earthly lives are taken into account. This was still so in the days of Aristotle. Aristotle has described this beautifully in his *Physiognomics*. He was still able to show how the external countenance is connected with the moral attitude, the moral tenor of a man.

And now let us think of cowards, faint-hearted men. They are those who took no interest in anything during the previous earthly life. You see, the study of karma has a certain significance for taking one's place in life in connection with the future. After all, it is only a craving for knowledge that we satisfy—though not only this craving—when we trace back a present earthly life to earlier lives. But if we go through our present earthly life with a certain amount of self-knowledge, then we can prepare for the *next* earthly life. If we drift superficially through life, without taking interest in anything, then we can be sure that we shall be a coward in the next earthly life. This is because a detached, inattentive character forms few links with its environment, and consequently the head-organisation in the next life has no relation with the forces of the earth. The bones remain undeveloped, the hair grows slowly: very often such a person has bow-legs or knock-knees.

These are things which in a very intimate way reveal the connection between the spirit and soul on the one side and the natural-physical on the other. Yes, my dear friends, from the very details of the shape of the head and of the whole structure of the human being, we can as it were look over into the previous earthly life.

These things are not said, however, in order that the observation itself shall be made through them. All the observations of which I have told you here, as a preparation for studies of karma, have not been made in an external, but in an entirely inner way, through spiritual-scientific methods. But precisely these spiritual-scientific methods show that the human being in his external form *cannot* be studied as is done in modern physiology and anatomy. There is really no sense in simply becoming familiar with the organs and their interconnections. For the human being is a *picture*. In part he is the picture of the forces holding sway between death and a new birth, and in part a picture of his previous earthly life. There is no sense in working at physiology and anatomy as they exist to-day, where the human being is taken and one organ after another in him is studied. The head, for instance, is much more closely connected with the previous earthly life than with the body which the human being receives in his present earthly life.

We can therefore say: certain physical processes are to be understood only when we look back to previous earthly lives. A man who learnt to know the world in a previous earthly life has quick-growing hair. A man who learnt to know little of the world in a previous life, has slow-growing hair. The hair grows very slowly; it lies along the surface of the body; whereas those who interested themselves intensely in life during a previous earthly life, who interested themselves all too intensely and poked their noses into everything, have loose, straggly hair. This is an absolutely correct connection. The most manifold bodily configurations can be referred back to experiences in one of the preceding earthly lives. This holds good into the very details of the constitution.

Take for instance, a man who ponders much in one incarnation—who thinks and ponders a great deal. In his next incarnation he will be a thin, delicately made man. A man who ponders little in one earthly life, but lives a life more concerned with grasping the outer world, tends, in the next life, to accumulate a good deal of fat. This, too, has a significance for the future. Spiritual "slimming cures" cannot well be managed in one earthly life; for this one must resort to physical cures—if indeed they are of any help! But for the next earthly life it is certainly possible to undergo a "slimming cure" if one ponders and thinks a great deal, especially if one thinks about something that calls for effort, of the kind I described yesterday. It need not be meditated, but simply pondered about a great deal, with the willingness to make many inner decisions.

There is an actual connection of this kind between the spiritual and moral way in which a man lives during one earthly life, and his physical constitution in the next earthly life. This cannot be emphasised sufficiently.

Take another case. Suppose, for instance, that in one earthly life a man is a thinker. I do not mean a professor—(this is not a joke!)—but a man who, possibly, walks behind a plough and who yet can think a great deal. It does not matter at all in what circumstances of life a man thinks, for he can be a real thinker when he follows a plough or is engaged in a handicraft of some sort. But because in his thinking the forces which fall away when earthly life comes to an end are mainly engaged, and he leaves unused those which are carried over into his next incarnation and take part in the building up of his head, such a man will appear again in a new earthly life with soft flesh, with delicate soft flesh.

The peculiar point, however, is this.—When a man thinks a great deal, then, in his next earthly life, he will have a good skin; the whole surface of the body, the skin of the body, will be very well constituted. Again, when you see people whose skin has spots, for instance, then you can always infer from this that they did little thinking in their past life. (Of course, one needs other grounds for this inference as well; it is not possible to deduce with absolute certainty from one symptom. Nevertheless, in general, the indications which I have given to-day about the inter-connection of the soul and spirit with the physical are correct). When you see people with some impurity in their skin, you can always conclude that they did little thinking in their past earthly life. People with many freckles have certainly not been thinkers in a previous earthly life.

These are the things which show at once that Spiritual Science does not pay attention merely to spiritual abstractions, but also to the working of the spiritual in the physical. I have often emphasised that what is harmful about materialism is not that it pays attention only to matter; the harmful element, the tragedy of materialism, is that it cannot really know anything about matter, because it does not recognise the spiritual workings within matter.

It is precisely in the study of the human being that attention must be paid to matter, for in matter, above all in the human form, in the whole human being, the working of the spiritual is expressing itself. Matter is the outer revelation of the spiritual.

You can glean from the "Leading Thoughts" which have lately appeared in the News Sheet issued with the periodical *Das Goetheanum*, that the head of man is observed in the proper way only when Imaginative cognition is applied even to its external appearance. For the human head in its formation, in the formation of the ears, particularly also in the formation of the nose and eyes, is actually according to the pattern of Imagination. It consists of outwardly visible Imaginations.

This is also connected with the life of the human being. There are human beings in whom the lower part of the trunk is longer than the upper part; that is to say, the part from the lowest point of the trunk up to the breast is *longer* than the part from the centre of the chest up to the neck. If the part from the centre of the chest to the neck is *shorter* than the lower part of the trunk, then we have to do with a human being who, in the life between death and a new birth, has made the ascent to the mid-point very quickly. He passed through this period very quickly. Then he descended slowly and comfortably to the new earthly life.

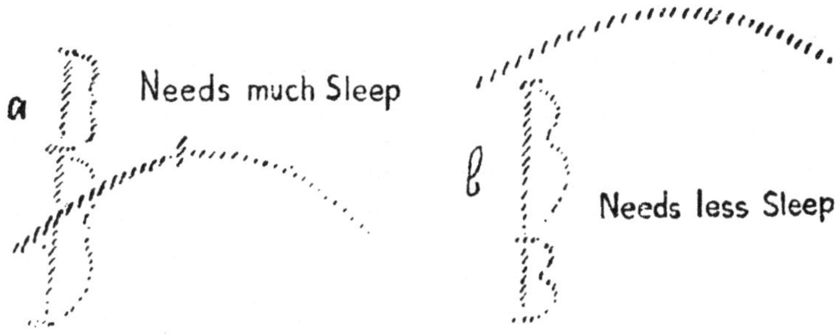

Where, on the other hand, the upper part from the neck to the middle of the chest is longer than the lower part from the middle of the chest to the end of the trunk, we have to do with a human being who passed slowly and sedately as far as the middle of his life between death and new birth, and then descended more quickly into earthly life.

In the physiognomy, indeed, in the proportions of the trunk, we find the after-effect of the way in which the human being passed through the first period of his existence between death and a new birth, in comparison with the latter period.

Truly, what is physical in the human being is through and

through a copy of the underlying spiritual. This has a consequence in life. For those who have the long lower trunk and short upper trunk are of a type showing from the outset that they need a great deal of sleep; they like to have long sleep. (The diagram is, of course, rather exaggerated). With the other type, who have the short lower trunk and long upper trunk, this is not so; they do not need so much sleep.

Thus, according to whether a human being needs sleep or not, which again expresses itself in the proportions of his trunk, you can see whether he has gone through the first part of the life between death and a new birth quickly or slowly, and also whether he has gone quickly or slowly through the second part of this life.

But this again is connected with the previous incarnation. Take the case of a man who was dull—not so much in disposition as because of his education and his mode of life. I do not mean that he was altogether lacking in interest, but he was dull; he could not really do anything properly, he never set about getting a real grip of things; he may have been attentive enough to poke his nose into everything, but it did not go beyond curiosity and a superficial understanding. He remained dull. Such a man has no interest for the first part of his life between death and a new birth. He develops an interest only when he has left behind the midnight summit of this life and begins his descent.

On the other hand, a man who is accustomed to penetrate everything both with his mind and with his feeling—he takes great interest in the first half, in the ascent, and then quickly completes the descent. Thus again it can be said: When you meet a man who is a sleepy-head, then this is to be traced to a dull life, such as I have described, in the previous incarnation. A man who is not a sleepy-head, who may even have to do something in order to go to sleep—we know there are books which can be used for the purpose of sending one to sleep!—a man who needs these things has not been dull, but attentive; he has been active with his mind and his feeling.

We can go further. There are men . . . how shall I speak of

them? Let us say they are ready eaters; they are fond of eating. Others are not so fond of eating. I do not want to say gluttonous people and non-gluttonous people for this would hardly be in place in a serious study. But I will say: there are people who are fond of eating and there are others who are less fond of it. This too is connected in a certain sense with what the human being experiences in his passage between death and a new birth, before and after the midnight summit of existence. The middle point here is the midnight summit of existence.

There are human beings who, as I will put it, ascend very high into the spiritual, and there are others who do not rise so high. Those who ascend very high will eat in order to live. Those who do not rise so high will live in order to eat.

These are certainly differences in life, and if we look at the way in which a man behaves in such actions as are connected with the fostering or non-fostering of his physical existence, we can say that here is something which enables us to perceive how his karmic life is flowing over from a previous existence.

Those who have acquired powers of observation in this direction perceive, for instance, in the way a man takes something at table, in the way he helps himself, a gesture which points very strongly indeed to the way in which the past earthly life is shining over into the present.

To-day I am speaking of the physical. To-morrow I shall speak more about the moral sides, but the physical must certainly be kept in mind, otherwise the opposite will become less intelligible. Men who help themselves vehemently, who when they so much as take a pear into their hands at table do it—well, with enthusiasm—are those who clung more to the trivialities of life in the previous incarnations who could not rise above trivialities; who were stuck in habit, convention, etc., unable to get a moral grasp of life. This, too, has great practical significance. As we are not used to such considerations, these things will often seem curious and we laugh about them. But they are to be taken with the deepest seriousness, for you see, there are in society to-day certain classes of people who spend their time and energy in the trivial customs of life; they do not willingly make anything their own which goes beyond the ordinary, habitual customs of life.

Nor must these things be applied merely to modes of behaviour. They can likewise be applied, for instance, to speech. There are languages in which you cannot say anything arbitrarily because everything is strictly prescribed in the construction of the sentence; the subject cannot be put in another place, and so on. There are other languages where the subject may be placed wherever you like, and the predicate too. These languages are of such a character that they help human beings to individual development.

This is only an example of how trivial habits are acquired, and how the human being cannot get out of triviality. An earthly life spent in such triviality leads to one in which the human being is gluttonous. He does not rise high enough in the life between death and a new birth—he becomes gluttonous.

In our day the time should dawn when men no longer reckon only with one earthly life, as was the case in the materialistic epoch of evolution, but take into account the whole of earthly evolution, in the knowledge that what is done and achieved by a man in one earthly life is carried over into the next earthly life; that what happens in one epoch is carried over into another by human beings themselves. As this awareness has to come, it is necessary that such knowledge should find a place in the education of growing children as well as of adults.

I should like to speak of two more types. There is a type of human being who can take everything seriously, and here I do not mean merely the external kind of seriousness. There may quite well be thoroughly serious people, who may even have a strongly tragic vein in their souls, but who all the same can laugh. For if a man is not able to laugh, if everything goes by him—and there are countless things in life to make one laugh—if he lets everything go by and cannot laugh at anything, then he must be dull. After all, there are things to laugh at! But a man may be able to laugh heartily at something that is funny, and still be, fundamentally, a serious man.

Then there is another type of person who does nothing but laugh, whom everything incites to laughter, who laughs when he is telling anything, whether or not it happens to be funny. There are people whose faces distort into laughter the moment they begin to relate anything, and who speak of even the gravest matter with a kind of grin, with a kind of laughter. I am describing extremes here, but these extremes exist.

This is a fundamental trait of the soul. We shall see to-morrow how it has its moral side. To-day I shall deal mainly with the physical side. This trait, in its turn, leads back to the karmic stream of evolution. A man who has a trait of gravity in his life, even if he can laugh too, has strong, steady forces working out of his previous incarnation into his present earthly life. In meeting a serious man of this kind, a man who has an understanding for the grave side of life, who stops to observe the grave side of life, we can say: one can feel in this man that he is bearing in his being and nature his past earthly life. A serious conception of life arises when the past earthly lives continue working, working on in the proper way. On the other hand, a man becomes an incessant chatterbox, laughing even when he is talking of the gravest matters, when past earthly lives are not working on in him. When a man has gone through a series of earthly lives—or at least through one—in which he has lived as if half asleep, then, in his next earthly life, he becomes a person who is never serious, who is unable to approach the things of life with the necessary seriousness. Thus from a man's attitude it can be seen whether he has spent his past earthly lives to good purpose, or whether he has more or less slept through them.

All this leads us to realise how false it is to take a mechanical view of a human being when he comes before us in his human guise, or even to see no further than the stereotyped pattern of his organism. This is quite wrong.

The human being in his form, and right down into his possibilities of movement, must be regarded as an image of the spiritual world.

First of all there is the head-organisation. This is essentially determined by the previous earthly lives. We observe a human head in the right way when we learn to know all there is to be learnt about Imaginative ideation. Here, in connection with the human head, and nowhere else, we can apply, in the sense-world, Imaginative ideation, which is otherwise used for gazing into the spiritual world. We must begin with Imagination if we wish to look into the spiritual world. Then, first of all, the spiritual-etheric pictures of the spiritual beings appear before us. In the physical world, with the exception of the human head, there is nothing that is reminiscent of Imagination. But in the human head, right into its inner organisation, right into the marvellous structure of the brain, everything is really a physical mirror-image of the Imaginative.

Then, proceeding further, you may begin to study in the human being something that is really much more difficult to observe, although it is generally thought to be easy—that is, to gain an understanding of how the human being takes breath, how he sets his rhythmic system in movement, and how the breath leads over into the blood circulation. This tremendously living play, which penetrates the whole body, is far more complicated than it is thought to be. The human being takes in the breath, the breath transforms itself into blood circulation, but on the other side the breath again passes over into the head and is related in a definite way to the whole activity of the brain. Thinking is simply a refined, delicate breathing. The blood circulation, again, passes over into the impulses of the movements of the limbs.

This rhythmic system of the human being does not express itself in a static condition but in a continuous mobility, and this difference must be clearly observed. The head of man is best studied by considering it as a self-contained formation *at rest;* by studying its interior, the various parts of the brain, for instance, and how one part lies alongside another.

Nothing can be known about the head if, say, the blood circulation in the head is studied by means of anatomy or physiology; for what the blood circulation achieves in the head is not connected with the head itself; it is connected merely with what the head needs from the rhythmic system. What can be seen when a portion of the cranial bone is raised, and the circulation exposed, is not really connected with the head. The head must be studied as an organ which is at rest, and where one part lies alongside another.

This method is not applicable to the rhythmic system, which has its seat in the breast. Everything there must be studied in its mobility, in the mobility of the blood circulation, of breathing, of thinking, of self-movement. This process can even be traced much farther into the physical.

Consider the breathing process as it passes over into the blood-process, and thence works over also into the brain. Carbonic acid is formed in the first place: that is to say, an acid is formed in the human organism. But when the breathing process passes over into the brain and into the nervous system, salt substances are formed out of the acids; salt substances are deposited.

Thus we may say: when the human being thinks, *solids* are precipitated. In the circulation, we find *fluidity*. In the breath, the *gaseous*. And in the principle of mobility when this passes over into movements, we find the *fiery*. The material elements are contained in all this, but the elements in *mobility*, in a constant state of arising and passing away. This process cannot really be grasped by sense-observation. Those who set out to grasp it, anatomically, by means of sense-observation, never really understand it; much must be added out of the inner creative force of the spirit if this process is to be understood. If we listen to explanatory discourses on the rhythmic process, as they are given in ordinary lectures on anatomy and physiology, we feel that it is all very remote from reality. (Those of you who have had this experience will be able to substantiate what I am saying). Yes, whoever listens to all this with an unbiased mind, and then watches the audience, actually feels as if the barrenness offered to the listeners must cause their very death; as if they must remain fixed to the desks, unable to move, unable even to crawl away! For this system of circulation ought to be described with such living vitality that the hearers, being continually carried from the sensible into the supersensible, from the supersensible back again into the sensible, enter into a kind of *musical* mood during the description.

When this is done, the human being develops inner habits of soul through which karma can be understood. We shall speak of that to-morrow. But what we have here is a sense-picture of *Inspiration.* Whereas in the study of the head we have a sense-picture of *Imagination,* so we have a picture of *Inspiration* in a study of the rhythmic system of the human being, *if* this study has the right character.

We pass now to the metabolic-limb system. In what modern anatomy and physiology have to say of the metabolic-limb system, we do *not* come to the forces of this system, but only to what falls away and is discarded by it. Everything that in the modern view is the content of the metabolic-limb system does not belong at all to the real human structure and organisation, but is expelled. The content of the bowels is only the extreme instance. Whatever else is physically perceptible in the metabolic-limb system does not belong to the human being but is deposited by him; some of it remains within him for a longer time, some for a shorter time. The content of the bowels remains a short time; what is deposited by the muscles, nerves, etc. remains longer. Any physical substance that can be found in the metabolic-limb system does not belong to the human being; it is excretion, deposit. Everything that belongs to the metabolic-limb system is of a *supersensible* nature. So that in studying the metabolic-limb system of man we have to pass over to what has a purely supersensible existence within the physical.

We must therefore picture the metabolic-limb system in such a way that physical arms, etc., are in reality spiritual, and within this spiritual the Ego unfolds.—When I move my arms or my legs, deposits are continually taking place, and these deposits are observed. But they are not the essential. You cannot refer to the physical when you want to explain how the arm or the hand grasps something; you must refer to the spiritual. The spiritual that runs all along the arm—*that* is the essential in the human being. What you perceive is merely a deposit of the metabolic-limb system.

How, then, can we even start on a study of karma if we believe that what we see in the metabolic-limb system is the human being? The human being is not this at all. We can only start on a study of karma when we know what the human being really is. We must include something that is to be found, certainly, in the sense-world, but which is, nevertheless, a supersensible picture of Intuition.

And so, my dear friends, you can say: A study of the *head* is an Imaginative process, projected into the sense-world; a study of the *rhythmic system* must be truly Inspired, though active in the realm of sense-observation, within the sense-world; a study of the *metabolic-limb system* must be Intuitive, a supersensible activity in the sense-world.

It is very interesting to find that in the study of the human being we have images for Intuition, Inspiration and Imagination. In a proper study of the metabolic-limb man we can learn what Intuition really is in the supersensible. In a proper study of the rhythmic man we can learn what Inspiration really is in the supersensible. In a proper study of the head we can learn what Imaginative observation is in the supersensible.

Study of the Head: Imaginative, projected into the sense-world.
Study of the Rhythmic System: Inspired, working in the sense-world.
Study of the Metabolic-Limb System: Intuitive, super-sensibily in the sense-world.

This is what is indicated in the latest 'Leading Thoughts', and it is something which everyone who carefully studies the existing Lecture-Courses can indeed find for himself.

To-day, my dear friends, we have tried to consider karmic connections in relation to the physical. To-morrow we will pass on to a closer study of karmic connections in relation to the moral and spiritual nature of man.

IX

We shall continue for a time to study the laws prevailing in the development of human karma, and I shall say something to-day about the inner aspect of the shaping of karma, of the part of karma that is connected especially with the moral, ethical and spiritual life.

You must remember that directly we look beyond the physical world—and this is always so in studying karma—the karmic connections are *spiritual.* Even when they take effect in the physical, for example in illness, whatever is karmic in an illness has a spiritual cause. So that under all circumstances we come to the spiritual whenever we approach the study of karma. To-day, however, we shall turn our attention more particularly to the ethical aspect of karma, to the workings of karma in the life of soul.

I have already told you that the forming of karma is connected with those Beings who in very ancient times of evolution were actually present on the earth and who departed from the earth at the time of the separation of the moon, taking up their abode in the cosmos as Moon-inhabitants, Moon Beings.

What we call Moon—of which the physical part as ordinarily described is no more than an indication—must be regarded as the bearer of certain spiritual beings, the most important of whom once lived on earth as the great primeval Teachers. It was they who established among men on earth that ancient wisdom of which I have so often spoken. These Beings were on the earth before the separation of the moon. In those times they infused the primeval wisdom into man who acquired it through a kind of inner illumination. And the way in which these Beings worked was altogether different from the way in which men can work on the earth to-day.

The activity of these ancient, primeval Teachers among men must in truth be described as a kind of magic, taking effect inasmuch as the influence of the human will upon happenings in the external world was infinitely greater than is possible to-day. Nowadays the will can work on the external world only through physical means of transmission. If we want to push some object we must put our will into operation through the arms and hands. But in the days of the primeval Teachers the human will still had a direct and immediate action upon processes in the outside world, upon the very processes of nature. It was a kind of action that we should now call magical. But in point of fact the last vestiges of this power of the human will persisted until comparatively recent times. Rousseau, for example, tells us that in certain warmer regions he was able to paralyse and even kill toads which came near him, simply by fixing them with his gaze. This power of the human will which in warmer climates persisted until the 18th century, has diminished through the course of the ages and has now vanished. But in ancient Egypt man was still able to influence and promote the growth of plants through his will. And when the primeval Teachers were on the earth, even inorganic processes of nature could be brought under the sway of the human will.

These things of course depended upon a true, instinctive insight into the connections of world-existence which remain completely hidden from the crude, material science of modern times. It is evident, however, that the influence of warmth upon the working of the human will must be taken thoroughly into account, for Rousseau, who was able, in warmer regions, to kill toads with his gaze, subsequently tried in Lyons to stare at a toad in the same way, supposing that it would at least be paralysed. But the toad was not paralysed; on the contrary it fixed its eyes upon him and he himself became partially paralysed and had to be restored to life by snake-poison administered by a doctor.

This way of activating the will is of course dependent upon an instinctive knowledge of the whole environment of man.

Out of their own spiritual foundations the primeval Teachers possessed a totally different, far deeper and more penetrating knowledge of nature than is within the reach of man to-day. They were endowed with powers which cannot be comprised in natural laws. Nor was this necessary when the primeval Teachers were working on the earth, for nothing in the least resembling modern natural science was then in existence. It would have seemed utterly pointless and nobody would have understood its purpose. For in those days all such activity was founded upon a far deeper, more inward knowledge and understanding than is possible to-day.

These primeval Teachers transferred the scene of their work from the earth to the moon and as everything in the cosmos is interconnected, a mighty task is now allotted to them within the nexus of cosmic happenings. They are Beings who have a great deal to do with karma, with the forming and shaping of human karma. For an essential part of the weaving of karma is to be observed when, after having laid aside his etheric body a few days after death, the human being lives through his sleeping life (not his waking life) backwards. When he passes through the gate of death he has, first of all, a clear retrospective vision of what he has experienced in life—a grand and majestic panorama in pictures. After a few days this panorama slowly fades away as the etheric body dissolves in the cosmic ether, and then an actual journey backward begins.

Earthly existence flows in such a way that although we grasp it in remembrance as a unity, this is an illusion. Life does not flow onwards uninterruptedly. We live through the day consciously, the night unconsciously; the day consciously, the night unconsciously, and so on.

When in remembrance man thinks back over his life, he forgets that the nights are always there between the days. During the nights a very great deal happens to the soul, to the astral body and ego, only man knows nothing about it. What happens to him while he is unconscious during the nights in earthly existence, this he lives through in a backward course after death, so that time actually seems to him to be flowing backwards; in full consciousness he lives backward through the nights.

As approximately a third of life is spent in sleep, this backward journey is also lived through in a third of the time of the earthly life. If, therefore, a man has reached the age of 60, some 20 years have been spent in sleep and the backward journey lasts for about 20 years. Then he enters the Spirit-land proper, into a different form of existence. This backward journey, this vision of what has happened during the nights, is lived through after death in such a way that the great and significant difference between its experiences and those of ordinary sleep is strikingly apparent.

With the exception of the dreams rising out of sleep which do not, after all, reproduce the experiences of earthly life very faithfully but in an illusory, fantastic shape—with the exception therefore of the dreams welling up from the night-life, the human being has little consciousness of all the manifold happenings in which he is involved. In earlier lectures here I have described what happens to the human being during sleep; but after death he experiences it with extraordinary clarity and definition. This life in the soul-world after death is much richer in impressions than earthly life. The pictures a man experiences and how he himself is involved in them—all this comes to him with extraordinary intensity; there is nothing dreamlike about it. It is experienced, if I may put it so, as a kind of photographic negative. If you caused suffering to some person during your earthly life, you experienced this infliction of suffering as it proceeded from yourself. You experienced what proceeded from yourself, was done by yourself. But journeying backward after death you do not feel what *you* experienced during earthly life, but you slip as it were into the other person and feel what *he* experienced as the result of your action.

To take a drastic example.—If you gave someone a box on the ears, you do not experience what you felt in earthly life as you planned and carried out this act, but on the backward journey you experience, instead, the feelings of the other person whose ears you boxed. You live through it as your own experience, and indeed with extraordinary concreteness, with greater intensity. No impression on earth is as powerful as the impressions along this backward course after death for a third of the time of the earthly life. During this period the whole karmic fulfilment of what was done in life is experienced—from the standpoint of the other man. You live through the whole karmic fulfilment, but not, of course, as earthly experience—that will come in the subsequent life on earth. Even though it is not as intense as regards the action as it will be in a later incarnation, you experience the impression more strongly than could be the case in any earthly life.

This is a very striking fact. It is the intense reality of the experiences that is so remarkable.

But even if the human being were able to unfold in his ego and astral body the degree of strength that is his when he passes through the gate of death, he would experience this whole backward journey at most as a very vivid dream. And he might expect it to be so if, after death, he were merely to look at the earthly life and what it has made of him. But this backward journey is not a vivid dream; it is an experience of far greater intensity than any experience in earthly existence. Only now there is no physical body, no etheric body, through which man's experiences are mediated to him on earth.

Just think what you would experience on earth with your ordinary consciousness if you had no physical body and no etheric body. You would flit over the earth with now and again a dream arising; then you would sleep again, and so it would continue.

It is easy to conceive that after his earthly life a man who had reached the age of 60 lives through a dream continuing for 20 years; but what he lives through is by no means a dream, it is an experience of the greatest intensity. What makes this possible? It is because the moment a human being has passed through the gate of death, has laid aside his etheric body and begins his backward journey, the Moon

Beings draw near him and with their ancient magical powers they pass into him, into his experiences, and impregnate his pictures with cosmic substance.

If I may use an analogy, what happens is just as if I were to paint a picture. In the first place it is simply a picture and doesn't cause actual pain—provided it is not too hideous—and even then the impression is only a moral or aesthetic one. It hurts nobody. But suppose I were to paint a picture, let us say, of three of you here and the picture were permeated with some magic power causing these three to step from the picture and carry out everything they had planned against others. You would react with more force and vigour than anthroposophists are wont to reveal! So it is after death. The experiences are full of living force, living activity, because these Moon Spirits permeate the pictures with their own substantiality; they saturate these pictures with a super-reality of being.

After death, therefore we pass through the region of the Moon Beings and what we experience as the balancing-out of our own deeds is stamped with mighty force in the cosmic ether. This backward journey—when it is described not merely in principle as in the book *Theosophy*, but when one tries to describe it as concretely as I want to do now—this backward journey after death is extraordinarily interesting and a highly important section of life.

In our time the experiences that may come to a human being during this period after death are particularly complicated. Just think how essentially the whole constitution of soul of these Moon Beings differs from that of the inhabitants of the earth. These Moon Beings with whom we have so much to do after death once imparted to men that primeval wisdom which in our time has completely faded away. As I have often explained, men could not have attained their freedom if the mighty wisdom of these primeval Teachers had remained. It has faded away and been replaced by something else, namely, abstract thinking. The human being to-day thinks in concepts which no longer have any very real relationship with the spiritual world. Let me repeat an example I gave on another occasion.—Aristotle has bequeathed to us ten concepts which were really a survival of ancient wisdom: Being, Quantity, Quality, Relation, Position, Space, Time, Possession, Action, Suffering. He called them the 'Categories'. They are ten simple concepts. These ten concepts are generally enumerated in our text-books of Logic. In classical schools they have to be learned by heart; professors of philosophy are familiar with them. But nothing more is known than just the ten concepts by name: Being, Possession, Position, Space, Time, and the rest. To what does such knowledge amount? These ten concepts seem tedious and dry to a modern man. But to one who perceives their significance they are no more tedious than are the 22 or 23 letters of the alphabet: a, b, c, d, e, f, g, . . .

Just think of it.—If you knew nothing more about the alphabet than a, b, c, d, e, f, g, up to z, if you knew this and nothing more, what would you make of Goethe's *Faust*? You would open the book and find these 22 signs scattered about in manifold permutations and combinations. *Faust* contains nothing but these 22 signs inter-connected in different ways. And if you knew nothing more, if you had never learnt to read but merely opened the book and saw these signs, just think how different it would be from what it is now, when you can take *Faust* and read it. That is a different matter altogether! No book in the world contains anything except these 22 signs and yet just think what you can make of them! The whole world of the mind is open to you because by juggling with these 22 letters you can apply them.

But the logicians who have accepted the ten Categories to-day: Being, Quantity, Quality, Relation, Space, Time, Position, Possession, Action, Suffering—these men know as little to what these Categories really apply as someone who has never learnt to read and simply recognises a, b, c, d, e, f, knows of all the books of the world. It is exactly the same thing. For these ten concepts of Aristotle's Logic have to be understood in such a way that they can be applied in manifold permutations, just as the letters are manipulated in the physical world by multifarious combinations and permutations. *Then, with these ten concepts, we read in the spiritual world.* They are the letters.

But in our time the concepts are known by name and that is all—which is equivalent to knowing nothing more of the alphabet than the letters in their sequence. Think what you would miss if you could not read but only knew a, b, c, d! Correspondingly, men miss everything that is in the spiritual world if they are unable to manipulate and apply the ten concepts of Aristotle in all manner of ways, in order to read in the spiritual world.

In this connection something very droll has been happening among philosophers for a long time. About the middle of the Middle Ages there lived a very astute and clever man, by name Raymond Lully. From tradition he still knew something about this permutation of the categories of logic, of the fundamental concepts of logic, and he gave out what he knew—clothing it in the form of pictures as was customary in those times. What he really wanted to say, or rather, what he would have said if he had expressed the reality, was this: My contemporaries are all blockheads, because they only know a, b, c, d; they do not know how to read with the fundamental concepts, the root concepts. A man must understand in his head how to combine these fundamental concepts as letters are combined into words and sentences. Then he can read in the spiritual world.—Raymond Lully did not say this in such direct words for that was not the custom in his days. He said: Write the fundamental concepts on slips of paper, then take a kind of roulette, spin it and the concepts will be thrown about among each other; and then read. Then there will be results.

This, however, was only an analogy, for he did not really mean anything like a dead, mechanical roulette; he meant the *spiritual head* which must manipulate and combine these concepts. But those who heard of it took the analogy literally and have laughed about it ever since, considering it to be a piece of childishness on the part of Raymond Lully.

The childishness, however, is purely on the side of modern philosophy which does not understand what was meant.

Practically everything that in olden days was brought to humanity by the primeval Teachers whom we know as the Moon Beings, has been lost. But during his backward journey in the first period after death the human being becomes acquainted in a very special way with this knowledge. He knows then how these ancient Sages thought, what kind of wisdom they possessed. Hence the graphic, concrete reality of his experiences during this period.

But in our time things have become complicated and confused owing to a kind of lack of understanding. Human beings, who since the fading of the primeval wisdom have been living here on earth with their abstract concepts, have not the power to understand the inner soul-constitution of these primeval Teachers since they entered the Moon-existence.

When a modern scholar is passing through this period of his life after death, he speaks a very different language from these primeval Teachers who, as I shall describe to you in more detail, have a very great deal to do with the shaping of karma. These primeval Teachers and the men of to-day who die imbued with modern culture and the fruits of modern civilisation do not really understand one another.

It is extremely difficult to form a clear conception of these things, for observation of what is happening to human beings in this connection is by no means easy. But in characteristic cases observation *is* possible: for instance, one can study two men who died not so very long ago and who have gone their way backward after death, two men who were steeped in modern culture and who nevertheless were very different from each other.

We can take a man who was brilliant in his own way, a scientist of average calibre like Du Bois-Reymond, or someone of the same type, and observe his backward journey after death. Another personality, too, can be observed in the same way. A very interesting personality as regards this backward journey through the soul-land is the one who hovered before me while I was composing my Mystery Plays and who took shape in the character of Strader. Strader in the Mystery Plays is an image of an actual person who in his youth entered the monastic life but subsequently abandoned it and worked in the field of rationalistic philosophy as a professor in a University. This man—he was responsible for a number of writings—has all the abstraction of a modern thinker, but his thoughts are extraordinarily penetrating, full of warmth and vigour. It does one good to find this quality of heart in a modern thinker.

The full-blooded vigour of Hegel, for example, who could present the highest abstractions with tremendous depth of emotion but also with utmost concreteness, is of course no longer possible to the same extent in a man of to-day. Hegel was a thinker who was able to imbue concepts and ideas with such concrete reality that he could, so to speak, hack wood with them. But the man to whom I am now referring revealed something of the same heart-quality in handling abstract concepts. As I said, his life hovered before me when I was shaping the figure of Strader in the Mystery Plays.

When this man died his backward journey was particularly interesting to me. A fact to be taken thoroughly into account was that all his thinking had a certain theological bent. Like that of a modern scientist, or at least a natural philosopher, it was entirely abstract, but all the time there was this nuance of theology (coming of course from earlier incarnations) and his thinking was lit by a gleam of consciousness that it is possible to speak, at least, of the reality of a spiritual world.

Hence this man's thinking has more affinity with the soul-constitution of the Moon Beings than has the thinking of an average scientist like Du Bois-Reymond, for example. When such men are passing through the soul-world, through the Moon sphere, one can perceive a marked lack of understanding—it is like someone who lives in a foreign country and never learns the language; the others do not understand him and he does not understand them. This, broadly speaking, is the fate of a man who is a typical product of modern civilisation when he enters upon this backward journey after death.

But it was rather different in the case of this personality, the prototype of Strader.—I have to resort to earthly language although it is utterly inadequate when applied to what I am here describing.—When, after death, this personality was journeying backward through the course of his life, it could be observed that the Moon Beings took a certain interest in the way he was bringing his thoughts, his abstract thoughts, into the soul-world. And he, in his turn, experienced a very remarkable awakening, an awakening in which he seemed to be saying to himself: 'Ah, now I see that all I fought against is, in reality, quite different.' (He had fought against many things that were traditional).—'I see now that it only gradually came to be what it is, because the ancient truths have become abstract words. I was often fighting against windmills; now, however, I see realities.'

Something of extraordinary interest is happening here—and a whole number of such men in modern life might be cited as examples. There is something extremely interesting in this backward journey after death where the foundations of karma are laid.

An even more striking figure in this connection is the philosopher Jacob Frohschammer, who wrote *Die Phantasie als Weltprinzip* (Imagination as a World-Building Principle). I have often mentioned him. There was still a great deal of inner substance in his abstract concepts, but, like the man just described, he was an abstract thinker. He could, however, so little tolerate the abstractions of modernism—I do not now mean 'modernism' in the terminology of Roman Catholicism—that he simply refused to acknowledge concepts as world-building forces; he would acknowledge only *imagination.* He said: imagination is working everywhere; the plants grow, the animals exist and so forth, through imagination. In this respect Frohschammer's book is extraordinarily interesting.

It is wonderful to observe how such a personality, who has still retained much of what was alive in cultural life before the modern, abstract way of thinking became customary, is able to blend with the substance of the Moon Beings. Investigations of this kind are profoundly interesting because a closer insight into the laws of the evolution of karma grows out of them. And when one is drawn by a certain sympathy to such a personality—as I myself was drawn to the prototype of Strader in the Mystery Plays—it is the warmth of soul by which one is united with him that makes it possible to share the experiences of this very significant journey after death.

The fact that the impressions are so strong for the man who is passing through these experiences has an after-effect, too, upon the person who is following them with knowledge. And that in itself is a very remarkable thing. For it becomes evident how much more impressive are the experiences after death than those of earthly life. I ask myself to-day in all earnestness: If I should wish to add a fifth Mystery Play to the four already written, would it be possible for me again to include the figure of Strader, now that for some considerable time I have watched these pictures of what Strader's prototype experienced after death?... It would be quite impossible, because the moment I want to present the earthly figure, where the impressions are far less intense, the pictures of the impressions experienced by Strader's prototype after death are there before me. And they are far, far stronger; they blot out what was there during the earthly life.

I can observe this quite clearly in myself. As you may imagine, I took an extraordinary interest in the life of this man, for he was the prototype of Strader. He has since died and the impressions coming to him, after death, are incomparably more interesting to me than anything I can find out or describe about him while he was alive.

When I think about my Mystery Plays I realise that because of the vivid impressions of this prototype of Strader in the life after death, the character of Strader is the one that fades away from me most completely of all. This does not apply to the same extent to the other characters in the Plays.

You see there how what is here on earth aligns itself in true observation with what is beyond the earth, and how the effect of such things enables one to realise the tremendous intensity of the life after death on this backward journey. The sheer intensity of it blots out the impressions of earthly life.

Still more can be said about these matters. I am not speaking here of anything that has been invented, but of realities. We may know a man very well in his earthly life and then experience what he has to undergo in the backward journey after death. Everything takes a different form because of the intensity of the pictures. If we have been exceedingly interested in a man's earthly life—as I was in that of a man who died a number of years ago—then our whole relation to the earthly life changes; it has an entirely different character when we subsequently share in the experiences of the personality in question during the backward journey after death. And many things in the earthly relationships are only now revealed in their whole truth.

This is all the more the case when the relationships in the earthly life were not of a spiritual nature; when they *were*, when they were essentially spiritual, there is, as it were, a continuous, onflowing development. If, however, there had been, for example, a human relationship without agreement in ideas and thoughts, then in certain circumstances this relationship may be transformed after death into something quite different, into an entirely different life of feeling and the like. The cause of this change is the vividness of the pictures which then appear.

I am describing these things in order to call up before you a concrete image of types of realities differing from those of earthly existence. There are many different types of realities. And when, so to speak, the deeds of the Moon Beings flow into the pictures which a man himself shapes, this reality is such that it appears even more wonderful than the subsequent reality when the man is passing through the spiritual world proper and in union with the Hierarchies is concerned with the elaboration of the results of his earthly life; this state of existence runs a much simpler course because it is a kind of continuation. But the radical transformation of the human being after death, due as it is to the fact that he enters into relation with Beings who left the earth long ago and founded a kind of Moon colony in the cosmos—this is something that with tremendous forcefulness discloses to us a reality which, because it follows immediately after the life on earth, is closely related to and yet essentially different from earthly reality.

When human beings cling too strongly to earthly things it may be difficult for them to find their bearings in the sphere of the Moon Beings. Something happens then which I will describe in the following way. Picture to yourselves the earth here, the moon there.—Now the active moon-influences which are, in reality, reflected sun-influences, penetrate just

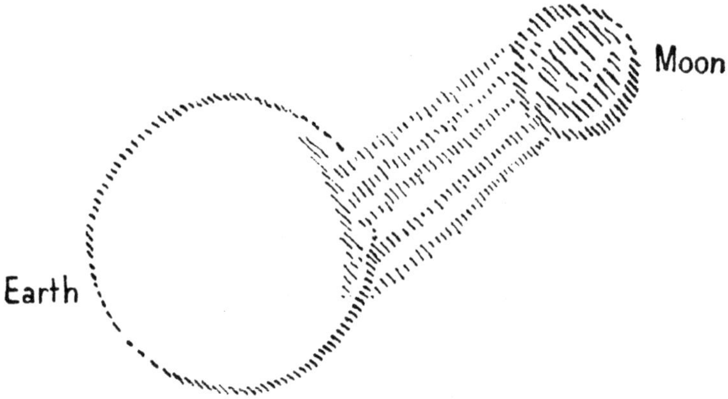

so far into the earth . . . At this point they cease. The moon-influences do not penetrate very deeply into the earth, actually only as far as the roots of the plants spread in the soil. The moon-influences are not really active below the stratum of the roots of plants. There is only a shallow layer up here where the moon-influences are held fast. Sun-influences, of course, penetrate deeply into the earth. The warmth of the sun in the summer is preserved; when you lay potatoes in the soil the sun's warmth is still there during the winter. The sun-influences penetrate deeply into the earth, the moon-influences only as far as the level of the roots of plants . . . a shallow layer.

The moon-influences, rising up like mist from this shallow layer, may cause human beings who have to pass after death into the Moon sphere—the soul-world—but are unable to understand the Moon Beings, to be trapped by this shallow stratum of moon-influences and they can actually be seen by sensible-supersensible perception wandering about as ghosts, as spectral shades.

The legends and poems which tell of these things are based upon reality, but in order to form a sound judgment in this domain we must be entirely free from superstition, we must proceed with critical deliberation and accept only what can be put to the test.

In this backward journey after death which lasts for a third of the time of the earthly life, karma is prepared. For the Moon Beings mingle in these 'negatives' of a man's deeds, also of his deeds in the life of thought. The Moon Beings have a good memory and they inscribe into the cosmic ether every experience they share with the human being.

We pass through the life between death and a new birth and then, on the return journey when we come back once more into the Moon sphere we find everything inscribed there. And we bear it all with us into our life in order to bring it to fulfilment by means of our earthly will.

This, my dear friends, is what I wanted to place before you to-day as a theme of study.

X

In the last lecture we spoke of how the seed of karma is formed in the period immediately following a man's death. And I tried to describe to you with what living force and intensity the experiences undergone during this period work upon him and also upon one who is able to follow the life of a human being through this period—which, as you know, lasts for about a third of the time of the earthly life. We must, of course, bear in mind how the terrestrial world in which the fulfilment and development of karma take place, works upon man, and in what a different way he is influenced by the *extra*-terrestrial world.

When we survey the scene of our karma—the earth—it is obvious that everything belonging to the earth, all the beings of the kingdoms of nature, exercise a very real influence upon man. This influence makes itself felt in his life even when his cognition is not directed to his earthly surroundings. He must be nourished, he must grow; to this end he must take into himself the substances of the earth. These substances work upon him through their qualities and inner forces quite independently of anything he may know about them. And expressing it rather radically, we may say that no matter what attitude a man adopts in his life of soul towards the kingdoms of nature surrounding him in earthly existence, he is related in a very definite way to the facts and realities of his physical environment.

This can be observed in many domains of life. How would it be, for instance, if the quantity of foodstuffs we consume were determined by what we know about the effects of the various foodstuffs upon the organism? Obviously we cannot wait until we possess such knowledge; we are obliged to eat. Our relationship to our earthly environment is entirely independent of our knowledge, independent too, in a certain sense, of our life of soul.

But now think of the utterly different character of our relationship to the world of stars. Influences of the world of stars cannot be said to have the same instinctive basis as the influences of the kingdoms of nature. The starry worlds fill man with wonder, he can be moved and inspired by them. But just think to what an extent his life of soul is involved in everything that concerns the world of stars, how his life of soul is affected. Take the nearest heavenly body that is related to man—the moon. That the moon has an influence upon man's life of phantasy and imagination is common knowledge. And even those people who repudiate everything else in respect of influence of the celestial bodies upon the human being will not deny that the 'magic of moonlight'—to use a romantic phrase—has an effect upon phantasy.

But it is impossible to imagine that even this crudest and most obvious influence of the world of stars could take effect if man had no life of soul. Without the life of soul there could be no such relationship as exists between man and his earthly environment, where in truth nothing essential depends upon whether he admires or does not admire, shall we say, a cabbage—it is simply there to be eaten—or upon what he knows of its effect upon his organs; what he has to do is to eat it! In this case, knowledge is merely an accessory. Knowledge does indeed, raise man's life of soul above the life of nature; but man lives his life within the realm of nature, and the spiritual life itself is an accessory. But if the spiritual life is excluded we cannot conceive that any influence could be exercised upon man by the world of the stars—let alone by the world lying still further beyond: the world of the Hierarchies, of the higher Spiritual Beings.

On the lowest level, so to speak, of the Hierarchies are those Beings of whom I said in the last lecture that inasmuch as they themselves live within the experiences of man after death, they impart tremendous power and intensity to these experiences. If these Moon Beings who were once the great primeval Teachers of humanity on earth did not live, as it were, within man's very being after death, his experiences would be like dreams. But they are anything but dreamlike; they are stronger, more full of reality than the so-called normal experiences of earthly life. Karma is actually prepared by means of these experiences, because we live with such intensity in others, not in ourselves, and have to establish the balance for our deeds. We experience things as the others experienced them, and with tremendous intensity. In this way our karma is prepared. And then comes a transition. Having shared these experiences with the Moon Beings, man passes on to experiences shared with Beings who have never been on the earth. The Moon Beings of whom I spoke in the last lecture were at one time on the earth. But now, in a later period between death and a new birth, man ascends to Beings who were never on earth. The Beings belonging to the first group of the higher Hierarchies are those we know by the name of the Angels. These Beings guide and accompany us from one earthly life to another. Among the ranks of the higher Beings they are the nearest to us and they are also very near to us throughout our earthly life.

When we reflect about the external circumstances of our earthly life, about things we have seen or heard, about what we have gleaned from the world of nature or from history, or about what other people have said to us . . . when our thinking is occupied exclusively with what comes to us from outside during earthly life, then that Being of the Hierarchy of the Angels to whom we belong has little to do with our thoughts; for the Angels never dwelt on the earth—unlike the primeval Teachers who although they were present in etheric bodies only, did nevertheless inhabit the earth. The Angels were never earth-dwellers. Our relation to them is therefore different from our relation to the Moon Beings of whom I have been speaking to you.

But for all that, as we follow the paths which lead us after death in a certain sense past the planets, and come, first of all, into the domain of the Moon Beings, we are also in the realm of the Angels. Thus while we are living together with the primeval Teachers of humanity who have now become Moon-dwellers, we are living, too, with the Angels.

Then, as our path leads further, we enter the sphere which in all spiritual science that has ever existed, is known as the sphere of Mercury. None of the Beings in this region were ever on the earth. Here live only Beings who were never earth-dwellers. When we pass into the sphere of Mercury between death and a new birth, we come into the realm of the Archangels. And when subsequently we pass into the sphere of Venus we come into the realm of the Archai.

In passing through these realms of the Third Hierarchy we approach what is in reality the spiritual sphere of the Sun. And the spiritual Sun-sphere is truly, in the most sublime sense, the dwelling-place of those Beings who in the ranks of the higher Hierarchies are named Exusiai, Dynamis, Kyriotetes. Thus it is the Second Hierarchy which, in reality, is the soul, the spirit, of the Sun-existence. We enter this sphere and spend in it the greater part of the time between death and a new birth.

Now these Beings can of a truth be understood only when we remember that their existence is entirely remote from what makes us into earth-men and holds us within the bounds of natural law. In the realm of true Sun-existence there are no natural laws as we know them on earth. In the realm of spiritual Sun-activity, spiritual laws—including, for example, the laws of will—and natural laws, are one. In that realm, natural laws do not in any way run counter to spiritual laws, for natural law and spiritual law are completely at one.

Let us be quite clear as to the consequences of this.—We live here on earth and have our various experiences. Perhaps we strive for goodness, we endeavour not to deviate from a path we consider morally right. With these intentions we perform certain deeds. We see someone else to whom such intentions cannot possibly be ascribed, to whom we can attribute only evil purposes. We wait a few years, continuing to unfold side by side with the other man's evil purposes, what we consider to be our own good intentions. But now we perceive that nothing has been achieved; our good intentions have had no effect and, in addition, ill-luck may have befallen us, whereas the other man whose purposes we deemed evil is living by our side in what appears to be good fortune.

This is something that leads so many people who have eyes only for earthly life, to rebel against it and to declare that in this earthly life there is no evidence of a power that deals justly with good and evil. And indeed no really unbiased observer will be able to say that a man who says this is entirely in the wrong. For would any reasonable person be prepared to insist that every occurrence in a man's life is connected, in respect either of merit or guilt, with what has come from his intentions in this earthly life? When we consider how earthly life takes its course we can only say that it is impossible to find any kind of balance there for the moral impulses issuing from the soul. Why is this impossible?

It is because we are not in a position, of ourselves, to translate our intentions, those innermost forces which by freely willed assent hold sway in our life of soul, into the reality wherein we live on earth. There, in the outer world, natural laws prevail and events occur for which the influences of many different human beings are responsible. We cannot but realise that in earthly life there is an abyss between the impulses of will in our souls and what we see taking effect in external life as our destiny.

Just ask yourselves how much of what is destiny in this external life and therefore significant for you is a direct realisation of the intentions you bear within your soul? The terrestrial world is not the realm in which the spiritual laws in accordance with which man allows himself to be governed, or governs himself, are at the same time natural laws. In this earthly world, spiritual laws are not identical with natural laws; spiritual laws hold sway in man's inner being only. And if we face the world fairly and squarely, we can only say: if someone misconstrues my good intentions, deeming them evil, if he does not recognise my good intentions and judges them by what my destiny may be after a few years . . . if, therefore, someone says that my good intentions are, in reality, bad, and when ill-luck befalls me a few years later justifies himself by saying: 'See what has happened now; I said all along that his intentions were bad . . .' then this would be an impossible way of living. The spiritual must work from soul to soul. But in the external, earthly world, the spiritual does not yet work as a force of destiny.

Thus we must keep vividly in mind that in earthly life there is an abyss between the moral and psychical on the one side and the natural and physical on the other. This abyss is caused by the fact that spiritual laws are not identical with natural laws.

Now if men leave entirely out of account the world which leads on from terrestrial existence—the world from B to C, from death to a new birth—whether they simply disregard it or whether they think that owing to the boundaries of cognition nothing can be known of it—what will such men say?

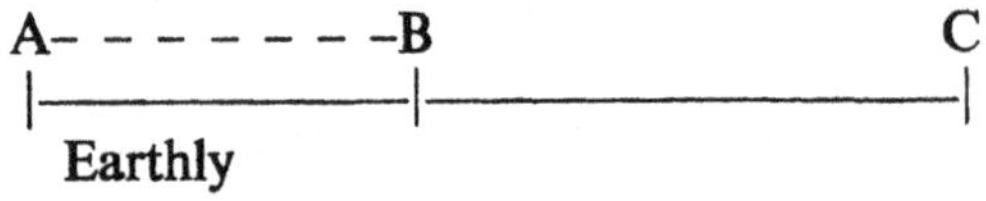

They will say: 'Natural laws and what the human being does and experiences because his life is involved in them—that is actually, that is real. Our knowledge, our science can encompass it. But the outcome of the intentions which are present within us as experiences of soul-and-spirit—that we cannot know.' Nothing, indeed, *can* be known, if the life from B to C is ignored. That these things living within the soul will in some way find fulfilment can only be a matter of *belief*. In the measure in which, since ancient times, knowledge of the span from B to C has faded, in that same measure has this separation arisen between knowledge and belief.

But we cannot speak of karma as we speak of knowledge and belief. For karma is the expression, the manifestation, of law—not of something that is mere belief—just as is the case with natural law.

Returning now to man's life between death and a new birth, after the earliest period which I have already described to you, our study brings us to a world where dwell the Beings of the Second Hierarchy, the Exusiai, Dynamis, Kyriotetes, and instead of earthly existence we have a Sun-existence. For even when we pass beyond the region of the stars, the sun still radiates, though not in the physical sense; and it continues to radiate as we live through the time between death and a new birth. Whereas here on earth the sun shines down upon us with its physical influences, in the life between death and a new birth the sun shines upwards to us; that is to say, we are borne and sustained by the Beings of the sun, by Exusiai, Dynamis, Kyriotetes. But in the world wherein we are then living, the natural laws which obtain in earthly life have no meaning at all, for everything is governed by *spiritual* laws, laws of soul-and-spirit. In that world there is no need for grass to grow; no cow needs grass to eat; for neither cows nor grass exist. Everything is spiritual. And within this Spirit-realm we can bring to realisation the intentions in the soul which cannot be realised in the earthly realm, so little realised that in extreme cases the good can lead to unhappiness and the evil to happiness. Everything in the realm of the sun finds fulfilment and expression according to its inner worth, its intrinsic nature, and it is therefore impossible for the good not to take effect in proportion to its power of goodness and the evil in proportion to its power of evil.—There is a very special reason why this is so.—From the Sun-existence which enshrines the Second Hierarchy, the Exusiai, Dynamis, Kyriotetes, a kindly, gracious welcome is extended to all the good intentions and purposes that were harboured in our life of soul on earth. This could also be expressed by saying that whatever has lived in a man's soul with any nuance of goodness is received in this Sun-existence with graciousness, but the evil is utterly rejected; it cannot enter.

In a series of lectures* I was able to give in the Goetheanum before its destruction by fire—the French Course as it is called—I spoke of how a man must leave behind his bad karma before a certain point of time is reached between death and a new birth. Evil cannot enter the realm of Sun-existence. There is a proverb which, to the modern mind, refers of course only to the physical effects of the sun. This proverb says that the sun shines equally upon the evil and the good. That is indeed so; but the sun does not admit evil into its realm. If you can perceive spiritually what is good in a man's soul, you will see it bright as sunlight—bright in the spiritual sense. If you perceive what is evil in him, it is dark, like a spot where no sunlight can penetrate. Whatever is evil in a man must be left behind when he enters the Sun-existence. It cannot go with him.

But think of it: in his earthly life man is one whole. His physical existence and his existence of soul-and-spirit are linked together, they form a unity. Although it cannot be proved with crude instruments, it is a fact that not only does the blood of a man who harbours only evil, flow differently, but the very composition of the blood is different from that of a man who has goodness in his soul!

Picture to yourself that in the life between death and a new birth a really evil man arrives at the threshold of the Sun-existence. He must leave behind him all that is evil. Yes, but this means that a considerable part of him remains behind, for the evil is bound up with him, is one with him. In so far at least as the evil is one with him, he must leave part of himself behind. But if at this threshold a man has to leave behind something of his own being, what is the consequence? The consequence is that he is maimed, stunted, and he passes into the Sun-existence as a kind of spiritual cripple. The Sun-existence can have an effect only upon what a man brings of himself into this realm. And in this realm those Beings who can work together with him between death and a new birth are led to him.

* *Cosmology, Religion and Philosophy*. Ten lectures, September, 1922.

Let us take an extreme case—the case of someone who was so evil, so utterly inhuman that he wished ill to all men. Let us imagine him to have been evil to a degree in which evil does not really exist . . . but hypothetically at any rate we will imagine him to have been an unmitigated villain. What will become of such a man who has identified his whole being with evil? What will become of him when he arrives at the point where he must leave behind everything of himself that is evil, or connected with evil? He will be obliged to leave the whole of himself behind! He will have passed through the realm of the Moon Beings, will have encountered the Being of the Hierarchy of the Angels who is specially connected with him, and also other Beings of that Hierarchy. But now, having reached the end of this realm, and pursuing his way through the spheres of Mercury and Venus, he approaches the realm of the Sun. Before entering this realm of Sun-existence he must leave all of himself behind, because he was wholly evil. What is the consequence? The consequence is that he does not pass into the Sun-existence at all. And if he is not to disappear from the world altogether he must at once prepare to reincarnate, to enter again into an earthly life.

In the case of a hardened evil-doer, therefore, you will find that very soon after his death he comes back again to earthly life.

There are, in reality, no such unmitigated villains in existence, because in a certain sense there is *some* good in every human being. All of them, therefore, can enter a little way into the realm of Sun-existence. Whether a man penetrates far or only a little way into this realm depends upon the extent to which he has crippled himself in soul-and-spirit. And this also determines what measure of power he is able to draw from the Sun-existence for his next earthly life. What a human being has within him can be founded only upon forces gathered from the Sun-existence.

You know the scene in the second part of *Faust*, where Wagner produces Homunculus in the retort.—Now to be able actually to create a being like Homunculus, Wagner

11—KR * *

would have needed the knowledge possessed by the Sun Beings. But Goethe does not depict Wagner as such a man; if Wagner had possessed that knowledge, Goethe would not have used the words "soulless groveller" in connection with him. Wagner is undoubtedly very clever but he lacks the knowledge possessed by the Sun Beings. That is the reason why Mephistopheles—a spirit-being who has this knowledge—must come to his aid. Wagner could have achieved nothing without the help of Mephistopheles. Goethe divined quite clearly that only so could there be produced in the retort a being like Homunculus who can then himself actually accomplish something.

We must be quite clear that the *human* cannot proceed from the earthly but only from the Sun-nature. What is earthly in man is only an image. Man bears the Sun-nature within him; the earthly is but an image, a picture, of his true being.*

So you see, the World Order commits us into the care of the sublime Sun Beings during our life between death and a new birth. And together with us, these Sun Beings work upon as much of our being as we have been able to bring into the realm of Sun-existence. The rest remains behind and must be gathered in again when we return to earthly life.

Man passes out into cosmic existence—I shall describe the further stages in the lecture the day after to-morrow—and then he returns to the earth. On the path of return he passes once more through the Moon region. There he finds the evil he left behind and he must receive it into his being, it must again become part of himself. He receives it in the form in which he experienced it immediately after having passed through the gate of death; and now he makes it so truly a part of himself that it comes to realisation in earthly existence.

Let us think once again of the rather unpleasant example I gave a little while ago.—If during my life on earth I have given someone a box on the ears, then after my death, in the

* See: *Man as Picture of the Living Spirit*. Lecture given by Rudolf Steiner, 2nd September, 1923, in London.

course of the backward journey, I live through the pain he felt. This experience too I find again on my return and strive for its realisation. If, therefore, something befalls me that is the consequence of what the other human being experienced, I myself have striven to this end on departing from the last life on earth. And when I return to the earth I bring with me the impulse for its realisation.—But let us leave that for the time being.—I shall speak in the next lecture about the fulfilment of karma. What I want to impress upon you now is that what I find again as I return, has not passed through the Sun-existence. I have taken through the Sun-existence only that in me which was related to the good.

Having built up in the realm of the Sun a somewhat stunted human being, I now take into myself once again what I left behind. What I now take into myself forms the basis of my earthly-bodily organisation. As I brought into the realm of Sun-existence only the part of myself that was able to enter this realm, I can only bring back, quickened and spiritualised by the Sun-existence, the part of my human being that was able to accompany me through that realm.

Let us therefore make this distinction:

(1) A part of man that has passed through the realm of Sun-existence appears on earth.

(2) A part of man that has *not* passed through the realm of Sun-existence appears on earth.

What I have been saying hitherto concerns man's life between death and a new birth and its after-effects in the earthly life. But the sun also works upon the human being while he is on the earth. And the other realms too, especially the realm of the Moon, work upon man in earthly existence. There is, firstly the influence of the Sun-existence between death and a new birth, and, secondly, the influence of the Sun-existence during life on earth. Similarly, if we take together the workings of Moon, Mercury and Venus, we have, firstly, the influence of the Moon-existence between death and a new birth, and, secondly, the influence of the

Moon-existence upon the human being while he is on earth.

During earthly life we need the sun, in order that we may have a *head*-life. What the sun sends to us in its rays calls forth the head-life from our organisation. This is the part of man that is conditioned by the Sun-existence, that is dependent upon the workings of the head. I say "the head", meaning the whole life of the senses and of ideation. The other part of man, the part that is dependent upon the influences of the spheres of Moon, Mercury, Venus, is connected, not with the head-life, but with the life of procreation in the widest sense.

There you have something very remarkable. The Sun-existence works upon man between death and a new birth, making him truly 'man', elaborating in him what is connected with the good. During earthly life, however, the sun can work only upon what is connected with the head. Of a truth this head-life has not very much to do with the good, for a man can also use his head to make himself into an out-and-out scoundrel. He can let his very cleverness make him an evil-doer.

Everything in earthly existence that promotes continuity of evolution is based upon the life of procreation. This life of procreation is under the influence of the moon and during the period between death and a new birth is connected with the part of man that does *not* share his existence in the cosmic spheres.

If you keep this in mind it will be easy for you to understand how what is connected with it makes its appearance in the human being during his earthly life.

We have, firstly, the part of man that has passed through the Sun-existence. In earthly life the Sun-existence works upon the head only; nevertheless what is connected with the Sun-existence remains in the being of man as a whole; it remains as his *predisposition to health*. That is why the predisposition to health is also connected with the head. The head becomes ill only when the illness is projected into it from below, by the metabolic process or by the workings of the rhythmic system.

On the other hand, the part of man that does not pass through the Sun-existence is connected with his *predisposition to illness.*

And so it will be clear to you that illness is woven into man's destiny *below* the realm of Sun-existence and is connected with the effects of the evil which are experienced as soon as he has passed into the life between death and a new birth. The realm of the Sun is connected with the predisposition to health. And only when influences from the Moon-sphere penetrate into the Sun-sphere in man's organism can that part of him which in earthly life is connected with the Sun-sphere—namely, the head—suffer any condition of illness. You see now that real insight into those great karmic connections is possible only when we follow the human being into the realm where spiritual laws are natural laws, and natural laws are spiritual laws.

(1) A part of man that has pased through the realm of Sun-existence appears on earth.	It is the part of man that is dependent upon the workings of the head.	Predisposition to health
(2) A part of man that has not passed through the Sun-existence appears on earth.	It is the part of man that is connected with the life of procreation.	Predisposition to illness

You must forgive me for using trivial words in describing matters that are anything but trivial, and for speaking the language of ordinary life. To do so is not unnatural for one who stands within the spiritual world. When we talk with human beings here on earth, we recognise by the way in which they speak that they stand within the realm of nature. Their very language betrays it. But when one comes into the realm I described in the last lecture—the realm into which man passes directly after death—and has converse there with the Beings who were once the primeval Teachers of mankind, or with the Beings of the Hierarchy of the Angels, then there is something strange in this converse. For in that realm—how shall I put it?—folk talk as though they were speaking of natural laws, but these are natural laws in which magic is operating and which are governed by the spirit. These Beings understand magic; but of natural laws they know only that men have such laws on earth. They themselves are not concerned with these natural laws. Nevertheless the processes and happenings in yonder realm appear in pictures which resemble the processes taking place on the earth. Hence the spiritual workings resemble the workings of nature, but are stronger, of greater intensity, as I have described.

When man leaves this sphere and enters the realm of Sun-existence, then no more at all is heard of the natural laws belonging to the earth. The language of the Beings in this realm has reference to spiritual workings, spiritual causes only. In that world nothing is heard of natural laws.

After all, my dear friends, these things must be made known some time or other. For when on earth it is constantly insisted that natural laws are absolute, universal—or even, foolishly enough, eternal—one would fain reply: But there are realms in the universe through which man has to pass in the life between death and rebirth where these natural laws are passed over with a smile because they have no significance there; they exist at most as tidings from the earth, not as any real factor in life. And when man passes through this realm between death and a new birth, and has lived long enough in a world where there are no natural laws but only spiritual laws, he ceases to think of natural laws as something to be taken seriously. Natural laws are not taken seriously between death and rebirth. Man lives in a realm where his spiritual intentions can be realised, where realisation is in sight.

But if in the realm of Sun-existence there were only the Second Hierarchy, if we were to experience in that realm only the kind of realisation that is possible there, then, having passed through this state of existence and desiring to enter earthly life again, we should stand at this point (see diagram) burdened with our karma, knowing that no progress is possible unless what has been brought, spiritually, to realisation, can be led over into the physical. Spiritually, our karma has been brought to realisation when we descend to earth; but the moment we enter earthly existence, the spiritual laws and spiritual aspects must be transformed into the physical. Here is the region where the Seraphim, Cherubim and Thrones transform the spiritual into the physical.

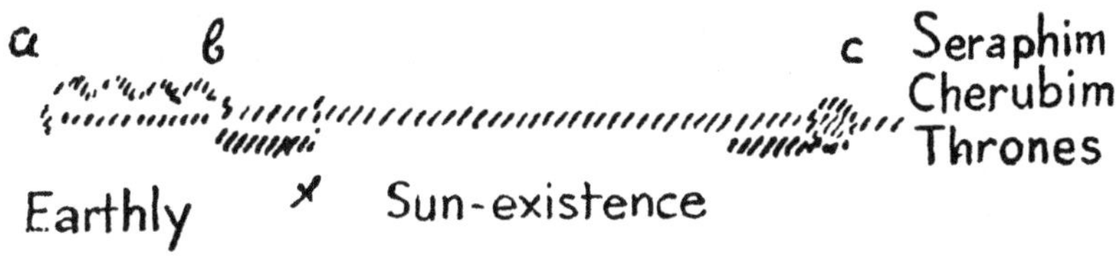

And so in the next earthly life, what has already been brought to spiritual realisation comes also to physical realisation in karma. Such is the onward course of karma.

XI

If we are to understand the real nature of karma, it is of paramount importance to turn our attention to the extent to which the cosmos participates in the evolution of mankind.

In order, therefore, to be able to envisage those Beings of the spiritual cosmos who play a part in man's evolution, let us consider, to begin with, man's connection with the beings belonging to the earthly realm. Man on earth is surrounded by beings of the mineral, plant and animal kingdoms, and must be regarded as having all these three kingdoms of nature within him—in a higher form. In a certain respect man is related to the mineral kingdom through his physical organism but he elaborates what is otherwise to be found in the external mineral kingdom into a higher form of existence.

Through his etheric body man is related to the realm of the plants, but again he elaborates this within himself. The same holds good of man's relationship through his astral body to the beings of the animal world. When, therefore, we think of the spatial environment of man we must realise that he bears the mineral, the plant and the animal kingdom within him.

Just as man bears within him these external kingdoms of nature, so does he bear within him—but in respect of time, not of space—the kingdoms of the higher Hierarchies. And we can only understand human karma in all its aspects when we know how the various realms of the Hierarchies work upon man through the course of his earthly life.

In considering how the mineral kingdom works upon man, we have to do with the processes connected with nourishment. For whatever means of nourishment man draws from kingdoms higher than the mineral, are reduced, in the first place, to the mineral condition. Passing on to the plant kingdom, we know that man has within him life-forces, vital forces. Again, in reference to the animal kingdom we know that through his astral body man raises mere life into a higher sphere, into the sphere of perceptive experience. In short, we can follow the sequences of processes in the three kingdoms of nature as well as within the human organism.

In the same way we can follow the workings of the higher Hierarchies in man's life of soul-and-spirit. The mineral nature, the plant nature, the animal nature in man can be understood in the light of the processes operating in the three kingdoms of nature in space. Equally, we must understand the higher forces operating in the life of man.

To begin with, we will consider human destiny and endeavour to understand how the kingdoms of the Hierarchies work into it. But here we must study, not what is present *simultaneously* in man, namely, physical body, etheric body and astral body but in connection with the working of the Hierarchies we must study what transpires in man's earthly life in the succession of time—regarded, of course, from the spiritual point of view.

In our anthroposophical studies we have always recognised distinct periods in the course of human life: from birth until the change of teeth at about the 7th year; from the change of teeth to puberty; from puberty to the 21st year where the differentiation is less perceptible; then from the 21st year to the 28th; from the 28th year to the 35th; from the 35th year to the 42nd; from the 42nd year to the 49th; from the 49th year to the 56th; and so on. Concerning what lies beyond the 56th year I shall speak in the next lecture. To-day we shall consider the course of human life up to the 56th year.

We have therefore three periods of life up to the 21st year, then three further periods, and so on.

Man says "I" of himself. But many forces play upon this "I". Outwardly considered, the "I" is worked upon by mineral forces, plant forces and animal forces; inwardly, in the aspect of soul-and-spirit, the "I" is worked upon by the third Hierarchy, by the Angeloi, Archangeloi, Archai, by the second Hierarchy (Exusiai, Kyriotetes, Dynamis), and by the first Hierarchy (Seraphim, Cherubim and Thrones).

These Beings do not, however, all work into the course of man's life in the same way. Even externally there is a difference in the influences taking effect in the human being according to his age. When, for example, we observe a little child at the very beginning of earthly life, we find what is characteristic of the animal kingdom especially marked in him; a growing, thriving, upbuilding process.

When we consider the last portion of life, the years that lead into old age, we find evidence of a mineralising process; the organism becomes sclerotic, brittle. Because this mineralising process is more subtle and intimate in man it works more strongly in him than in the animals—with the exception of the higher animals. The difference there is due to conditions into which we cannot enter now, but which will be dealt with on some later occasion. Whereas in the animal the ebbing of the life-forces begins directly the up-building process is complete, the human being carries over important phases of his development into the period of decline which in reality begins already in the thirties. A very great deal in the evolution of humanity would simply not exist if human beings developed in the same way as the animals, carrying nothing over into old age. Human beings can carry very much into old age, and many momentous achievements of culture are due to what has thus been carried over into old age, into the period of physical decline when the mineralising process is particularly in evidence.

Outwardly, then, it is clearly perceptible that at the beginning of earthly life the animal nature predominates, at the end of earthly life the mineral nature, and in the intervening period the plant nature.

But in respect of the working of the higher Hierarchies upon man the difference is even more emphatic. In earliest childhood the Third Hierarchy—Angeloi, Archangeloi, Archai—work with particular strength upon the life of soul-and-spirit. The activity of this Third Hierarchy embraces, properly speaking, the first three periods of life. The Angeloi, Archangeloi and Archai work throughout this period. In the little child and the young human being the organism is all the time being built up by the soul-and-spirit. This activity embraces almost everything: and into it works forces from the world of the Third Hierarchy, the Angeloi, Archangeloi, Archai.

At the 14th year the Second Hierarchy (Exusiai, Dynamis, Kyriotetes) begins to work. So that here, again through three periods, between the 14th and 35th years, I must write: Exusiai, Dynamis, Kyriotetes. You will see, my dear friends, that in the period between the 14th and 21st years the Third and the Second Hierarchy together exercise their influences upon the human being. It is not until the 21st year that the Second Hierarchy begins to work by itself.

At puberty, great cosmic processes, which until this age are not present in the human being, begin in some measure to be active in him. Little reflection is needed to perceive that when he becomes capable of procreation the human being is able to receive into himself from the cosmos those forces which co-operate in the creation of a new physical man. Before the age of puberty these cosmic forces do not work in the human being. A change takes place in the physical organism at puberty whereby it is imbued with mightier forces than it previously contained. These stronger forces are not present in the child before that age. In the child are the weaker forces which, to begin with, work only upon the soul in earthly life, not upon the body.

In the 35th year a period begins when the human being becomes weaker in respect of his inner soul-forces, less able than he was before to withstand the onset of the destructive forces of his organism. Before the 35th year the organism itself provides essential support, for its inherent tendency is to upbuild. This tendency continues on into the thirties but then a destructive tendency begins to predominate. This process of destruction cannot be counteracted even by the forces emanating from the Beings of the Second Hierarchy. Henceforth the soul must receive *from the cosmos* enough support to prevent the normal course of life being ended by death at the age of 35. For if until the 21st year only the Beings of the Third Hierarchy were to work and then from the 14th to the 35th year only the Beings of the Second Hierarchy, we should be ripe for death at the age of 35, that is to say at the very middle of earthly life proper—unless the physical body were still to hold together from sheer inertia. Death does not occur at this time because actually from the 28th year, not only from the 35th, and again through three periods, the Beings of the *First* Hierarchy, the Seraphim, Cherubim and Thrones, work upon man.

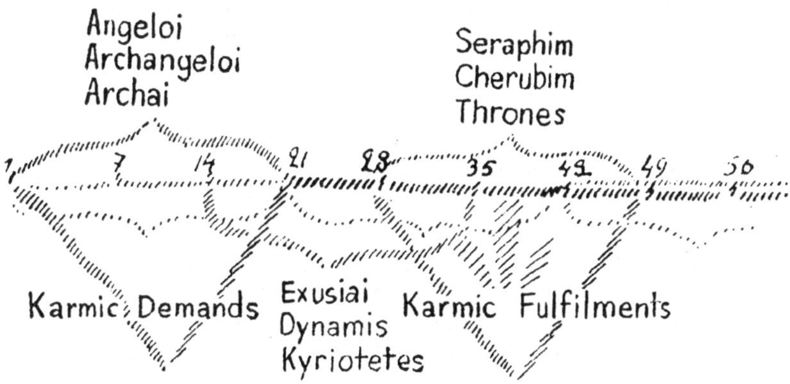

Again there is a period, between the 28th and the 35th years, when the *Second and the First Hierarchies* are working together. Thus in point of fact the Second Hierarchy works by itself during the period from the 21st until the 28th year of life.

As I said before, we will consider the later period of life in the next lecture. You will naturally say: But is a human being who has passed his 49th year forsaken by all the Hierarchies? We shall consider that on another occasion. What has been said to-day need not therefore be taken as applying only to those who are under the age of 49 and not to the others. To begin with, however, we must learn to know how the Hierarchies pour their forces, their particular strength into human life as it runs its course.

Naturally you must not think that such matters can be adequately studied by setting them out diagrammatically. This is never possible when we have to do with any higher form of life.

For many years I have been speaking of man as a threefold being: the man of nerves-and-senses, the rhythmic man, the metabolic-limb man. A professor once inferred from this—what will professors not infer!—that I divided man into three—head, chest, abdominal system. This was because he thought of everything side by side. I have of course always emphasised that although the nerves-and-senses system is concentrated mainly in the head, it extends through the whole organism. The same is true of the rhythmic system. The three members must not be thought of in spatial juxtaposition. You must also conceive the sequence of which we have been speaking, in the same way: the working of Angeloi, Archangeloi and Archai is limited, in the main, to the first three periods of life, but the aftermath of these periods continues through the whole of life, just as the nerves-and-senses system is concentrated mainly in the head but is present through the whole organism. We can feel with the big toe, because it too contains nerves-and-senses life.

Nevertheless this threefold membering of the human being is a reality; so too is the other threefold membering of which I am speaking to-day.

When you study these periods in human life, you will be able to say: on the spiritual side, the human "I" is subject to any number of influences proceeding from the spiritual world, just as on the physical side it is subject to influences coming from the animal, plant and mineral kingdoms. As human beings we stand with our "I" in the midst of what is coming to us in a most complicated way from the cosmos. And this activity which extends spiritually from the cosmos, from the Hierarchies, to man, is also concerned with the shaping of karma during physical life on earth.

It is the Angeloi, Archangeloi and Archai who bring us from the spiritual world into the physical world, and it is they who mainly accompany us through the first three periods of life. They work most strongly of all upon the nerves-and-senses system. In all the complicated and wonderful development taking place in our sense-life and in our intellectual life up to the age of 21—in all this, the Angeloi, Archangeloi and Archai participate.

Countless happenings take place behind the scenes of the ordinary consciousness. And it is precisely in these happenings that the Beings of the higher Hierarchies participate.

Then again from puberty, from about the 14th year onwards, Beings whose forces are stronger than those of the Angeloi, Archangeloi and Archai, begin to take hold of the rhythmic system. The real task of the Beings of the Third Hierarchy, the Angeloi, Archangeloi and Archai, is to influence our life of soul. From pre-earthly existence we bring with us into the first three epochs of life such strong forces that the soul is able to work powerfully upon the body. During this period, only the comparatively weaker forces of the Third Hierarchy are required to come to our help.

Now the forces which the Angeloi, Archangeloi and Archai need in order to guide and direct human life up to the 21st year, stream to them from the spiritual radiations of Saturn, Jupiter and Mars. When physical science comes to describe the cosmos, it is extremely naïve. From Saturn, Jupiter and Mars radiate forces of which the Angeloi, Archangeloi and Archai have the very deepest understanding.

When man is passing through the life between death and a new birth, he enters, first of all, into the Moon-sphere, where he comes into contact with Beings who were once on earth and who are stern judges of the good and the evil he brings with him. For the time being he must leave behind in the Moon-sphere the evil that is part of him. He cannot bear it into the Sun-sphere.

Then he passes through the Sun-sphere and still farther out into the cosmos. The forces of Mars, Jupiter and Saturn begin to work upon him. He passes through the whole of life between death and a new birth, and only on the path of return, when he has come again into the Moon-sphere, do Angeloi, Archangeloi and Archai approach him, saying, as it were: We have learned from Saturn, Jupiter and Mars that thou art crippled.—I have said that the evil must be left behind, but this means that man leaves something of himself behind. He enters as a cripple into the Sun-sphere as well as into the regions beyond. And there the gaze of Saturn, Jupiter and Mars falls upon him.

Truly, my dear friends, this life between death and a new birth is complicated! As soon as we pass through the gate of death, what I have described takes place in the Moon-sphere. Man must leave behind whatever of his being has identified itself with evil. It is as though the physical body were obliged to leave its limbs behind. Because he has identified himself with evil, man enters the Sun-sphere and all the rest of the cosmos in a maimed, mutilated condition, for he has been obliged to leave behind certain parts of his being. And when, having passed through the Sun-sphere, he enters the spheres of Mars, Jupiter and Saturn, he feels how Mars, Jupiter and Saturn gaze upon him with the penetrating eye of justice; for as the weavers of cosmic justice they watch him in order to behold how much of his being he may bear upwards. They gaze upon him. Each one of us perceives how much good or evil has become part of us, what we have been able to bear upwards, as well as what is lacking, that is to say, what we were obliged to leave behind; each one of us realises to what extent we are identified with evil, how much is lacking in us. The gaze directed upon us by the Beings of Mars, Saturn and Jupiter makes us realise our imperfections and shortcomings.

When a man returns again, Saturn, Jupiter and Mars have in the intervening time communicated to the Angeloi, Archangeloi and Archai what they beheld and experienced when he passed before them with all his imperfections. The Beings of the Third Hierarchy weave this into him, so that there is inscribed in his being what he has to do in compensation. In these first three epochs of life when Angeloi,

Archangeloi and Archai work upon the human being with particular strength, the *demands of karma* are inscribed into the nerves-and-senses system, into the head-system.

When the 21st year has been passed (—how things are with human beings who die before that age will be explained in later lectures—) the karmic demands upon life have already been stamped into a man. If one is able to read what is there in some human being of 21, one can perceive what karmic demands are inscribed into him; for it is in this period up to the 21st year, that these demands are inscribed. They lie mainly in the hidden, occult foundations of the nerves-and-senses system, in that which spiritually underlies the nerves-and-senses system.

When, on the other hand, we direct our attention to the further course of life, when we observe the human being between the ages of 28 and 49, we find that it is less a matter of the inscribing of karmic *demands*, but rather of the *fulfilment of karma*, the discharging of karma. For it is particularly in this period of life that what has been inscribed into a man's being in the first three epochs of life must be brought to karmic fulfilment.

So that here (see diagram) I can write: *fulfilment of karma* (28th to 49th years). During the period from the 21st year to the 28th year, karmic demands and karmic fulfilment are in balance.

Now there is one remarkable phenomenon to which attention must be paid in our time. In the present epoch of evolution there are a great many human beings whose last incarnation of importance occurred in the first centuries after the founding of Christianity, up to about the 8th or 9th century. (—This does not imply that there has been no other incarnation in the intervening time, but if this was the case it was an unimportant one.—) If we were to make a survey of the human beings living in our time and sharing in its culture, we should find that by far the greater number of them had their last important incarnation in the first seven or eight centuries after the founding of Christianity.

Now this period was one that had a striking effect upon

the human beings then living. This can be perceived to-day when one observes certain people in respect of their karma. Again and again, my dear friends, I have set myself the task of studying a number of people from this particular point of view, people who have acquired a certain amount of contemporary culture, intellectual culture, and also, speaking comparatively, considerable learning. Think of the large numbers of people nowadays who have become teachers in secondary schools, civil servants, and the like. They have learned a great deal, they have been to secondary schools, even to universities, and have really become exceedingly clever. (I do not mean this ironically, I only ask you to take it in connection with what I have said at other times about such things.) There are untold numbers of clever people to-day. The majority, indeed, are so clever that one can hardly tell them anything, for they know it already! Everyone has his own point of view; everyone passes judgment on what he hears.

That is how things are in our time, but only in our time. In earlier epochs it was quite different. Then there were individuals who had knowledge and the others listened to them. Clever people were by no means as numerous as they are to-day, when even in youth they are already clever. Just think of how many people under the age of 21 write—I will not say poetry, for this they have always done—but newspaper articles, even serious critiques.

In our time, then, intellectuality is very highly developed. In the case of most individuals this intellectuality is influenced, fundamentally, by their incarnation during the first seven or eight centuries after the founding of Christianity. In these centuries the feeling in the human soul for what came from pre-earthly existence into earthly life was all the time growing weaker. Men were beginning more and more to take an interest in what comes after death and were less and less concerned with what had preceded earthly life. In this connection I have frequently pointed out that we have no adequate expression for eternity but only for the half of eternity which has a beginning and never ends. For this part of the eternity of man's existence we have the word 'immortality', but unlike ancient languages we have not a word for the other half of eternity, which has never had a beginning. But eternity embraces both 'immortality' and 'un-bornness'. We have come into this world as beings to whom birth means only a metamorphosis, just as we depart from the earthly world through death which again signifies only a metamorphosis, not an end.

The strong consciousness that was alive in man until the early Christian centuries: 'I have descended from the spiritual world into physical existence'—this consciousness grew fainter and fainter and man began to confine himself to that other thought: I am here! What went before does not interest me. What does interest me is what follows after death.—This was the consciousness that grew stronger and stronger during the first Christian centuries. The feeling for pre-earthly existence grew dim in those who at that time were passing through their last incarnation of importance, and that is why intellectual cleverness now is entirely directed to the earthly. Great though it is, it is directed entirely to the earthly. Striking and tremendously significant discoveries can be made in this domain when one embarks on investigations into karma. I will mention two cases.

The first is that of a man who taught history in a secondary school, an extremely clever man and really impressive as a teacher. Until the time when the karmic demands were still working and then through this neutral zone here (see previous diagram)—that is to say until the beginning of the thirties—his cleverness was very evident. He was one of the many really clever men of our time. But the moment he entered this phase here (28th to 49th year) his cleverness was no longer a support and his moral impulses were in jeopardy. There was nothing left but intellectuality, which was then undermined. When the forces which are not bound up with the nerves-and-senses system but in the later part of life with the metaboilc system began to work, the lower nature of the metabolic-limb system undermined what had previously come to a very fine form of expression in the nerves-and-senses system. The man in question, who in respect of intellect had begun his life really well, actually ended in degeneracy; there was a moral *débâcle*. That is one example.

And now another example—of a personality who was even more intelligent than the one I have just mentioned—but again merely intelligent. He was extremely short-sighted and was possessed of really remarkable intelligence. Up to the age of 30, this personality too, because of his intelligence, had a strong influence upon his fellow-men. When, however, he had passed his 30th or certainly his 35th year, when the nerves-and-senses system was no longer working so powerfully but when the metabolic-limb system became especially active in this later phase of life, this man, who had previously been so able and clever, became utterly trivial and banal, absorbed in petty squabbles. I had known him in his youth and confess that I was astonished when I found him subsequently among people who were taken up with all kinds of party factions. Observation of the path that leads from karmic demands to karmic fulfilments disclosed that the forces of intelligence in men of our time, prepared as they were in the earlier incarnation during the first Christian centuries, were not strong enough to enable the soul to reach the realm of the First Hierarchy in the period when the soul becomes weaker and the body puts up greater resistance.

And then it became evident to me that the large numbers of men to-day who are so clever, who can, above all, be made so clever through their education—these men in the first epoch of life develop the capacity to reach up with the forces of their intelligence to the Third Hierarchy, to the Angeloi, Archangeloi and Archai. This they achieve. And in this epoch of life they are personalities of great promise.

When they come into the realm of the Second Hierarchy, they are, as it were, given over to this Hierarchy. The Second Hierarchy reaches down to men; practically all human beings become capable of procreation. This cosmic Hierarchy reaches downwards. Here there is no real abyss between man and the Hierarchy.

When, however, man reaches his 28th year and must begin to find a relation to the still higher Hierarchy, the First Hierarchy, he must find this relation with his whole nature, right down into the metabolic-limb system. Here he needs stronger forces of inner support in the spiritual realm; and the seed which was planted in him during an earlier life, in an epoch when men ceased to think about pre-earthly existence, proves unable to supply these forces.

In connection with karma, one would fain impress upon all true educators and teachers the urgent necessity of imbuing intellectuality with such spiritual strength that when the human being is passing through the later years of life, what has been permeated with moral force in his intellect may be able to hold the balance against the forces which draw him away from the First Hierarchy. (See arrow in diagram.)

It is a matter of no small interest in this age of ours to compare the second part of human life with the first, and those who have an aptitude for observing life should certainly begin to practice observation from this standpoint. For the things of which I have spoken occur in ordinary life; the examples I have given are taken from everyday life and could be multiplied a hundred—nay, a thousandfold; they are to be found everywhere. But something else of the same kind can also be found at a higher level of life. I have always been interested in the spiritual development of human beings and when I look at many who were creative in early life, who made a great impression on their contemporaries, perhaps as young poets or artists in some sphere, of whom it was said when they were 24, 25, 26, 27 years old: "What wonderful talent!" . . . well, they grew older; after the poetic and artistic achievements of youth the stream dried up and they were of no account at all in the sphere where they had once been of real significance.

If you go through the names of those who made reputations as young poets or artists and then lost all right to be included in the annals of literature or art, you will find abundant proof of what I am saying. But what I have told you will, at the same time, show you how the different epochs in human life reveal in manifold ways how karma and the impulses of karma take effect.

Everything that is merely intellectualistic and materialistic can really only influence a human being inwardly in his youth. The spiritual that is infused into the intellectuality—that alone can hold its own through the whole of earthly life—in accordance with karma. Therefore when we observe the kind of destinies I have described, we must look back to previous incarnations which failed to turn men's eyes to that vista of the spiritual which can be revealed only when the gaze is directed to the life before birth, not merely to the life after death.

Life in our time is often fraught with this tragedy and there is so much that does not stand the test of the years. In youth, ideals are plentiful; in old age few remain. Older people rely more upon the State and upon their pensions than upon the sustaining power of life itself; they need support from outside because they cannot find what brings them into relation with the First Hierarchy.

You see, therefore, that if we are to study karma in the right way, we must pay attention to these different, but interpenetrating, members of man's being.—When man is passing through the first three epochs of life he lives in relation to the Third Hierarchy. Then, inwardly and unconsciously, he begins to be related to the Second Hierarchy and finally to the First Hierarchy. Only on the basis of this knowledge are we able to judge to what extent a man enables the karmic impulses within him to come to expression. For this knowledge of man's relation to the higher Hierarchies, this knowledge alone can reveal human life in concrete reality.

Angeloi, Archangeloi and Archai say to us in our subconsciousness during the first three epochs of life: All this thou hast brought over from earlier epochs, from earlier earthly lives. This thou must take upon thyself.—In our subconscious experience of destiny this is said to us. And in truth, throughout these three epochs of life this message of destiny constantly resounds within us. From the Hierarchy of the Angeloi there rings forth: This is what Saturn, Jupiter and Mars have meted out to thee. Their forces have revealed it to us.

Then there follows all that comes from the Second Hierarchy, from the realm of the Sun; and finally what comes from the First Hierarchy, from the sphere of Venus, Mercury and Moon. And just as it is especially the Angeloi whose call resounds in our subconsciousness during the first three periods of life: Saturn, Jupiter and Mars have told us that this is ordained for thee . . . so from the 28th year onwards it is the Seraphim who also speak in the unconscious realm of the soul, saying: All this remains with thee because thou canst not fulfil it, because thou art unable to reach up to us; this remains with thee and thou must bear it into the next earthly life; thou canst not balance it because thou hast not the strength.

Under the level of man's consciousness speak the forces of karma, the forces that shape destiny. They speak from all the three higher Hierarchies. And if we have a delicate faculty of perception for what enters our life as destiny, then we can also look behind this vista of destiny and begin to apprehend with reverence and awe how through the course of our life the Beings of all the three Hierarchies are weaving this destiny. And in truth only then do we learn to look at life in the right way.

For who would be satisfied, if, when asking us about a man of whose life on earth he wants to know something, and presumes we can tell him, we merely answer: 'Oh, he is called Joseph Müller.' All that we can tell him is just the name! But the questioner had expected that he would hear something more than a name: events in the man's life, something that throws light on the forces and impulses that influenced his earthly life! No one who really wants to know something about a human being can be satisfied with merely knowing his name. But in this materialistic age of ours people are, unfortunately, satisfied with the designation 'Man'. In respect of all that lies behind the ordinary consciousness wherein work Angeloi, Archangeloi, Archai, Exusiai, Dynamis, Kyriotetes, Cherubim, Seraphim, Thrones—people to-day are satisfied with the general designation 'Man'. They do not look at the concrete realities. But this they must learn to do; they must turn their eyes again to these concrete realities of human life.

XII

In my last lecture here I spoke of how man is related to the Spiritual Hierarchies during the different periods of his life.—I should like to repeat that the aim of all these lectures is to lead us to a better and better understanding of how karma works in human life and in human evolution. Everything is really a preparation for this.

I told you that from a man's birth until about his 21st year, the Third Hierarchy is related to him in a special way; at the age of puberty the Second Hierarchy—Exusiai, Dynamis, Kyriotetes—begins to work. These Hierarchical Orders continue to work from puberty until the 21st year in the first period of their influence; in the second period they work until the 28th year, and in the third period until the 35th year. But from the 28th year onwards, an inner relationship begins with the First Hierarchy—Seraphim, Cherubim, Thrones. These Beings of the First Hierarchy continue working, in the first phase of their influence until the 35th year (during which period they co-operate with the Second Hierarchy), in the second phase until the 42nd year, and in the third phase until the 49th year.

Now the influences exercised directly by the Hierarchies during the various periods of man's life interweave, as it were, with the influences which play, as reflections, into these periods of life from the Spiritual Beings of the planetary spheres. As we look at the outer, physical radiance of the planets, we know that each of these heavenly bodies is but the sign that in the direction where we behold it there is a colony of spiritual Beings in the cosmos.

Our constitution as human beings is such that within the physical body we have an etheric body. The moment a man acquires the faculty of supersensible, Imaginative Knowledge, he is able to perceive everything that can be revealed to him through the etheric body. And then, as he looks back over the tableau of his earthly life since birth, all the events he has lived through and the forces that have influenced his development and determined his organisation of body, soul and spirit, lie manifest before the eye of soul in a mighty panorama, as if time had become space.

At this stage of Imaginative Consciousness on the path of Initiation, life can be surveyed in this way.

When, however, the stage of Inspiration, Knowledge through Inspiration, is reached, a higher revelation is added to the memory-tableau of the earthly life. This higher revelation is possible because in Inspired Consciousness the Imaginations are suppressed and the pictures of the events of earthly life, even when they have been perceived through the etheric body, are no longer there.

If by means of a diagram I were to represent this backward survey as a stream (drawing it as if presented to physical sight, not to the eye of soul) you must picture that the several phases are blotted out in Inspired Consciousness and manifestation of a different character revealed.

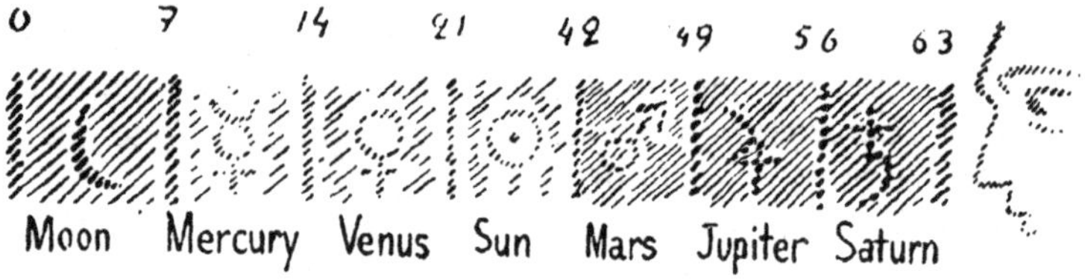

First of all, something is made manifest as a kind of revelation within this first phase and if we can find our bearings in the sphere of Inspiration, we become aware of what it is that is actually appearing.

Please understand me.—We gaze at a tableau of the whole of earthly life. Part of this tableau is obliterated, blotted out as it were, when Inspired Consciousness has been attained on the path of Initiation—in this case the phase in the memory-tableau from birth until the 7th year. This is blotted out and in its place the deeds resulting from the connection between the Moon Beings and man after death lie manifest before the eye of soul.

I told you, for example, how the life after death undergone by the personality who was the model for Strader in the Mystery Plays, was experienced. What happens in such a case is that one looks, first of all, at the memory-tableau; then, in Inspired Consciousness, this memory-tableau is obliterated. When the part of the tableau corresponding to the period from birth until the 7th year is obliterated, the deeds of which I have told you are made manifest—the deeds wrought by the Moon Beings in connection with the human being after death. Such experiences are possible when the course of life from birth until the 7th year becomes transparent and the Moon Beings and their deeds are revealed. Vision of the revelations connected with this phase of life is possible for every Initiate and is indeed the easiest to attain.

As you will readily understand, Initiation is possible at any age in life, with the exception of early childhood. Children up to the age of seven are not, as a rule, initiated. And if what I am now describing is to be seen and understood, one must, in the present earthly life, have passed beyond this age. Everyone who is initiated has passed the age of seven. That is why vision of what is disclosed by this first phase of life is comparatively easy to attain. What is here revealed are, as we have heard, the experiences undergone by a human being after death during the backward journey which lasts for a third of the time of his earthly life.

A second revelation is possible when that part of the backward survey which corresponds to the years between 7 and 14—that is to say, to the time of puberty—becomes visible to Inspired Consciousness. The experiences lived through by the human being after death as he ascends from the sphere of the Moon to that of Mercury are then revealed.

Having traversed the sphere of the Moon, man ascends to the sphere of Mercury. But in order to establish relationship with human beings in the Mercury-sphere, the phase of life between the 7th and 14th years, between the time of the change of teeth and that of puberty, must be obliterated from the memory-tableau.

If in Inspired Consciousness, the next phase of life is obliterated, enabling what can become visible here to shine through, the experiences undergone by man in the sphere of Venus after death are revealed.

Thus in looking back with the Inspired Consciousness of Initiation over these first periods of life, one beholds what is happening in the macrocosm, the spiritual macrocosm, to the Dead, the so-called Dead.

You will realise from what I am saying that infinite wisdom is contained in the terminology used by ancient science. For the element of love is associated with the name of Venus. Vision of the Venus-sphere corresponds to the period of human life following the onset of puberty.

Then there is a period lasting from the 21st until the 42nd year of life. When this period is revealed in Inspired Consciousness, one experiences—or can at any rate experience—what a dead man undergoes in the period that is by far the longest in his life between death and a new birth, when he is living together with the Sun Beings. The Sun-existence between death and rebirth is now revealed.

The Sun is a heavenly body of such might, embracing such a multitude of spiritual forces and spiritual Beings, that in order to perceive all the influences of the spiritual Sun-sphere upon the human being between death and rebirth, a period three times as long as the others must be obliterated from the memory-tableau, namely the whole period between the 21st and 42nd years. You will realise from this that Initiates themselves must have passed the age of 42 before they are able to look back upon man's connection with the Sun Beings between death and a new birth. This connection cannot be perceived in its fullness before then. To grow older, you see, has an important bearing upon spiritual vision itself. There are realities for the perception of which a certain maturity of years, not only a certain degree of Initiation, must have been reached.

We come now to the period between the 42nd and 49th years. This is the point to which I tried to lead in the last lecture, for when man reaches his 49th year the possibility of direct relationship with the Hierarchies ceases. You will have gathered this from what I have said. We shall consider presently how it is with men who have passed the age of 49.

If our attention is focussed upon influences which interweave with this phase of the tableau—we ourselves must of course have reached the age of 50 or more—and we look back at the span of time between the 42nd and the 49th years, we can behold the experiences a man undergoes after death in connection with the Beings of the Mars-sphere.

But in this sphere the spiritual world begins to impart a strongly individualised character to the karma of the human being when he is on earth. You have heard that a man's karma is prepared during the period which immediately follows death and lasts for a third of the time of the earthly life. Karma is then gradually elaborated, and I have already indicated how this takes place. Karma is elaborated, wrought out, in union with higher Beings.

Now there are men whose karma is elaborated mainly in the Mercury-sphere, or in the Venus-sphere, or in the Sun-sphere; and again there are others whose karma is elaborated mainly in the sphere of Mars. Human beings who by virtue of their earlier earthly lives bring into the spiritual world something that must be elaborated chiefly in the sphere of Mars, give evidence of this during their next life on earth. Let me give you an example.—

At the time when the influence of Mohammedanism upon civilisation had already spread across Asia, Northern Africa and into Spain, there lived a personality whose spiritual development proceeded, to begin with, in Northern Africa, in a School which in spite of having become decadent, was similar to the School in which, very much earlier, St. Augustine had spent the same phase of his life. The study in which this personality engaged in Northern Africa was entirely similar in character and trend.

We must picture to ourselves that in those days the

pursuit of knowledge was something very different from what it is to-day. Little is to be heard at the present time about the kind of study that was pursued so many centuries ago in Northern Africa by St. Augustine, or, later on, by the personality of whom I am now speaking. But at that time, particularly in Northern Africa, studies connected with the Mysteries were still possible although the Mysteries were in the throes of decline. The personality to whom I am referring had pursued such studies, had imbibed all that could be learned from them concerning the independence of the human soul, the realms experienced by the soul when liberated from the body, and so forth. Then this personality joined in the Mohammedan campaigns and went over to Spain. There he absorbed much Mohammedan-Asiatic learning in the form into which it had already been re-cast in Spain; also much of the lore that had been spread far and wide by the Jews—it was not, however, the Cabbalism that was so universally cultivated later on, in the Middle Ages, but an older form of Cabbalism. And so in the early years after the Mohammedan campaigns we find this personality steeped in Mohammedanism but working along particular lines: reckoning, calculating, according to Cabbalistic principles.

All this was lived through again in a later incarnation as a woman, when it was inwardly deepened, received by the heart rather than by the head.

Then, later on, in the 18th century, this same individuality passed over into a man who has become a world-famous figure in French culture, namely *Voltaire*. This individuality appeared again in Voltaire.

When our gaze is directed to the experiences lived through by this individuality between death and a new birth, before he became Voltaire—experiences that were the outcome of his previous earthly lives—we find that the fruits of his studies in Northern Africa, with their subsequent Cabbalistic trend, were wrought out in the sphere of Mars during the second half of his life between death and rebirth. And with the results of the metamorphosis that can be wrought in the Mars-sphere, Voltaire came again in the 18th century as Voltaire. I am therefore able to bring him forward as an example of the elaboration of karma in the sphere of Mars between death and a new birth.

Now the Mars Beings imbue everything with an element of aggressiveness—be it in the domain of physical, psychical or spiritual qualities. Nay more, they make a man combative, warlike by nature. This warlike element is compatible not only with attack but also with retreat—otherwise wars could not be waged! I think this was obvious enough during the World War.

Look at the whole life of Voltaire.—It was a life in which splendid qualities of soul were developed, but it was a life of attack, of aggression, and also of withdrawal and retreat—at times engaging in attacks with almost foolhardy daring, at others evincing actual cowardice in retreat.

It is much better to study these things from examples where the whole character and tenor of the life can be discerned than to study them in theory. That is why I am taking examples of this kind.

And now when a man penetrates with the Inspired consciousness of Initiation into the phase of life between the 49th and 56th years—he must be considerably older than was necessary for the vision connected with the earlier periods—he attains knowledge of what the Beings of the Jupiter region can bring about in human beings during their life between death and a new birth.

Acquaintance with the Beings of the Jupiter-sphere makes a very remarkable impression.—One must of course have passed the age of 56 before this experience is possible.—The first impression is one of astonishment that Beings like those belonging to the Jupiter-sphere can exist at all.—I mean that as a man on earth one is astonished, not as a man between death and rebirth; for then, of course, one is actually connected with these Jupiter Beings. They are Beings who need not 'learn' anything, because the moment they take form—I cannot say 'the moment they are born' as you will presently see—they are already wise, supremely wise. They are never stupid, never unwise. They are as men on earth would often like to be—men who do not appreciate the blessings of being taught and would prefer to be wise directly they are born. These Beings on Jupiter are not 'born'; they simply arise out of the whole organism of Jupiter. Rather in the way that we see clouds forming out of the atmosphere, so do these Beings arise out of Jupiter, and once they are there they can be regarded as embodied wisdom. Neither do they die; they are merely transformed, they undergo metamorphosis. Jupiter is in essence *weaving wisdom*. Picture yourselves standing, let us say, on the Rigi, and looking down at the clouds. And now imagine that you are looking, not upon weaving clouds of water-vapour but upon weaving wisdom itself, weaving thought-images which are actually *Beings*.—Then you will have an impression of Jupiter.

Again let me give an example of the way in which karma can be elaborated in this Jupiter-sphere.

There was a personality who lived in the later period of Mexican civilisation and was connected with the utterly decadent, pseudo-magical Mystery cults of Mexico; with an intense thirst for knowledge he studied everything with close and meticulous exactitude. My attention was attracted to him through having made the acquaintance some years ago of a curious man who is still engaged in a primitive form of study of the decadent superstitions of the Mexican Mysteries. Such lore is of negligible importance, because anyone who studies these things at the present time is studying pure superstition; it has all become decadent to-day. But the other personality to whom I am referring imbided with fervent enthusiasm all that could be learnt from the still flourishing Mexican civilisation before the discovery, the so-called 'discovery' of America. In those days Mexican civilisation was still influenced by the Mysteries but was already in the throes of decline. When mention is made to-day of Taotl, Quetzalcoatl, Tezcatlipoka—the Beings of the Mexican Mysteries—little more is known than the names and a few scattered images. But this personality still knew that Taotl is a Being who as a cosmic, universal Spirit weaves in the clouds, lives in the lightning and the thunder. He knew too that under certain given conditions this Spirit could be invoked into consecrated water by enactments of sacred ritual. And he knew that Quetzalcoatl was a Divine Being who could take hold of man in his circulating blood, in the working of his breath. Living reality of Being was experienced in the Mexican Mysteries by the personality of whom I am speaking. He was reborn in a later age without any intermediate life as a woman. He had been a man in Mexico and was born again as a man. But in his life between death and rebirth this individuality passed through the supersensible world in such a way that in the development of his karma—this in turn was the outcome of still earlier incarnations not in Mexico but elsewhere—he bore through the Jupiter region all that he had experienced in Mexico: knowledge that had degenerated into superstition but was nevertheless replete with vitality, saturated with the fruits of older civilisations. In the Jupiter-sphere all this assumed the form of wisdom, but a wisdom that is in truth automatic, unconscious, when compared with the wisdom man should make his own by individual effort.

When in the elaboration of karma between death and a new birth, the living, weaving wisdom of the Jupiter-sphere pours over what has been experienced by a man in a previous earthly life, wisdom and its light can still shine forth in the subsequent life. But the wisdom, then, is founded on the experiences of earthly life.

The individuality of whom I am speaking was born again in modern civilisation as *Eliphas Levi.* Eliphas Levi, therefore, had spent his previous incarnation in the Mexican civilisation, had then passed through the sphere of Jupiter with its wisdom, and in this sphere of Jupiter everything was worked through once again. But Mexican culture is a decadent culture and if you read the books of Eliphas Levi to-day you will find evidence of great wisdom spread out as it were over something extremely primitive. And one who has insight into these things will say: all this is Jupiter, but inferior Jupiter!

When it is possible to survey the period of life from the 56th to the 63rd year—and I myself am now in this position—one gazes at the influences exercised upon man between death and rebirth by Saturn, by the Beings of Saturn. This is an even more startling vista, a vista that causes bewilderment, nay indeed actual pain.

The Beings associated with Saturn are Beings who by their very nature take no heed at all of what they do in the immediate present; they act as it were unconsciously, under the sway of much loftier Beings into whose world they enter on reaching maturity. But as soon as they have done something, it stands there in powerful, living remembrance.

Try for a moment to imagine yourselves in this position . . . I am not referring to any particular vocation or profession . . . but just picture yourselves doing something, no matter what, and not noticing anything at all while you are actually doing it; but once you have done it, it stands there in living remembrance as an intensely vivid picture. Take a singer: he sings but is unconscious that he is doing so; he is simply being used by the Gods to sing. Imagine a large audience listening to him; as long as he is actually singing he is aware of nothing at all; he knows nothing, either about himself or about what he is experiencing. But the moment it is all over and the concert ended, the whole event is there and does not fade away; it remains and forms part of the content of his very life. On Saturn, man *is* the past, only the past.

Think of yourselves walking over the earth. As you walk you see nothing of yourself. But when you have gone a little further and look back, you see a little snowman—he is a figure of yourself as you were before you took the last step. Again you observe nothing, but walk on, and another little snowman stands behind you. And so it continues, with more and more little snowmen standing behind you. To all of them you say "I".—Now transpose this imagery into the spiritual and you have the key to the nature of the Saturn

Beings. Between death and a new birth man has to encounter these Beings—Beings who live wholly in the past. And there are men who in the elaboration of their karma have a particularly strong connection with these Saturn Beings.

The destiny of such men can be intelligible only when one looks back upon the period of life between the 56th and 63rd years. Again I will give an example in order to show you how karmic events in life point back to happenings in the supersensible world between death and a new birth.

When I was speaking to you not long ago about the Hibernian Mysteries, I told you how difficult it is to approach these Mysteries, how they seem to thrust one back; and I spoke of the wonder and the sublimity of what was experienced in these Hibernian Mysteries in Ireland. I described how the pupil, having first learned to know the utmost depths of doubt and uncertainty in life, was led before two statues. The first consisted of a substance that was elastic throughout and the pupil was exhorted to touch or to press this statue again and again. The indents made in the statue gave rise to a feeling of overwhelming dread: it was as if one had constantly to cut, I cannot say into a corpse, but into living flesh—a horrifying experience for any sensitive person.

The second statue retained every indent made upon it by pressure and its form was only restored, made intact, after an interval of time, when the candidate for Initiation was led before the statue again.

I told you how those who were initiated in these Hibernian Mysteries experienced the glory and majesty of the microcosm, that is to say of man himself, and of the great world, the macrocosm. The impressions were tremendously powerful, of indescribable sublimity.

One of those who had participated with intense fervour in the Hibernian Mysteries and had reached a high degree of Initiation, was destined after death to penetrate deeply into the Saturn-sphere.—His earthly life within these Mysteries was the outcome of still earlier incarnations.—He had been profoundly moved by the grandeur and majesty of what he had experienced in the Mysteries of Hibernia.—When I was describing them to you I told you that in spiritual vision, without any kind of connection in physical space, the Initiates beheld the actual Event of Golgotha.—

The individuality of whom I am speaking lived through all these experiences again with great intensity of feeling and was subsequently born again in our own period of civilisation.

Picture to yourselves what this personality acquired by virtue of the fact that the karma of his last life had been elaborated, wrought out in the Saturn-sphere. Everything presented itself to him in the light of the past. He beheld his experiences in the Hibernian Mysteries in the light cast by the Saturn Beings over the far, far distant past, and majestic pictures of pre-earthly times, of Moon periods and Sun-periods came alive in him.

When he was born again, all that before this earthly incarnation had been bathed in the past, coloured by the past, transformed itself into mighty pictures—idealistic, albeit visionary pictures which cast their light into the future and came to expression in a transcendental romanticism.

In short, this individuality who had once been initiated in the Hibernian Mysteries, was born in our epoch—our epoch in the wider sense—as *Victor Hugo.* In its romanticism, in its whole configuration, Victor Hugo's life bears the stamp of karma wrought out in the Saturn-sphere.

These are small contributions towards an understanding of how karma originates and takes shape. As I said, the best way of getting to understand karma is to study concrete examples. For the study of how karma is elaborated in the case of men like Voltaire, Eliphas Levi, Victor Hugo, is full of the deepest interest and leads to a knowledge of the connection of the human being on earth with the macrocosmic, spiritual being engaged in the elaboration of karma between death and a new birth.

XIII

The ability to perceive karmic connections in human life demands a clear understanding of laws and conditions of existence with which, generally speaking, the man of modern times is entirely unfamiliar. For into the karmic connections extending from one earthly life into another, spiritual laws are working, spiritual laws which will be totally misconstrued if they are associated in the very slightest degree with causation similar to what is meant when we speak in the ordinary way of 'cause' and 'effect' in the world.

In order to understand the real nature of karmic connections we must, in the first place, have a clear and exact perception of what is happening within man behind the sphere of his ordinary consciousness. And it is only by observing the being of man as revealed to supersensible cognition, to Initiation-knowledge, that such understanding can be attained.

Let us therefore consider to-day how the attainment of Imagination, Inspiration and Intuition makes it increasingly possible for man to recognise how he lives, as man, within the whole cosmos. This will enable us to continue the study of certain matters that were touched upon in recent lectures and will eventually lead to an understanding of karma.

It has often been said, even in public lectures, that at the stage of Imaginative Cognition a tableau of the present earthly life spreads out before man. A vista of his life lies before him in mighty pictures and he is able to behold things that cannot be yielded by memory in the ordinary sense.

In this vista which opens out as a result of the striving for Imaginative Knowledge, man is, to begin with, entirely within his physical and etheric bodies, but through the appropriate exercises he makes himself completely independent of everything by which impressions are transmitted to him from his physical body. In the activity of Imaginative Cognition man is therefore independent of his sense-impressions, and also of his intellectual knowledge. He lives entirely in the etheric body and the memory-tableau lies outspread before him.

We can therefore say: man is now living in the supersensible, inwardly detached from his physical body. And in point of fact it would not be so difficult as it actually is for the majority of people to acquire this faculty of Imaginative Knowledge, if only there were a stronger inclination to break through the inner link between the life of soul and the physical body.

It is, of course, comparatively easy to break through the link with direct sense-perception. But remember that a man is also connected with his physical body through the attitude and tenor of soul he acquires in his earthly life. After all, our moods of soul are also dependent upon the physical body, are essentially influenced by the physical body. When a man ascribes one thing or another to his capacities, his talents or other qualities of soul, this is all connected with his experiences in the physical body. If he is to acquire the faculty of genuine Imaginative Knowledge he must free himself from all this; and if he succeeds, even if only for a moment, he knows what Imaginative Knowledge is and the life-tableau begins gradually to unfold.

It is necessary to bear in mind the difference between the condition of being bound up with the physical body and thus living within it, and the condition of being independent of the physical body but for all that remaining within it. There is a real difference, and it is the latter condition that obtains in the activity of Imaginative Knowledge. We remain within the physical body, we do not leave it, but we are nevertheless independent of it.

When you remain with your soul and spirit within the physical body, then you fill the physical body, even if you are not bound up with it. I will illustrate this diagrammatically.—

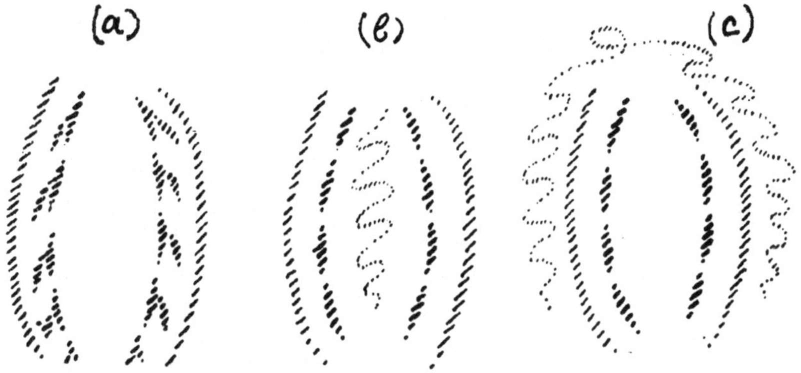

Let us think, first, of man's ordinary, everyday condition. Take this (a) to represent the physical body (inner curves), this the etheric body (outer curves) and this the soul and spirit (short branching lines).

The etheric body is connected everywhere with the physical body through the muscles, bones and nerves. These connections are everywhere, proceeding from the etheric body to the physical body. Now picture to yourselves that you have a porous clay vessel and you pour liquid into it. The liquid fills the pores and runs out into the porous clay. But it may also happen that your vessel is not porous and in that case none of the liquid is absorbed; the liquid will then be in the vessel but there will be no channels into the clay walls. In the activity of Imaginative Knowledge man is in this sense within his body but the etheric body does not enter into the muscles, the bones and so forth. This condition can be indicated by (b) in the diagram. Physical body; then etheric body which is now on its own; and within, the soul and spirit. All that has happened is that the etheric body is now inwardly detached. The result of this detachment will of course be perceptible when returning to the previous condition. It is therefore only natural that when a man really tries to make himself free of his physical body but remains within it, as is the case in the activity of Imaginative Cognition, he is aware not only of exhaustion but of actual heaviness. He becomes intensely aware of his physical body because he has now to make his way into it again.

This is the condition obtaining in the activity of Imaginative Cognition but not in that of Inspiration, Inspired Knowledge. In the activity of Inspired Cognition—which begins, as I have described to you, with consciousness that has been emptied of images—man is outside his physical body with the soul and spirit. Thus (c) in the diagram represents the soul and spirit outside the physical and etheric bodies.

The outer configuration must therefore be the same as in sleep. Knowledge through Inspiration is possible only when with his ego and astral body a man can be outside the etheric body.

And now, when he returns into his physical and etheric bodies, he notices the presence there of something else; the physical and etheric bodies are not at all as he is accustomed to know them; something is there within them. This is very important, because knowledge of it gives an indication of the whole process of Initiation.

At first, a certain difficulty is experienced in coming back into the physical and etheric bodies after the state of Inspiration, because there is the feeling of diving down into something quite different.

Remember what I told you yesterday about the backward survey of the memory-tableau. If this memory-tableau is blotted out in the activity of Inspired Knowledge, we perceive what it is that is present there within the physical body. And when the memory-picture of the phase between birth and the 7th year, until the time of the change of teeth, is blotted out, we perceive that within this physical body there was an Angelos, an Angel! We actually behold there a Being of the Third Hierarchy. So that what happens is this. We succeed in getting outside the physical body and then return into it as into our house and home . . . and lo! we meet our Angel there when we look back upon the phase of life from birth until the 7th year.

Knowledge of such truths existed in the days of the ancient, instinctive clairvoyance, knowledge which took different forms in the various epochs of evolution; and these truths were taken into account in establishing certain customs and usages.

In olden times men were fully conscious that the giving of names should conform with spiritual realities. Generally speaking, people to-day are indifferent about the kind of names their children receive. For some the only consideration is whether the name has a pretty sound. There is often an element of coquetry in giving a name to a child; people 'fancy' the name. But in olden times men were mindful of the child's relation to the spiritual world and chose the name accordingly. In an epoch, for example, when a prophetic being was venerated under the name of 'Elisha', girls were sometimes named 'Elisa-beth', that is to say, the 'house of Elisha'. In this way expression was given to the hope that by placing a child in the world with this name, the grace of the prophet would be ensured. And so the names were given with this aim in view.

What were the grounds for this? It was known that when man has been outside his body and then returns into it, he sees himself as the bearer of spiritual Beings. And the whole conception that little children, especially, are guarded by their Angel originates in the fact that when with Initiation-knowledge we look back upon the phase of life from birth to the 7th year, we experience what I described yesterday by saying that when this phase in the memory-tableau is blotted out, the Hierarchy of the Angeloi, that is to say, the deeds and activities of the Moon-sphere shine through.

Again, when we look back upon the phase from the 7th to the 14th years and then return into the body, we find an Archangelos. This Archangel is of course also present within the human being from birth until the 7th year, but we do not find the Archangel when we are looking back only at the phase between birth and the 7th year.

And so when we return into the body after having been outside it, we become aware that there, within the body, are

Beings of all the higher Hierarchies. But this form of self-knowledge, the knowledge that the body is the bearer of the Beings of the higher Hierarchies, cannot be acquired in any other way than by having first been outside the body and then returning into it again.

This can be understood only when it is connected with another fact. I have told you that the many stars in the heavens are but the outer signs of colonies of gods. Where the stars sparkle in the heavens there are, in reality, colonies of spiritual Beings. But you must not imagine that these gods have their consciousness *only* in Venus, or only in the Sun, or in Mercury, or in Sirius. They have their main habitation, the focal point of their existence in these several spheres, and this is true of all spiritual Beings of the cosmos who have anything to do with the earth. But it is impossible to say of their existence in the cosmos that they have their dwelling-place only in Mars, only in Venus, and so forth. Paradoxical as it will seem, I am nevertheless obliged to say that the Divine Beings who belong to the earth and who people Mars, Venus, Jupiter or another of the planets—also the Sun—would be blind if they inhabited only one of these spheres. They would live, they would be active—just as we can walk about and take hold of things even if we have no eyes; but they would not see—I mean, of course, in the way in which Divine Beings 'see'—they would lack a certain faculty for perceiving what is happening in the cosmos. But this, my dear friends, will lead you to ask: Where, then, is the eye of the gods, where is their organ of perception? This organ of perception is provided by the Moon, our neighbour in the cosmos—in addition to all its other functions. All the Divine Beings belonging to the Sun, to Venus, Mercury, Mars, Jupiter, Saturn, have their eye in the Moon and are at the same time in the Moon.

And now think of some of the things of which we have spoken here from time to time. Take only one fact. The Moon was once part of the earth, and separated from the earth only in the course of time. Before the separation of the Moon, therefore, the eye of the gods was bound up with the earth; the gods beheld the cosmos from the earth. Hence at that time the great primeval Teachers too were able to impart their wisdom to mankind. For in that they were living on the earth, and the Moon was still within the earth, they could gaze into the cosmos with the eye of the gods. When the Moon departed, remembrance of this vision of the gods remained with them for a time; thus they could behold, in remembrance, what was now seen with the eye of man, and could communicate this to the gods. But the primeval Teachers themselves had then to make their way to the Moon, where they are to this day, and to found a colony there in order to be able to see with the eye of the gods.

And now turn your minds to something else. From the Moon, Jahve reigned over the heart and soul of the Jewish people, and those of the primeval Teachers who were still associated with the cult and the teaching of Jahve united with him in the Moon, in order to look out into the cosmos through his eyes. In time to come the Moon will again be united with the earth and then it will be possible for man on the earth to gaze into the cosmos with the eye of the gods. Vision of the cosmos will then be a natural human faculty.

It is only by understanding these things that we can come to know the nature of the universe. For only when man views the universe in this way can he have any true conception of the function of the Moon.

And now we have the reason why freedom, free spiritual activity, can be unfolded in earthly life. As long as the Moon was connected with the earth, as long as the primeval Teachers taught men out of their store of remembrance, and as long as this teaching was preserved in the Mysteries—actually until the 14th century A.D.—all wisdom consisted in what had been seen with the eye of the gods. Only since the period I indicated to you, only since the year 1413, has it become utterly impossible for the earth to see with the eye of the gods. So that with the development of the Consciousness Soul, freedom begins to be within the reach of men.

But in point of fact man is on the earth only in the activity of sense-perception and intellectual knowledge, for the latter is also bound up with the physical body. The truth of the matter is as follows. Let us picture the human being. It is only in his sense and intellectual knowledge that he extends beyond the Hierarchies who are within him. In respect of all that lies behind his intellect, he is filled with the Third Hierarchy; in all that lies behind his feeling, he is filled with the Second Hierarchy; in all that lies behind his willing, he is filled with the First Hierarchy.

We are therefore in very truth within the Hierarchies and it is only in respect of our sensory organs and intellect that we extend beyond their realm. It is actually as though we were swimming, with the head rising a little out of the water. With our senses and our intellect we rise out of the ocean of the activities of the Hierarchies.

All this we find when, having experienced the reality of perception outside the body, we return again into the body. And then we find that in very truth man is the House of the Gods.

Something else will now be clear to you. When the gods desire cosmic vision, they gaze through the eye of the Moon. But when they desire to behold the cosmos from the earth—whereby an entirely different aspect is revealed—then they must look from out of man. The human race is the other eye of the gods!

In very ancient times it was natural for man to be able to see with the eye of the gods because the Moon was within the earth. And he will be able to do so again when in future time the Moon and the earth are re-united. Through Initiation, however, through becoming aware on returning into the body that the gods are present there, and through coming to know these gods, man learns to behold the world through the "eye of man." Thus *Initiation reveals to man what in earlier times was revealed to the gods through the eye of the Moon.*

What we do with our everyday consciousness, the intentions we form, and so forth—all this depends upon ourselves; but our karma is shaped and fashioned by the *Hierarchies* within us. They are the architects and shapers of an entirely different World-Order, a World-Order belonging to the soul, to the moral sphere of life. This is the other aspect of man, the aspect of the Hierarchies who are within him.

As long as we remain at the stage of Imaginative Knowledge we are convinced, as we look back over our own earthly life, that we are a unity; we are also convinced that certain actions in life are free, because they proceed from this unity. With Imaginative Knowledge we perceive little of our karma. When we reach the stage of Inspired Knowledge, however, and then return into the body, we feel ourselves divided into a world of countless Hierarchies. We return into the body and at first do not know our identity. Are we the Angel, are we a Being of one of the Hierarchies, one of the Dynamis, or Exusiai? We are divided into a world of Beings, dazed by the multiplicity of our nature, for we are one with all these Beings.

At this point the appropriate exercises must make a man so inwardly strong that he can assert his unity over against this multiplicity. And then—it is of course all an after-effect of the life between death and rebirth—he perceives how karma is shaped by the interweaving activities of the many Beings within him. Countless Divine Beings take part in the shaping of human karma. It is therefore true to say that man leads an earthly life in the real sense only in respect of his intellectual and sensory activity. In the activity of his life of feeling and of will—yes, and even in a more remote and hidden activity of thought—man shares in the life of the gods. In a hidden thought-activity he shares in the life of the Angeloi, Archangeloi and Archai; in respect of what is hidden in his life of feeling he shares in the life of the Exusiai, Dynamis, Kyriotetes; and in respect of his will he shares in the life of the Seraphim, Cherubim and Thrones.

What we call human destiny is therefore an affair of the gods and as such it must be regarded.

But what does this mean for earthly life? If a man cannot accept his destiny with inner composure, if he rebels against his destiny, if—from his personal point of view of course—he is discontented with it, if he brings his destiny into confusion by subjective decisions, then it is as though he were continually disturbing the gods in the shaping of his destiny. Destiny can of a truth only be lived through in the right way when life is accepted with inner composure and tranquillity. To feel and perceive how destiny works is something that brings with it hard and heavy tests for human nature. If a man can succeed in taking his destiny earnestly, this experience will give him a strong and deep impulse to live in communion with the spiritual world. And life itself will unfold in him a feeling for connections of destiny, of karma.

Men of the modern age have to a great extent lost this sensitivity, this delicacy of perception; their perceptions have become crude. But suppose there is someone who looks back with more delicate perception upon the relationship he had with a human being who was an example to him in his youth—a teacher, perhaps. People do not always feel contemptuous about those who were their teachers; many look back with inner happiness to those who educated them. When this is so, the recollection can deepen into a very intimate experience. It may come to us that between our 7th and 14th years, for example, we always felt obliged to do whatever this revered teacher did; or we may realise that when this teacher told us something we felt as though we had already heard it, as though it were just being repeated. It is actually one of the most beautiful experiences in life when we remember something of this kind, feeling that it was repetition. And then it strikes us that something must underlie this experience. Healthy human reason will tell us that there is nothing to account for it in the present earthly life, and then the same reasoning faculty points us to previous lives. There are indeed many whose attention is directed in this way to earlier lives on earth.

Now what does it mean when we can look back to a teacher with feelings like these? It means that in our present life destiny has led this teacher to us. It is our karma to have such a teacher and it points to a previous earthly life.

As a rule—and this is shown by occult observation—as a rule it is not the case that in the previous earthly life the teacher was also our teacher; the relationship then was quite different. From a teacher we receive *thoughts*, *ideas*, even if they are clothed in the form of pictures; in true education we receive thoughts and ideas. When this is the case it points back, as a rule, to a relationship where feelings, not thoughts, were communicated by the person in question; there was less opportunity for receiving *thoughts* from him, but *feelings* were communicated—feelings which can be transmitted in so many different ways. And the same may apply to the present and a future earthly life.

Let us suppose that in this present life a man feels drawn by warm, inner sympathy to some other person with whom life does not bring him into specially close contact, whom he merely meets but to whom he is strongly drawn. In such a case it may happen that these feelings of sympathy lead to the other becoming his teacher in a later life.

What, then, has actually happened? When feelings of sympathy and attraction towards another person unfold in a man, this is the result of what the Beings of the Second Hierarchy—the Kyriotetes, Dynamis, Exusiai—unfold in and around the human being.

Then, in the next life, when the influence does not work by way of the feelings but by way of thoughts and ideas, this means that the Beings of the Second Hierarchy have given over what they wrought in a preceding life, to the Beings of the Third Hierarchy, to the Angeloi, Archangeloi and Archai; and it is they who are now working within the human being.

When, therefore, our karma unfolds from one earthly life to another, this means that actual deeds are passed on from one Hierarchy to another and that in the cosmos, in the spiritual cosmos, something of immense significance is taking place.

In looking at a man's destiny we gaze, as it were through a veil, into a wide vista of cosmic happenings. If we can become conscious of this, the impression will be one of tremendous power. You have only to picture it to yourselves, entering into it with the right feeling and understanding.

Imagine now that you are observing the manifestations of destiny in the life of a human being. This should never be done in a spirit of indifference, for in observing the destiny of a human being we are in truth beholding deeds which have poured from the highest Hierarchy into the lowest Hierarchy, and again from the lowest into the highest Hierarchy. We are gazing upon a weaving activity of life in the ranks of the Hierarchies when we study the destiny of a human being. It is something that must be contemplated with deep piety and veneration, because as we behold this destiny the world of the gods lies manifest before us.

This was the feeling I tried in some measure to convey when I was writing the Mystery Plays. Throughout the Plays you will find scenes that have their setting in earthly life and others that have their setting in the spiritual world. And I have also made it evident how not only the higher Hierarchies but elemental beings, also the Ahrimanic and Luciferic powers, mingle in the living, weaving deeds that flow from above downwards and from below upwards when the destiny of man is being fulfilled.

Think of the scenes when Strader and Capesius are within the supersensible world in quite different forms of existence but for all that the same individuals. This is only the other side of man's life which is just as truly part of him—the side that belongs to the world of the gods and not to the world of the minerals, the animals, the plants, the mountains, the clouds, the trees and so forth. To learn to contemplate the destinies of human beings with reverence and awe—that too is something that the times demand of us. It is a dreadful experience to read biographies from the pens of materialistically-minded authors to-day, for they write without an iota of reverence for the destiny of the one whose life they are narrating. Of a truth it would be well for biographers to realise that when they intrude into the life of a human being, even if only for the purpose of describing it, they are coming into invisible contact with all the Hierarchies.

Deliberations of this kind lead us to the 'feeling' side of Anthroposophy. We realise that everything offered to us in Anthroposophy must also move our feelings. For in Anthroposophy it is not merely a question of acquiring knowledge; feelings about the world are quickened within us, feelings which alone can enable us to find our rightful place in life. And without such feelings we cannot truly understand or perceive the laws by which the karma of man is pervaded.

14—KR * *

XIV

The study of problems connected with karma is by no means easy and discussion of anything that has to do with this subject entails—or ought at any rate to entail—a sense of deep responsibility. Such study is in truth a matter of penetrating into the most profound relationships of existence, for within the sphere of karma, and the course it takes, lie those processes which are the basis of the other phenomena of world-existence, even of the phenomena of nature. Without insight into the course which karma takes in the world and in the evolution of humanity it is quite impossible to understand why external nature is displayed before us in the form in which we behold it.

We have been studying examples of how karma may take its course. These examples were carefully chosen by me in order that now, when we shall try to make the transition to the study of individual karma, we can link on to them. To begin with I will give a general introduction, because friends are present to-day who have not attended the lectures on karma given during the last few weeks and months.

It is very essential to realise the importance and seriousness of everything connected with our Christmas Foundation Meeting. We must be deeply conscious of the fact that this Christmas Meeting constituted an entirely new foundation of the Anthroposophical Society. And there must be no returning to old customs, to old habits of thought in relation to the fundamental changes that have come about in the method of handling the truths of Anthroposophy. The contents of the lectures given here since Christmas should not really be passed on to any audience otherwise than by *reading an exact transcript of what has been said here*. A free exposition of this particular subject matter is not possible at the present stage. If such a course were proposed I should have to take exception to it. These difficult and weighty matters entail grave consideration of every word and every sentence spoken here, in order that *the limits* within which the statements are made shall be absolutely clear. If anyone proposes to communicate the subject-matter to an audience in some different way, he must first get in touch with me and enquire whether this would be possible. For in future a united spirit must prevail through the whole Anthroposophical Movement. Otherwise we shall fall into the same mistakes that were made by a number of members who thought it their duty to elaborate anthroposophical truths in terms of modern science, and we have experienced to the full how much harm was done to the Movement by what was then "achieved"—I say the word with inverted commas!

These conditions do not, of course, apply to entirely private communications; but even in such cases the person who makes them must be fully alive to his responsibility. For the moment things are spoken of in the way we are speaking of them here, there begins, in the fullest meaning of the words, *a sense of responsibility in regard to communications from the spiritual world.* It is difficult to speak of such matters here in view of the limitations of our present organisation which do not, however, admit of any other arrangement. It is difficult to speak about these matters because such lectures ought really to be given only to listeners who attend the series from beginning to end. Understanding will inevitably be difficult for anyone who comes in later. If, however, friends are fully conscious that such difficulties exist, a certain balance can be established. Provided this consciousness is present, then all will be well. But it is not always there . . . Nor will it ever be possible to think in the right way about these matters—which are among the most delicate in our Movement—if, as is still the case even since the Christmas Foundation, the same habits persist—jealousies, mutual rancour and the like. A certain attitude of mind, a certain earnestness are absolutely essential for anthroposophical development.

Before I assumed the office of President I spoke of such matters as a teacher. But now I must speak of them in such a way that they actually represent what proceeds from the Executive at the Goetheanum and must come to life within the Anthroposophical Society. I think that the meaning of what I have said will be understood. I have spoken as I have in order that the necesary earnestness may prevail in regard to lectures of the kind now being given.

Karma is something that is in direct operation through the whole course of man's life but lies concealed in the unconscious and subconscious regions of the human soul, behind the outer experiences.

Now a biography should evoke experiences of a very definite kind in the reader if he follows the narrative with genuine, warm-hearted interest. If I were to describe what the reading of a biography can awaken in us, it is this.—Whoever reads a biography with alert attention will find description after description of events and phenomena which are not really in keeping with an uninterrupted flow of narrative. When reading a biography we have before us a picture of the life of a man. But truth to tell it is not only the facts experienced in his waking consciousness that play into his life. Time takes its course thus.—First day, then night; second day, then night; third day, then again night, and so on. But in ordinary consciousness we are aware only of what has happened during the days—unless we write an anthroposophical biography which, in the circumstances of present-day civilisation, is an utter impossibility. Biographies give an account of what has happened during the days, during the hours of waking consciousness of the one whose biography is being written.

But that which actually shapes life, gives it form and implants into it the impulses that are connected with destiny—this is not visible in the events of the days but comes into operation between the days, in the spiritual world, when man himself is in the spiritual world from the time of falling asleep to that of waking. These impulses are at work in life but are not indicated in biographical narratives. To what, then, does a biography amount? In regard to the life of a man it is as if we were to hang Raphael's Sistine Madonna on a wall and paste strips of white paper over certain places so that only portions of the surface remain visible. Anyone looking at the picture would be bound to feel that there must be something more to be seen if it is to be a complete whole.

Everybody who reads a biography dispassionately ought in truth to feel this. In view of the conditions of culture to-day it can be indicated only by means of *style*, but that should be done. The whole style and manner of writing should indicate that impulses are flowing all the time into the life of a man from impersonal levels of the life of soul and spirit. If that is achieved we shall gradually come to feel that in a biography, karma itself is speaking. It would of course be pure abstraction to narrate some scene in a man's life and then add: This comes from a previous earthly life; at that time it took such and such a form and now it takes this. Such a way of speaking would be sheer abstraction, although a great many people would probably find it highly sensational! Actually, however, it would contain no higher spirituality than is to be found in the conventional biographies written in our time, for everything that is produced in this domain to-day is so much philistinism.

Now it is possible to cultivate the attitude of soul that is needed here by learning, shall I say, to love the diaries or daily notes written by individuals. If such diaries are not read (or written), thoughtlessly . . . some diaries, of course, are very humdrum and prosaic, but even so, as he follows the transitions from one day to another, a man who is not a philistine will be aware of feelings and perceptions which lead on to an apprehension of karma, of the connections of destiny.

I have known people—and their number is by no means small—who out of blissful ignorance thought themselves capable of writing a biography of Goethe. But the fact is that the more deeply one looks into the connections of existence, into the karmic connections of existence, the more do the difficulties increase.

Try to recall what I have been telling you here recently, and especially the lecture in which I urged you expressly to understand me with your hearts rather than with your intellects, and when I should speak again, to receive that too with your hearts. Remember the emphasis I laid upon this. For the fact of the matter is that an intellectual approach cannot lead to a real apprehension of karma. Anyone who is not inwardly shaken by many of the karmic connections disclosed here shows that any real perception of karma is beyond him and that he is incapable of pressing on to the *perception of individual karmic connections.*

But let us try now to find the transition from the studies hitherto pursued, to what can lead us to say of some happening in the life of a man that this is karma, in a definite form of manifestation.

When I recall all that I experienced in relation to Goethe during the seven years I was working in the Goethe and Schiller Archives in Weimar—in narrating the story of my life I am having to review it all in thought—I say to myself in reference to karma that one of the most difficult problems in any presentation of the subject is to describe the experiences through which Goethe passed between the years 1782 and 1800. To write this chapter in a biography of Goethe is one of the most difficult of all tasks.

Now we must learn to perceive, even if it has to be with higher, occult vision, how and where karma is working in the life of a man.

Between the moment of falling asleep and that of waking, man lives in his astral body and his ego, outside his physical and etheric bodies. With his ego and astral body he lives within the spiritual world. Again, it is one of the most difficult of all investigations that can be undertaken in spiritual science to make an accurate survey of what happens between falling asleep and waking. I shall describe it in outline to-day.

If you review all that has been brought before you in

Anthroposophy, you will feel that it gives the impression of being comprehensible; but the discovery of it is a matter of extraordinary difficulty in anthroposophical investigation.

If I were to draw a kind of sketch of the human being, this outline or boundary-line indicates his physical body. In this physical body is the etheric body, within that the astral body, and within that again, the ego, the 'I'.

Now think of man as he falls asleep. The physical and etheric bodies lie in the bed. What happens to the astral body and the ego? The astral body and the ego go out

through the head and, in reality, through the whole senses-system, that is to say, they pass out through the whole body but mainly through the head, and are then outside. Thus, leaving aside the ego, we can say: At the moment of falling asleep the astral body leaves the human being through the head. Actually, the astral body leaves him through everything that is a sense organ, but because the sense organs are concentrated chiefly in the head, the main part of the astral body goes out through the head. But as the sense of warmth, for example, is distributed over the whole body, and the sense of pressure too, weaker radiations also take place, in every direction. The whole process, however, gives the impression that at the moment of falling asleep the astral body passes out through the head.

The ego, which—speaking in terms of space—is rather more extensive than the astral body and not entirely enclosed within it, also passes out.—Such is man as he falls asleep.

Now let us turn to man as he wakes. When we observe him at the time of waking we find that the astral body approaches through the limbs, actually through the tips of the fingers and toes first, and then gradually spreads through the limbs. Thus at the moment of waking the astral body comes in from the opposite side. So too, the ego, only now the ego does not envelop the astral body but on returning is enclosed by the astral body.

We wake from sleep and as we do so the astral body and the ego stream into us through the tips of the fingers and toes. In order to fill the human being entirely, as far as his head, they really need the whole day; and when they have reached the head the moment has come for them to go out again. You will realise from this that the ego and astral body are in constant, perpetual flow.

At this point you may raise the question: Yes, but if that is so, half an hour after waking from sleep we have in us only a small part of our astral body (and here I include the ego as well) as far as the wrists above and as far as the ankles below. And that is actually so.—If somebody wakes at 7 o'clock—I will assume him to be a person of decorum—and stays awake, then at 7.30 his astral body will have reached about as far as his ankles and possibly his wrists. And so it goes on, slowly, until the evening.

You may say: But how is it, then, that we wake up as a whole man? We certainly feel that we wake as a whole man, all at once . . . yet properly speaking, only our fingers and toes were awake at 7.15, and at mid-day most people are within the astral body only as if they are sitting in a hip bath. This is really so.

The question that arises here must be answered by pointing to the fact that in the spiritual realm other laws prevail than in the physical world. In the physical world a body is exactly where it is—nowhere else. In the spiritual world it is not so. In the spiritual world our astral body works through the whole space taken up by the body, even when it has actually occupied only the fingers and toes. That is the strange fact. Even when the astral body is only approaching it can already be felt throughout the body. But its reality, its substantiality spreads out only slowly. Understanding of this phenomenon is of the greatest importance, above all in enabling a true judgment to be formed of the human organisation in health and disease. For think of it: throughout the hours of sleep, in what lies in the bed and is not man in the full sense but only the physical and etheric bodies, a kind of plant-mineral activity is going on, albeit within a human organisation. And this activity can be either normal or abnormal, healthy or unhealthy.

It is precisely in the morning hours, when the astral body begins to rise upwards from the limbs, that the unhealthy phenomena become manifest to a special faculty of perception. Therefore in forming a judgment of illnesses it is of the utmost importance to know what feelings the patient has when he wakes from sleep, when his astral body is forcing upwards what is unhealthy within him.

And now let us proceed.—On falling asleep, our ego and astral body pass out of our physical and etheric bodies into the spiritual world. The after-effects of what we have experienced during the day still remain. But thoughts do not remain in the form in which we harboured them, neither do they remain in the form of words. Nothing of this remains. Remnants, vestiges, still adhere to the astral body when it passes out, but no more than that.

Immediately the astral body has passed out of the human being, karma begins to take shape, although at first in the form of pictures only. Karma begins to take shape. What we have done through the day, whether good or bad, viewing it to begin with in accordance with customary ideas—directly we fall asleep, all this begins immediately to be *translated, integrated, into the stream of karmic development.*

This process continues for a time after we fall asleep and overshadows everything else that happens to us during sleep. As sleep continues, however, a man begins to dive down into the experiences undergone in his preceding earthly life (see arrows in diagram), then into those of the life before that, and so on, backwards. And when the time of awakening comes he has reached and passed his first, most distant earthly life as an individual. Then he reaches the state of being when he was not yet separate from the cosmos, a state of existence in reference to which one cannot speak of an earthly life as an individual. Only when he has reached thus far can he return again into his physical and etheric organisation.

Still another question arises here, moreover a very important one.—What happens when we have a very short sleep —for example an afternoon nap? Or indeed when we have a brief forty winks during a lecture, but really do go to sleep; the whole thing may last only two or three minutes, perhaps only a minute or half a minute. What happens then? If the sleep were real, we were in the spiritual world during that half minute.

The truth is, my dear friends, that for this short nap even during a lecture, the same holds good as for the all-night sleep of a lie-a-bed—I mean, of course, a human lie-a-bed! As a matter of fact, whenever a man falls asleep, even for a brief moment, the whole sleep is a unity and the astral body is an unconscious prophet; it surveys the whole sleep up to the point of waking . . . in perspective, of course. What is remote may lack clarity, as when a short-sighted person looks down an avenue and does not see the trees at the farther end of it. In the same way the astral body may be short-sighted, figuratively speaking, in the subconscious. Its perception does not reach the point where the individual earth-lives begin. But broadly speaking, the fact is that even during the briefest sleep we rush with tremendous, lightning-like rapidity through all our earthly lives. This is a matter of extraordinary significance. Naturally it is all very hazy; but if somebody falls asleep during a lecture, then the lecturer or those who share his power of observation have it in front of them. Think of it: the whole of earth-evolution, together with what the sleeper has experienced in previous earthly lives! When somebody falls asleep during a lecture everything lacks clarity because it happens with such terrific rapidity; one thing merges quickly into another, but it is there, nevertheless. From this you will understand that karma is perpetually present, inscribed as it were in the World-Chronicle. And every time a man falls asleep he has opportunity to approach his karma. This is one of the great secrets of existence.

One who can survey these things from the vantage-point of Initiation Science, with unimpeded vision, looks with deep reverence, a reverence of knowledge, upon what can live in a human memory, upon the *memory-thoughts* that can arise in the human soul. These memories tell only of the earth-life now being undergone, yet within them lives a *human ego*. And did these memories not exist—I have spoken of this previously—then the human ego would not be fully present. Deep down within us there is something that can ever and again evoke these memories.

But inasmuch as we are in communication with the external world through our senses and our mind, we form ideas of this external world, ideas that give us pictures of what is outside.

Drawing this diagrammatically, we say: here (*a*) man

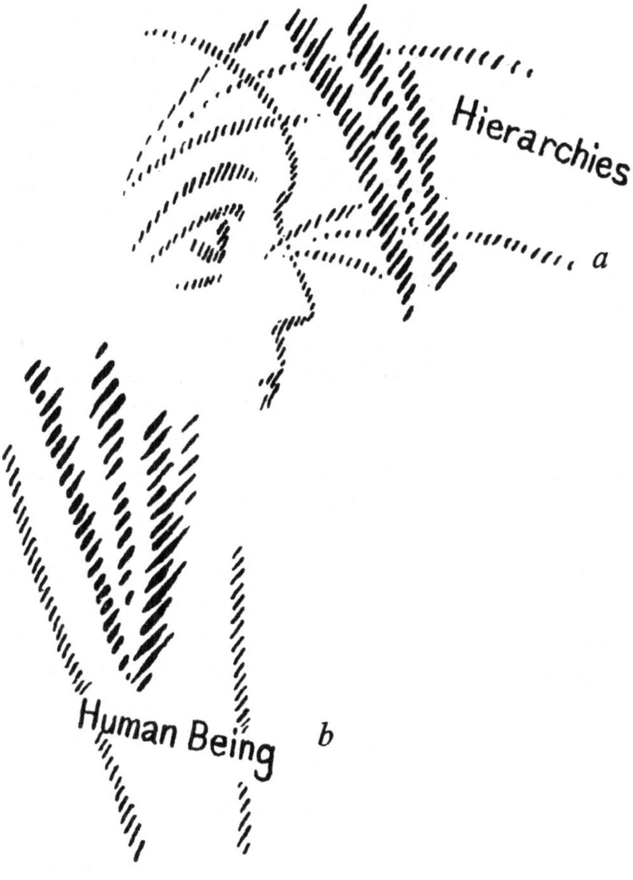

looks out into the world. Pictures arise in his thoughts, representing to him what he perceives in the external world. Here (*b*) man lives within his body. Thoughts well up, containing their own store of memories. Of our store of memories we say that it presents, as faithfully as our organisation of spirit-soul-body allows, what we have experienced in this present life on earth.

But now let us think about what lies on the other side, outside man. We do not as a rule reflect upon the fact that what we see there is but a section of earth-existence, in the first place, the surrounding earth and sky. If a man is born in Danzig, his eyes and other senses perceive different processes and phenomena from those of one born in Hamburg or in Constantinople. We can say: The world presents 'sections' of itself in infinite variety; for no two human beings are these sections identical, even though the two may have been born at the same place and die at the same place, living their lives in close proximity. The section of the world presented to the one is completely different from that presented to the other.

Let us be quite clear what this means. The world presents to us a certain part of itself and this we see. The rest we never see. It is extremely important to reflect upon how the world presents to a human being a sum-total of impressions upon which the experiences of his life depend. This will mean very little to a shadowy thinker, but one who thinks deeply will not put it lightly aside. As he ponders it all he will say: 'This fact is so puzzling that I am at a loss how to put it into words.—The cosmos, the world, presents to each human being only a portion of itself, a more or less coherent portion; therefore in this sense the cosmos particularises human beings. How am I to put this into words? In speaking of it as abstractly as this I am merely stating a bare fact which does not really amount to anything. I must be able to express the facts clearly, to formulate them. How am I to do so?'

Now we shall arrive at a way of formulating these facts if we again consider memory. What is it that wells up from the depths when we recall something in memory? What is it that rises up? It is what our own human being has experienced. Our real human being is somewhere deep down where we cannot take hold of it. It streams up in our memory-thoughts, streams up into our consciousness from our inmost being. What is it that streams into us from outside? Man himself is still so minute when all this is welling up from within him and everything in the cosmos out yonder is so vast, of such immensity! But these 'sections' of the cosmos are always entering into man. And the fact of the matter is that here too, thoughts arise.

We know that our memory-thoughts derive from what we have actually experienced. But thoughts also come into us from outside, just as memory-thoughts come from below. Here below (see diagram) is our own human being; and here, outside, is the whole world of the Hierarchies.

An impression of greatness and majesty comes to us when with Initiation-Science we begin to realise that these 'sections' of cosmic intelligence are outspread around us and that behind all this that makes an impression upon us from outside live the Hierarchies, as truly as our own individual being lives behind the memories that well up from within.

It all depends upon the vividness of some experience whether or no we can call it forth again in memory, whether or no there is any reason why one thought rises up from our store of memories, and another, or all the others, lie dormant. And it is the same here. Those who learn to know the true facts realise that at one time a Being from the Hierarchy of the Angeloi is appearing, at another, a Being from the Hierarchy of the Exusiai, and so forth.

Thus we arrive at the following formula.— *During our earthly existence we behold that which it pleases the Spirit-Beings to reveal to us.*

Inasmuch as a particular portion of the world is revealed to us during our life on earth, we learn to recognise that it is just this portion of the infinite range of possibilities contained in the cosmos that certain Beings of the Hierarchies have selected in order to disclose it to us from our birth until our death. One human being has this portion revealed to him, another that. Exactly what is revealed to individual men lies in the sphere of the deliberations of the Hierarchies.

The Hierarchies remember, just as man remembers. What is it that provides the basis for the memory of the Hierarchies? They look back upon our past earthly lives—that is what gives them the basis for their memory. And according to what they behold in these past lives they bring the appropriate section of the cosmos before our soul. In what we see of the world—even in that lies karma, karma as apportioned by the world of the Hierarchies.

Within: remembrance of the present brief life in our human memory. Out yonder: memory of the Hierarchies of all that men have ever done. Memory-thoughts rise up from within; memory-thoughts from the world of the Hierarchies enter in the form of what a man beholds of the cosmos ... and human karma takes shape. This thought is startling in its clarity, for it teaches us that the whole cosmos, working in the service of the Hierarchies, is related to man. Viewed in this aspect, to what end is the cosmos there? In order that the gods may have the means whereby to bring to man the primary form of his karma. Why are there stars, why clouds, why sun and moon? Why are there animals on the earth, why plants, stones, rivers, streams, why rocks and mountains, and all that is in the cosmos around us? It is there as a reservoir upon which the gods may draw in order to bring to our vision the primary form of our karma, according to the deeds we have wrought.

Thus are we placed into the world and thus can we relate ourselves to the secrets of our existence.

And so we shall be able to consider the various forms of karma. In the first place it is karma in its cosmic aspect that is being brought before us, but it will come to be more and more individual. We shall discover how karma works in its inmost depths.

XV

Our study of karma can lead us only slowly and by degrees to an understanding of this fundamental and complicated law. To-day I should like, first of all, to repeat that in the elaboration of karma during the life stretching between death and a new birth there is co-operation primarily between those human beings who are living this life between death and a new birth. We work together with those with whom we are specially connected by karma. In the elaboration of karma during this life between death and a new birth, groups of human beings united by their karma work together and it can truly be said that in this purely spiritual life there are clear differentiations between the groups. This does not preclude the fact that we also form part of the whole of humanity in the life between death and a new birth, and still more do we form part of the life of those who are incarnate on the earth. The fact that we belong to a particular group of souls does not exclude us from forming part of humanity as one whole. And into all these groups and down into the destiny of each individual there flows the work of the Beings of the higher Hierarchies.

Those Beings of the higher Hierarchies who elaborate karma by the side of man during the life between death and a new birth, work also into the life we spend between birth and death, where karma works itself out in the moral sense, as destiny. And to-day we must find an answer to the question: In what way does the work of the Hierarchies influence human life?

Speaking now with the help of Initiation-Science, we shall admit that this is a deep and searching question. For you can understand from what I have told you in the course of recent lectures, that the phenomena of nature too are connected with the karma of mankind.

The man who directs his gaze to the whole flow of cosmic and human events and not alone to the immediate facts presented by the world of nature, perceives the connection between the events which take place among larger or smaller groups of men at one epoch and the facts of nature at another. There are occasions when we can observe events in nature breaking into the orbit of human life on earth. We witness devastating volcanic eruptions and we know what is brought about by natural influences during floods or suchlike phenomena.

If we regard such events as belonging merely to the natural order, we are confronted with something that is incomprehensible in its relation to the general impression we have of the world. For here we behold events that simply break into the cosmic order, events which are so envisaged by man that he gives up all hope of understanding them and accepts the distress they bring as a stroke of destiny. The investigations of spiritual science are able, however, to take us a little further, for they open up remarkable information precisely in connection with these elemental events in nature.

When we let our mind's eye scan the face of the earth, we find certain areas of the earth literally covered with volcanoes. We find that other parts of the earth are liable to earthquakes or other catastrophes. And if we examine the karmic connections of such events as these in the same way as we have examined them in recent lectures from the point of view of the history of certain personalities, then we arrive at very remarkable results. We find the following: Up above in the spiritual worlds, human souls are gathered together in groups according to their karma; they are elaborating their karma in conformity with their past and future existence. And we see one of these groups of human souls in their descent from pre-earthly into earthly existence wander to regions situated, for example, in the vicinity of volcanoes, or to districts where earthquakes are liable to occur, in order there to receive their destiny from the elemental phenomena of nature.* We even find that during this life between death and a new birth when man's conceptions and feelings are of quite a different nature, that such places are deliberately chosen by the souls thus karmically connected, in order that they may experience this very destiny. For a thought which finds little enough understanding in our souls on earth, such as the thought: "I choose a great disaster on earth in order to become more perfect, I choose it because I am still so far from fulfilling what lies in my past karma"—such a thought for which, as I have said, there is so little understanding in earthly life, can be present in the life between death and a new birth, and has there an inherent value.

It can happen that we deliberately seek out a volcanic eruption, or an earthquake, in order to find in the path of disaster the path to perfection. Clear distinction must be made between these two completely different outlooks upon life,—one outlook being that of the spiritual world and the other of the physical world.

But in this connection there are other things to be considered. In the outer world, the everyday happenings of nature proceed with an ordered regularity inasmuch as the world of the stars is playing a part in them. For the world of stars with its mysteries works with a certain regularity. This above all is the case in connection with the sun and moon, indeed with all the stars with the outstanding exception of the enigmatic phenomena of meteorites and comets which burst in upon the regular, rhythmical order of the cosmos in a most mysterious way. But that which cuts across the regular course of natural existence in the way of thunderstorms, hailstorms and other climatological and meteorological events—all this interrupts the regular rhythm of natural happenings. We realise these things and, to begin with, resign ourselves to the outer course taken by natural phenomena. But later on, when a longing to understand spiritual things awakens within us, we listen to what is told us by

* See also: *The Deed of Christ and the Opposing Spiritual Powers.* Two Lectures by Rudolf Steiner, Berlin, 1st Jan. and 22nd March, 1909.

Initiation-Science, namely that besides this outwardly visible world there is also the supersensible world where dwell the Beings of the higher Hierarchies. And in our life between death and a new birth we enter the domain of these higher Hierarchies, just as in our life between birth and death we live among the three kingdoms of nature—the mineral, the plant and the animal kingdoms.

We listen to what is taught by Initiation-Science and try to envisage the existence of this second world, but we often stop short at the idea of the two worlds being there side by side, without connecting them together in our thought. We can form a true idea of the two worlds only when we are able to realise their existence simultaneously, and when with inner vision we can realise the way in which they work together and are interwoven. For this interworking must be known if we are to understand the shaping and forming of karma. In the life between death and a new birth, karma is prepared. But karma is worked out and elaborated on earth, too, with the help of the Beings of the higher Hierarchies who are also active during the life we lead between birth and death.

The question therefore arises: In what way do the higher Hierarchies work into earthly life?

In their work upon earthly life, these Beings of the higher Hierarchies make use of earthly processes. We shall best understand what this means if we look, to begin with, at all that is spread out before our senses, in the world of stars as well as in the physical world. Throughout our waking-day life, we see the sun up there in the heavens. Through the hours of the night we behold the radiance of the moon and of the stars. Think, my dear friends, of how we look out into the world, and how we allow what is above us, and what is around us in the kingdoms of nature, to work upon us. And let us remind ourselves that this world of the senses has in itself just as little meaning as a human corpse. The forces that are at work in the earth outside man are the forces that are in a corpse. But in a corpse we do not find the forces of the living man. In itself, the corpse is meaningless. It has significance only inasmuch as it is the remains of a living human being. It is not reasonable to imagine for a moment that a corpse could exist in itself as a collection of phenomena having an independent being of their own. A corpse can only reveal the *form* of something that is no longer visible. Just as one is led back from a corpse to a living human being, so too are we led by everything in the visible world of physical existence to the spiritual world. For this physical sense-existence has just as little meaning of its own as has a corpse.

Just as we are led in thought from the corpse to a living man, and say: This is the corpse of a living human being; so, in relation to nature, we say: This is the revelation of divine-spiritual powers.

No other way of thinking can be reasonable, indeed no other way is sound or healthy. To hold a different view would imply a morbid way of thinking.

But what is the nature of the spiritual world for which we are to look behind the physical world of sense? The spiritual world behind the physical world is the world of the Beings of the Second Hierarchy: Exusiai, Dynamis, Kyriotetes. The Second Hierarchy is behind everything on which the sun sheds its light. And what is there in the whole compass of our sense-experience that is not lit up and kept alive by the sun? The sun is the source of the light and the life of everything.

These Beings of the Second Hierarchy have their chief dwelling place in the sun. From the sun they rule over the visible world which is their revelation. Thus we can say: There we have the earth, with the sun shining down upon it, and behind and through the workings of the sun weave the Beings of the Second Hierarchy: Exusiai, Kyriotetes, Dynamis.

Upon the rays of the sun which are the deeds of the Second Hierarchy are borne all the sense-impressions that come to our senses through the hours of waking-day consciousness.

And so we speak truly if we say: Within and through and

behind the workings of the sun throughout our physical sense-existence is the supersensible world of the Second Hierarchy.

Now there is another and different condition of our earthly existence. We spoke of this different condition in the last lecture from a certain point of view. We have the condition of sleep. How does this condition of sleep present itself in its cosmic counterpart? Let us consider it for a moment. When our physical and etheric bodies are there in the bed, and our astral body and ego outside, then out in the cosmos we have to think of the sun at a position where the earth must first let the rays of the sun pass through it before they reach us. Now in all the ancient Mysteries a certain teaching was given which, if fully understood, produced a profoundly moving impression in those who become pupils in the Mysteries and gradually mastered the Science of Initiation. They reached a certain stage of inner development which they might have described in the following way.—I am now telling you what might have been said by one of these ancient Initiates when he had attained to a certain degree of Initiation.—He would have spoken somewhat as follows: "When I stand in the open fields in the daytime, when I direct my gaze upwards and give myself up to the impressions of the senses, then I behold the sun; I see it in its dazzling strength at noontide and behind the dazzling strength of the noontide sun I behold the working of the spiritual Beings of the Second Hierarchy in the substance of the sun. Before my Initiation the substance of the sun vanished from me at the moment of its setting. The shining radiance of the sun vanished in the purples of sunset. Before my Initiation I went through the dark path of night, and in the morning, when the dawn came, I remembered this darkness. Out of the dawn the sun shone forth again and took its course onward towards the dazzling brightness of noon. But now, having attained to Initiation, when I experience the dawn and behold the sun as it passes from dawn on through its daily course, a memory of my life during the night-time awakens within me. I know what I have experienced in this night life, I remember clearly how I beheld a blue, glimmering light arise from the evening twilight and gradually spread, travelling from west to east. And I remember how I beheld the sun at the midnight hour, at the opposite point in the firmament to where it had stood in its noontide, dazzling strength; I saw it gleaming there behind the earth, full of deep and solemn meaning. I beheld the Midnight Sun!"

Such has actually been the monologue of Initiates in their meditation, and it faithfully expresses their experience. The Initiate is conscious of these things. And when we read Jacob Boehme's book entitled *Aurora* then we cannot help being deeply moved by the realisation that the words which are written in this book are echoes of a wonderful teaching of the ancient Mysteries.

What is the "Dawn" to Initiates? It is an instigation to cosmic remembrance, to remembrance of the vision of the Midnight Sun behind the earth. With our ordinary sight we see the radiant yellow-white disc of the sun at noon, but with the vision of Initiation we see the bluish-violet sun at the opposite point of the heavens. The earth appears as a transparent body, with the sun gleaming on the other side of it with a bluish-red light. But this bluish-red sheen is not what it seems. I must utter the paradox:—it is not what it seems. When we are gazing at the Midnight Sun it seems at first that we are looking at something hazy in the distance. And when we learn with the help of Initiation more and more clearly to see what at first appears as a blur in the distance, then the bluish-red light will begin to take shape and form; it will spread itself over the whole of the sky but still on the other side of the earth and covered by the earth. It becomes peopled. And just as when we go out of our house on a starlit night and look up at the majestic spectacle of the starry heavens with its sparkling points of light, perhaps with the moon in the centre, so to the gaze of Initiation a whole world becomes visible on the farther side of the earth which is now transparent. It is a world that emerges, as it were, out of the clouds, becoming a world of living forms. It is the world of the Second Hierarchy, of the Exusiai, Kyriotetes, Dynamis. There they appear, these Beings of the Second Hierarchy. And as we watch more and more closely, if we can attain the stillness of soul that is required, then something else happens. All this reveals itself after preparation and meditation and only becomes a conscious experience at dawn, as an after-memory, when it is immediately present with us, when we know we have actually beheld it during the night. What appears on yonder side of the earth is in reality the weaving world of the Beings of the Second Hierarchy. And from out of this weaving, living world of the Second Hierarchy there now radiates a world of other Beings—raying to us through the earth. It is a truly wonderful world of Beings that works thus through the earth at night, hovering there in the firmament, now approaching man, now drawing away, now approaching him again. We see how the line of the weaving Beings of the Second Hierarchy ever and again fades out, while another Hierarchy approaches man, now hovering towards him and now drawing away from him again. And by-and-by we learn to know what all this really means.

We have been conscious the whole day long and now we lie down in sleep. This means that the physical and etheric bodies are left to themselves, working in sleep as a plant and mineral world. But by day we have *thoughts;* all day long, ideas have been passing through our being. They have left their traces in our physical and etheric bodies. We should not be able to remember the experiences of our earthly existence at all if these traces which we subsequently use in our memories did not remain. There they remain, these traces, in what is left of man as he lies asleep at night—in that part of his being which he has left behind. A mysterious process takes place there, above all in the etheric body. All that man has thought during his waking life from morning till evening begins to move and ring on waves of sound. If you think of a certain region of the earth where men are sleeping, and think of all that weaves and works in the etheric bodies as an echo of all that these sleeping men have

been thinking during the hours of their waking life, this will give you a picture of what has happened through the hours of the day.

And those Beings who hover over us, rising and descending, busy themselves through our hours of sleep with the traces that have remained in our etheric bodies. This becomes their field of action. It is an immediate experience in them and absorbs their attention. It is an immediate experience in them and absorbs their attention. When this is revealed to us, we say with a sense of deep reverence: "Thou, O Man, hast left thy body. And as it lies there it bears within it the traces of the day's experiences. It is the field where live the fruits of thy thoughts and ideas during the day. The Beings of the Third Hierarchy, the Angels, Archangels and Archai, now enter this field. While thou hast left thy physical and etheric bodies, these Beings experience what thou hast thyself experienced from the thoughts and ideas of thy waking hours."—Deep reverence fills us at the sight of some region of the earth where human bodies are left in sleep and whither the Angels, Archangels and Archai wend their way to all that unfolds as an echo of the life of day. And we here behold a wonderful life, born of all that is unfolded between the Beings of the Third Hierarchy and the traces of the thoughts we have left behind.

As we gaze at this field, we become aware how, as human beings, we have our place within the spiritual cosmos, and how, when we wake, we create work for the Angels during our hours of sleep. It is so indeed: during our waking hours we create work for the Angels during the time of sleep. And now we learn to understand something about our world of thought. We realise that the thoughts which pass through our heads contain the fruits of what we lay into our own physical and etheric bodies—fruits which Angels gather at night. For Angels gather these fruits and bear them out into the cosmos in order that they may find there their place in the cosmic Order.

One thing more we see as we behold these Beings of the Third Hierarchy—Angels, Archangels and Archai—coming forth from the Beings of the Second Hierarchy and their activity. We behold how behind this weaving, again Beings of sublime majesty and grandeur take part in the activity of the Second Hierarchy. We gaze at the Second Hierarchy, and we see how into this weaving life of the Second Hierarchy something else works from behind; and we soon become aware how this not only strikes, lightning-like, into the weaving and working of the Second Hierarchy, but striking right to the other side of the earth, it has to do, not with the part of man that is left on the earth, but with that other part of his being that has gone out, namely, the ego-organisation and astral body. And as we gaze at what has been left behind and behold it as a field where the fruits of thoughts throughout the day are being gathered by the Angels, Archangels and Archai for the purposes of cosmic activity, so too we see how the Beings of the Second Hierarchy, the Exusiai, Dynamis, Kyriotetes, uniting their activity with that of the First Hierarchy—the Seraphim, Cherubim and Thrones—concern themselves with the astral body and ego. And in his morning memory the Initiate says to himself: "I have lived from the time of falling asleep till the time of waking in my ego and astral body. I have felt myself enwrapped in all that the Seraphim, Cherubim and Thrones are unfolding, together with the Kyriotetes, Dynamis and Exusiai. Living in this world I gazed down at my physical body and my etheric body and hovering above them I perceived the Angels, Archangels and Archai, gathering the fruits of my thoughts. I felt myself one with the Beings of the First and Second Hierarchies, and I beheld the weaving and working of the Third Hierarchy in mighty spirit-clouds over my body."

And so, my dear friends, in this way you can get a clear picture of how the Beings of the three Hierarchies appear to the imaginative vision of Initiation, how they appear there on the opposite side of the earth in the picture of the physical world, but only when this physical world is plunged in darkness.

Knowledge and vision of these sublime truths penetrated more and more deeply into the hearts and souls of those who in days long since gone by, partook in the ancient mysteries of Initiation.

And once again this knowledge can find its way into the hearts and souls of those who are led to the modern science of Initiation.

Let us picture this majestic imagination which arises before the soul. We can picture the human soul liberated

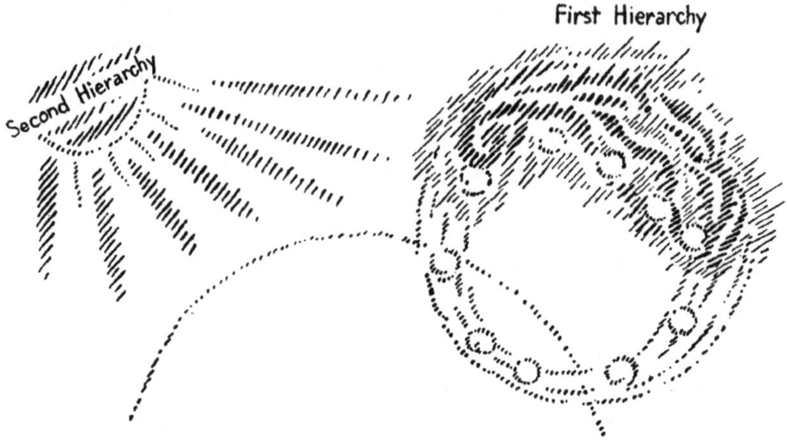

from the body, free from its physical and etheric bodies, weaving in the streaming forces of the Seraphim, Cherubim and Thrones, the Kyriotetes, Dynamis, Exusiai.

In the ancient Mystery rite this was wont to be presented to the uninitiated in plastic form and in colour. The purpose was to present in plastic form what the Initiate was able to see in such sublime grandeur on the other side of the earth. And, in order to show that this world is also the world where karma is elaborated in communion with the highest Beings, in front of the plastic form stood the highest Initiates, those who during earthly existence itself could already behold with that vision which otherwise comes to man only between death and a new birth. The highest Initiates stood in front of the plastic form and still another form was set up, with human figures all around it. There stood the lesser Initiates whose work upon their physical and etheric bodies was not yet complete. The spectacle thus placed before the eyes of men was a copy of what the Initiates beheld in the Mysteries. Such was the origin of the altar, where the ritual was enacted by the higher and lower grades of the priesthood as a copy of what is revealed in Initiation-Science.

In Roman Catholic Churches to-day, as you look from

the nave towards the altar, you have a faint copy of what was once inaugurated by Initiation-Science. And you begin to understand the origin of the cult. A ritual is not invented, for if it is invented it is not a true ritual. True ritual is brought into existence as a copy of happenings in the spiritual world.

If I may give an example, let me speak of one part of that great and all-embracing cult which has found its place in the Christian Community, and with which the majority of you are already familiar. Let me remind you of the ritual for the burial of the dead, as it is given in our Christian Community.

Watch the order of this ritual. There rests the coffin, containing the mortal remains of the dead. And before the coffin a ritual is enacted. Prayer is uttered by the priest. Other things could be introduced to make the ceremony more complicated, but the help it can be to humanity can also be clothed in simplicity. What is this ceremony? Let us suppose, my dear friends, that here we have a mirror and here again some object. You see the reflection of the object in the mirror. You have the two things—the original and the reflection. Similarly, when a ritual for the dead is enacted, there are the two things. The ritual enacted by the priest before the coffin is a reflection. It is a reflection, and it would be no reality if it were not a reflection. What does it reflect? The acts of the priest as he stands before the dead body have their prototype in the supersensible world. For while we celebrate the earthly rite before the physical body, and the etheric body is still present, on the other side the *heavenly* ritual is enacted by the Beings beyond the threshold of earthly existence. Over yonder, the soul and spirit are received by what we may call a ritual of welcome, just as here on earth we assemble before the dead for a ritual of farewell. A cult or ceremony is only true when it has its origin in reality.

Thus you see how the supersensible life works into earthly life and permeates it. If we celebrate a true ritual for the dead, a supersensible ritual is enacted simultaneously. The two work together. And if there is sanctity, truth and dignity in the prayers for the dead, then the prayers of the Beings of the Hierarchies in the supersensible world echo in the prayers for the dead and weave in them. The spiritual world and the physical unite.

Thus in all things there is accordance between the spiritual world and the physical world. The spiritual and the physical world interplay in the very truest way when there comes into being on earth a copy of what is woven as karma in the supersensible world between death and a new birth together with the Beings of the higher Hierarchies.

XVI

The day before yesterday I tried to picture for you the cosmic drama, as it were, wherein human beings are shown in their relation to Beings of the spiritual world, so that one can see how there stems from this relationship not only the working out of karma, but also the living out of karma during physical life on earth. To-day I should like to turn to a thought touched upon in that lecture. I said that the present period in human evolution confronts anyone who has the knowledge of Initiation-Science with problems of world-karma in the deepest sense of the words. And before proceeding to consider how knowledge of karma is acquired, we will study its world-historic aspects, which in the nature of things must closely concern the whole of civilised humanity at the present time.

Things are happening in the world to-day which stir even the everyday consciousness of man and the heart that is bound up with this everyday consciousness. A heavy cloud looms over the civilisation of Europe and from one point of view it is amazing to find what little willingness there is on the part of mankind in general to feel and realise what this cloud portends.

Think only of what is emerging as the result of views of life and of the world widely prevalent in humanity to-day. Look at what is being made of Christianity in the East of Europe! Information—not entirely to be discredited—has reached us that the works of Tolstoy are to be banned by the present Government of Soviet Russia with the object of keeping them out of the reach of future generations. Although such things do not always work out exactly as they are announced, we must not blind ourselves to the gravity of the present moment in world-history; we do well to listen to the warning which Initiation-Science would like to repeat day in and day out—that now is the time when the many petty concerns occupying men's minds ought to be silenced and the attention of numbers of souls directed to the great concerns of life. But in point of fact, interest in these great concerns is dwindling rather than increasing.

We see views of life and of the world arising to-day with a certain 'creative' force, although this actually takes effect in destruction; these views are the offspring of human passions and emotions, of an element in human nature working entirely in a Luciferic direction. It may truly be said that reality is denied and rejected by a large portion of humanity to-day. The essential nature of matter is not understood by materialistic thinkers. Matter can be understood only when the creative spirit within it is apprehended. Therefore anyone who denies the reality of the creative spirit within matter knows only a false image of matter and the consequent idolatry is a far greater menace than that of the primitive peoples who are said to represent civilisation in the stage of infancy. Fantastic ideas and conceptions of what is, after all, unreality, hold sway in mankind.—This is one side of the picture.

Such things have of course occurred in various forms throughout human history. But spiritual science teaches us to recognise their connections in the whole World-Order, and to realise with what earnestness they must be studied.

And so we must be mindful of what is brought into existence when certain social orders are created under the influence of materialistic, fantastic ideas—ideas which have sprung entirely from human aberrations, have nothing to do with reality and could never have originated elsewhere than in man himself.

Having turned our minds to a phenomenon of history which has, however, immediate bearing upon our present age, let us consider occurrences in elemental nature like those mentioned in the last lecture, when groups of human beings are suddenly snatched away from earthly existence as the result of an earthquake, a volcanic eruption, or the like. The news reaches us of a catastrophe of this kind and we hear that a large number of people have met their death or suffered grave disablement.—Again, there are events for which the devices of civilisation are responsible. We hear, for example, of a railway accident, where again the karmic threads of life are abruptly severed, but in this case as the result of man-made institutions.

If we are earnest in our study of karma, we must ask, on the one hand: What form does karma take in the case of adherents of a social order originating from sheer emotionalism, sheer fantasy in man himself and devoid of objective reality? And on the other, we must ask: What form does karma take when the thread of life is suddenly severed by a catastrophe of nature or one that is the outcome of civilisation?

Here is one of the points where Initiation-Science enters deeply into man's life of feeling and perception. Ordinary, everyday consciousness does not ask about the consequences of such happenings in the successive earthly lives of men. In the case of catastrophes of civilisation particularly, the question of human destiny in the wider sense is never asked. The destiny of a man who has been the victim of such a catastrophe is regarded by ordinary consciousness as finished and done with.

Initiation-Science observes on the one side what takes place in the foreground of earth life and, in the background, the deeds of gods in connection with the souls of men. And it is what proceeds in the background that provides Initiation-Science with a criterion for assessing earthly life. For as we shall see in our further studies of karma, a great deal has to be moulded, recast in one way or another in earthly existence in order that the divine things behind it may take effect in the lives of men—in accordance with the will of the gods.

For on looking into the background we perceive the karma that is woven between one human soul and another during the life between death and rebirth; we perceive how human souls work together with the Beings of the higher Hierarchies. We see, too, the activities of the Luciferic and

Ahrimanic powers. Within the living organism of gods behind the organism of the earth we perceive the justification for this intervention by the Luciferic and Ahrimanic powers; we realise that Lucifer and Ahriman play an essential part in the deeper, spiritual ordering of the world. But although this necessity becomes evident to us, we must nevertheless often stand aghast at the way in which Luciferic and Ahrimanic influences penetrate into the earthly world.

When our vision extends beyond the earthly into the spiritual world, many things must be viewed in the light of their inter-connections, which need not necessarily be the case in ordinary consciousness. If in times when Initiation-Science was regarded with the reverence that must prevail once again—if in those ancient times the question arose whether a person was in truth an Initiate, men knew the right attitude with which such a question must be approached. And when a man who took life earnestly met another like him and their opinions differed as to whether a third person was an Initiate, the question was wont to be put to the one who felt uncertain: "Have you looked into his eyes?" For in those olden times, when clairvoyance was a natural gift in civilisation all over the earth, Initiates were recognised by the deep, earnest look in their eyes.—And something similar will come again. Without losing sight of the humour of life, men must again be mindful of its gravity.

Many of these lessons can be learned from what is happening in our present time and has indeed happened in some form through all ages, but they stand before humanity now as a great and mighty riddle . . . And now let us think of the facts connected with a certain kind of event.

Numbers of human beings have perished in some region where a terrible earthquake has taken place. Contemplating the event in the light of spiritual science, it cannot be said that the thread of karma belonging to the present earthly lives of these men has in every case come to an end. Think of the thread of karma in those who have met their death: in the case of the aged, whose earthly karma in this incarnation would soon have been completed, the thread of life will be shortened possibly only by months or at most by a few years. Younger people in the prime of life who have thought a great deal about what they wanted to achieve in the time ahead of them for themselves, for their family, or for a wider circle of humanity, are robbed of many years of activity. Children in process of education as a prelude to manhood are torn away from earthly existence together with the elderly and aged. Babies just weaned or still unweaned are snatched away, together with the old and the young.

The great riddle is this: How does karma work in an event of this kind?

And now think of the difference between such an event in elemental nature and an event that is due, fundamentally, to civilisation, for example, a terrible railway accident. There is obviously a difference, a difference that becomes significant and fundamental when studied from the point of view of karma.

As a rule it will be found that when human beings perish together, let us say in an earthquake, there is some kind of karmic connection between them all—just as men who live in a particular district are, broadly speaking, karmically connected or at any rate have some link with one another. These people have a certain common destiny into which they have been impelled through having descended from pre-natal existence to a particular locality on the earth, and with this common destiny they are led along their path to the point where the threads of their lives are severed.

On the other hand, in the case of a railway accident it will generally be found that only a few of the victims are karmically connected with one another. What, then, is their situation? As a rule they are human beings between whom there is no definite link, who are brought together without any such connection as invariably exists between victims of a particular earthquake. The victims of a railway accident may be said to have been brought together at a certain spot by destiny. Do we not see karma working quite differently in these two cases?

With the help of Initiation-Science, let us think of a

catastrophe like that of a devastating earthquake. We are concerned there with human beings whose karma at birth did not entail the severance of the thread of earthly life by the time the catastrophe occurred. As the result of this event they were torn as it were out of their karma.

How could this be? It is the decree of the gods that karma shall come to fulfilment, shall be lived out to the full. Now upheavals in nature—earthquakes, volcanic eruptions, great floods and the like—are not an integral part of the onflowing evolution of the earth; something extraneous—although still under the sway of natural laws—intervenes here in the evolutionary process, something that in times when man was not subject to birth and death as we know them to-day was both necessary and propitious for evolution. To form a clear conception of what this means, we must turn our minds to the epoch of the Old Moon.

In the epoch of the Old Moon which preceded that of the Earth, man was not led into physical existence by a transition as abrupt as birth or conception, nor led out of physical existence by a transition as abrupt as death. The transition in each case was much gentler; it was a transformation, a metamorphosis, rather than a sudden change. The Moon-man was not as densely material as the man of to-day; nor in the spiritual world was he as bereft of spirit as he is to-day.

The beings inhabitating the Old Moon were subject to quite different natural laws, laws under which this Moon-life was involved in constant movement; it was inwardly mobile, in ceaseless, surging flow. This surging, flowing life has become rigid—but only partially so—in the present Moon, our companion in the universe. The rigidification in the Moon—it has really a kind of hornlike quality—points to the past inner mobility of the Moon which takes effect in the earth when elemental catastrophes of nature occur of the kind of which I have been speaking. The ordinary natural laws of the earth are not operating, but the Old Moon is beginning to stir, to rumble in the earth. The Moon revolving out yonder in the universe has the constitution that is proper for it to-day, but after its separation from the earth, forces were left behind; and it is these Moon-forces that rumble and stir in the earth when nature-catastrophes occur.

As you will remember, I told you that the Beings who were once the great primeval Teachers of humanity are connected with man's karma; it was they who brought the ancient wisdom to mankind. They did not live on the earth in physical bodies but in etheric bodies, and at a certain point of time they departed from the earth to establish their abode in the Moon; and there we encounter them during the first phase of our life between death and a new birth. These are the Beings who engrave a record of men's karma into the cosmic ether, in an unerring script of soul-and-spirit.

But in the cosmos a pledge has been taken—if I may put it so—a pledge that use shall be made not only of the relations between the present Moon and the earth but also of the Moon-forces that were left behind and are still astir within the earth. And it is here that the Ahrimanic powers can step in and take hold of the threads of human life. It can actually be seen how from the depths of the earth the Ahrimanic powers present a countenance of gloating satisfaction when such catastrophes of nature befall.

With the help of Initiation-Science we can perceive how up to the moment when the thread of life is abruptly severed, part of the karma of one who perishes in a catastrophe of this kind has been absolved. According to whether death occurred in old age, adult life or babyhood, a longer or shorter portion of life would have remained to him; life might have continued until the completion of its course, but as things are, the events that would otherwise have been spread across this whole span lay their grip in a single, sudden moment upon the physical organisation.

Think of this situation, my dear friends.—Suppose such a catastrophe befalls a man at the age of thirty. If he had not been a victim of the catastrophe he might, in accordance with his karma, have reached the age of sixty-five, living through countless experiences which now are no more than possibilities. But everything is contained in his karma, in the make-up of his etheric and astral bodies and of his ego-organisation. And what would have been happening up to the sixty-fifth year of life? After the culmination of the upbuilding process, the organism would have been involved in a process of slow and steady decline; a subtle, gradual decline would have been taking place until the sixty-fifth year of life.

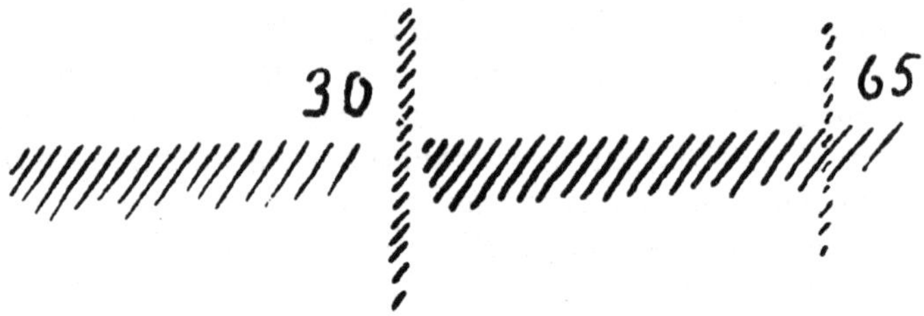

This steady decline which, in the slow tempo corresponding to such a lengthy period, would have lasted for at least thirty-five years, is fulfilled in a single moment, concentrated as it were into a single moment. Such a thing can happen to the physical body but not to the etheric body, the astral body or the ego-organisation.

When the circumstances are as described here, a man enters the spiritual world in quite another way than would have been the case had his karma been lived out to the full. Something is brought into the spiritual world that would otherwise not have been there: an etheric body, an astral body and an ego-organisation which might still have been living on earth. Instead of remaining in earthly existence they are taken into the spiritual world. What was destined for earthly existence is carried into the spiritual world.

And so we see an earthly element streaming into the spiritual world from all such nature-catastrophes.

Such is the situation of human beings who have been turned aside in this way from the karmic course of their life by the working of the Ahrimanic powers; such is their situation when they arrive in the spiritual world.

And now we must ask ourselves a question—for if we take

spiritual science earnestly we must learn to put questions from the standpoint of the spiritual world and of the spiritual Beings in that world, just as with our ordinary consciousness we put questions relating to the physical world and its beings. We must ask the question: How do the Beings of the three Hierarchies respond when human beings ascend to their realm bearing with them an earthly element, bearing this earthly element into the spiritual world?

It then becomes the task of these spiritual Beings to re-integrate into the World-Order what seems to have been turned to evil, to run counter to the World-Order. The gods have now to reckon with what confronts them in these circumstances, in order that they may transmute the Ahrimanic evil into a higher good.

This leads to the question: What is the situation within the World-Order of those human beings who are destined after their death to pass into the spiritual world in this way? The Beings of the higher Hierarchies are confronted with a particular state of affairs and have to say to themselves: In the previous incarnation of this human being and through the whole sequence of preceding lives, a world of facts was prepared, a world of experiences belonging, properly speaking, to the incarnation that has just ended. But only the first part of what was thus prepared has been able to come to expression; the second part has remained without fulfilment. Hence there is part of a life which ought, in reality, to correspond in respect of karma, to all that went before. There ought to be complete correspondence, but there is not . . . there is only a part which corresponds to some extent with the previous incarnation, but not with the whole of it.

As they survey this previous earthly life the gods must say: There is something that has not taken effect as it should have done. Causes are there which have not been utilised or turned to account.—And now the gods can take hold of these unutilised causes, guide them to the human being and so strengthen him inwardly for his next earthly life. The power of what existed as a cause in a previous incarnation can manifest all the more forcefully in the incarnation following the present one. If such a catastrophe had not befallen the man in question he might have appeared again in the world in his next incarnation with inferior faculties or very possibly with faculties of quite a different kind. A change has been wrought in him to the end that karma may be adjusted. But he also comes into the world endowed with special qualities; his astral body is reinforced, as it were, because unutilised causative forces are membered into it.

Will you then still be astonished by the legend of a philosopher who threw himself deliberately into the crater of a volcano? What can have been the motive of such a resolve on the part of one who was initiated into the secrets of world-existence? The motive could only have been a conscious intention to achieve through the agency of human will something that could otherwise have been achieved only through the agency of elemental nature: the sudden sweeping away of a process that would otherwise have worked itself to an end by slow degrees.

What is thus told of a philosopher may be due to a resolve to appear in the world in the next incarnation endowed with special powers. The world takes on a very different aspect when we enter into the deep problems of karma!

In principle, therefore, this is how things are in the case of nature-catastrophes. Let us think now of a catastrophe due to the institutions of civilisation, where human beings between whom there are no strong karmic links are as it were massed together by the Ahrimanic powers to suffer common destruction.

The situation here is altogether different. Again the Ahrimanic powers are in action; now, however, the human beings concerned are not, to begin with, grouped together by karmic ties, but for all that are led together. The consequences here are essentially different from those of nature-catastrophes.

A nature-catastrophe evokes in a man whom it befalls a vivid, intensified remembrance of what lies in his karma as causation. For when the human being passes through the gate of death he is made mindful of everything that is contained in his karma. And remembrance of karma is intensified, made more vivid in the soul as the result of a fatal nature-catastrophe.

On the other hand a railway accident, any catastrophe due to the institution of civilisation, brings about oblivion of karma. But because of this oblivion a man becomes highly sensitive to the new impressions coming to him in the spiritual world after death. And the result is that such a man is impelled to ask himself: What is to become of the unexhausted karma I bear within me?

Whereas in the case of a nature-catastrophe the *intellectual qualities* especially are intensified in the astral body of the victim, a catastrophe of civilisation leads to a strengthening, an enchancement of the *will.*

But now we will turn from these catastrophes and think of a state of affairs arising from fanatical emotionalism in a group of human beings, where the sole source of the impulses is man himself, where he lives in sheer unreality and works, moreoever, as a destructive force. Let us think of a structure of civilisation as fantastically distorted as that presented to us to-day in the East of Europe, and ask ourselves what happens when the men who help to produce such conditions pass through the gate of death.

Here too—as in the case of the other catastrophes—something is carried into the spiritual world, namely a Luciferic element which begets darkness and devastation.

From catastrophes of nature and of civilisation it is, in the last resort, light that is carried from the physical into the spiritual world. But from aberrations and misguided impulses in cultural life, darknesss is brought into the spiritual world. When men pass into that world through the gate of death they must make their way as it were through a dark, dense cloud. For the light which Lucifer kindled in human emotions on earth becomes dense darkness in the spiritual world when man enters it after death. And in this case, forces and passions engendered entirely by man himself and are concerns of his subjective life, are carried into the spiritual world.

These are forces which through Ahriman's power can be changed in the spiritual world in a way that enables use to be made of the Moon-elements still present in the earth. Lucifer is here stretching out a helping hand to Ahriman.

What is carried up into the spiritual world through impulses in civilisation arising from sheer emotionalism, from blind, misguided earthly consciousness—this, in different guise, is what bursts from the earth's interior in the form of volcanic eruptions, earthquakes and the like.

With this knowledge as a background we are led to the question of the karma of the earth and its peoples, the karma of individuals too, inasmuch as the karma of individuals is bound up with that of the peoples and of the earth itself. In putting the question we shall seek for the seeds in Luciferic activities at work in some region where ancient culture is cast on the rubbish-heap by the working of human emotions, where wild, misguided instincts set out to create something new but succeed in spreading only destruction. And we must ask ourselves: Where shall we see the forces seething in the wild passions of men burst forth one day on the earth, in flames or convulsive upheavals of the ground beneath us?

In respect of many an event of elemental nature, Initiation-Science may, nay must, put the question: When and where was this event set in train? And the answer is that it derives from the horrors and atrocities of enmity and warfare through the course of the development of civilisation. There you have the connection.—These happenings lie in the background of existence. In the light of such knowledge, events do not appear in isolation but are seen in their great cosmic setting. How do they find their place in the destinies of men? As I said already, of a truth the gods are there, gods who are linked with the evolution of mankind, and it is their unceasing task to transform these happenings into what is propitious and beneficial for human destiny.

In the interworking between the earthly and spiritual worlds the destinies of men are continually being wrenched from the pinions of Lucifer and the claws of Ahriman, for verily the gods are good! The unrighteousness originating from the activities of Lucifer and Ahriman behind the scenes of existence is led by the good gods into the path of righteousness again and the karmic connection is finally lawful and good.

Our gaze, which must of course be full of understanding for human karma, is now deflected from the destiny of men to the destiny of gods. For when we contemplate the horrors of war, the guilt and ugliness of war in their connection with death-dealing elemental catastrophes, we are watching the battle waged by the good gods against the evil gods—in two directions evil. We gaze beyond the life of men into the life of gods, beholding the life of gods as the background of human life. We watch this life of gods—not with dry, theoretical thoughts, but with our hearts, with deep, inner participation; we watch it in its connection with the individual karma of men on earth because we see human destiny inwoven with the destiny of gods.

When we contemplate these things, the world lying behind human life has for the first time drawn really near to us. For something is then revealed which cannot but stir the very fibres of our hearts. It becomes clear to us that the destiny of men lies embedded in the destiny of the gods, and that in a certain sense the gods yearn for what they have to take in hand for men while their own battle is being waged. And in making such conceptions our own we are led again to what is brought into the world through the Mysteries—as it was brought, too, in the days of the old clairvoyance.

One who had attained Initiation in the ancient Mysteries told how he was led, to begin with, into the world of the Elements; there he beheld his inmost being, with its moral attributes, turn outwards. But then—and he spoke of this experience in words of power and solemnity—he came to know the nether gods and the upper gods, the Ahrimanic and the Luciferic gods. The good gods, the Ahrimanic and the Luciferic gods. The good gods move in the field of *equilibrium*. And as the pupil of the ancient Mysteries came to know what must be known again by the pupil in our modern age, he was initiated, stage by stage, into the very depths of existence. When this is understood and its implications realised, the strange, yet all-illuminating conception is reached: To what end does calamity exist in the world? To the end that the gods may transmute it into well-being. Ordinary well-being does not lead into the life of worlds. Well-being that springs from calamities befalling man along his path through the physical world of sense—this alone can lead into the depths of existence.

In the study of karma we must never call theoretical concepts alone to our aid; we must call upon the whole man. For knowledge of karma can be acquired only when the heart, the feelings and the will participate. If, however, knowledge of karma is acquired in this, the right, way, human life will be deepened and due importance attached to the relationships and circumstances by which human beings are led together.

There will, of course, be moments when karma weighs heavily upon a man who does not lead a superficial life. But all such moments are balanced out by others when karma lends him wings on which his soul can soar out of the earthly realm into the realm of the gods. In our inmost being we must feel the reality of the connection between the divine world and the human world if we are to speak of karma in the right and true way.

What we are of ourselves, what is in us in a single earthly life passes away along the path from death to a new birth. What remains is that wherein the gods, that is to say the Beings of the Hierarchies, hold us by the hand. And no one will be able to cultivate the right attitude to the knowledge of karma who does not perceive in karma the helping hand of the gods.

Thus you must try, my dear friends, to grasp the knowledge of karma in such a way that it calls up the feeling: If I am to approach the holy ground of the spirit where something concerning karma can reveal itself to me, I must take the hand of the gods.

Thus real, thus immediate our experiences must become, if we are to win our way to true knowledge of the spiritual world—which is at the same time knowledge of karma.

Publisher's Note Regarding Rudolf Steiner's Lectures

The lectures contained in this volume have been translated from the German which is based on stenographic and other recorded texts that were in most cases never seen or revised by the lecturer. Hence, due to human errors in hearing and transcription, they may contain mistakes and faulty passages. Every effort has been made to ensure that this is not the case. Some of the lectures were given to audiences more familiar with anthroposophy; these are the so-called 'private' or 'members' lectures. Other lectures, like the written works, were intended for the general public. The differences between these, as Rudolf Steiner indicates in his *Autobiography*, is twofold. On the one hand, the members' lectures take for granted a background in and commitment to anthroposophy; in the public lectures this was not the case. At the same time, the members' lectures address the concerns and dilemmas of the members, while the public work speaks directly out of Steiner's own understanding of universal needs. Nevertheless, as Rudolf Steiner stresses: 'Nothing was ever said that was not solely the result of my direct experience of the growing content of anthroposophy. There was never any question of concessions to the prejudices and preferences of the members. Whoever reads these privately printed lectures can take them to represent anthroposophy in the fullest sense. Thus it was possible without hesitation—when the complaints in this direction became too persistent—to depart from the custom of circulating this material "for members only". But it must be borne in mind that faulty passages do occur in these reports not revised by myself.' Earlier in the same chapter, he states: 'Had I been able to correct them [the private lectures] the restriction [for members only] would have been unnecessary from the beginning.'